TEACHER SAYS

30 Foolproof Ways to Help Kids Thrive in School

Teacher Says

30 Foolproof Ways to Help Kids Thrive in School

Evelyn Porreca Vuko

A Perigee Book

A Perigee Book
Published by The Berkley Publishing Group
A division of Penguin Group (USA) Inc.
375 Hudson Street
New York, New York 10014

First Perigee paperback edition: August 2004

Visit our website at
www.penguin.com

Library of Congress Cataloging-in-Publication Data

Vuko, Evelyn Porreca.
Teacher says : 30 foolproof ways to help kids thrive in school /
Evelyn Porreca Vuko.—
1st Perigee ed.
p.   cm.
"A Perigee book."
Includes bibliograhical references.
ISBN 0-399-52997-7
1. Education—Parent participation.   2. Motivation in education.
3. Child rearing.   I. Title.

LB1048.5.V85 2004
371.19'2—dc22   2003063947

Printed in the United States of America

10   9   8   7   6   5   4   3   2   1

For Jim,
For his devotion and his rescue services

Acknowledgments

Though many special people played an important role in this book, the following deserve special mention:

My dearly departed dad, Charles A. Porreca, Sr.
My mother, Evelyn Arnone Porreca
Marguerite Kelly, *Parent's Almanac* columnist for the *Washington Post*
My agents, Stephanie Kip Rostan and Jim Levine
My editor, Sheila Curry Oakes
My readers, Barbara-March Smith and Ann Prosten
My *Washington Post* editor, Peggy Hackman
Los Angeles Times/Washington Post News Service editor, Kate Carlisle
Nina Graybill, *Esquire*
Thanks to all my contributors, especially Patricia Lemer, Lisa Mc-Phearson Robinson, Carol Kranowitz, Diana Henry, Johnny Lott, Donald Michels, Joye Newman and Mary Rentschler.
My own superb teachers: Prem Rawat, Dorothy Wolfe, Margaret P. Close, Sister Mary Anthony Weinig, SHCJ.
Thanks and hugs to my precious students who've allowed me the honor and pleasure of teaching them, especially when the last thing in the world they felt like doing was learning.

Contents

Introduction

It happens every time. The breath sucks in, the eyes sparkle, the mouth drops open, and off a kid blasts into learning. It's thrilling enough to watch when it happens to one child, but when a classroom takes flight, it makes you shout with joy. And it has inspired me to stay as close to teaching as I can for more than thirty years.

The spark of learning may look, smell, and taste like spontaneous combustion, but it definitely is not. It's the target I aim for, plan for, and labor to the bone for whenever I work with a child. With this book, I strive to put you there, too, so you can look beyond your limitations and race with all synapses firing straight for discovery. This is heady stuff to imagine doing with your child, but the potential is there.

If you are a pivotal adult in the life of a child, he or she will naturally look to you for answers and solutions. *Teacher Says* is your resource for learning new ways to deal with old problems, along with some pioneering methods that harness vision, senses, and muscles to help kids learn. Arranged by grade level from kindergarten through high school, each chapter provides practical suggestions engineered to take you and your child from a standstill to an active strategy at warp speed. If you want to delve deeper, books, materials, organizations, and Internet addresses are provided within the chapters, in the bibliography, and in the resources section at the end of the book. Don't expect to find methods that spoil or coddle here because kids see right through them. *Teacher Says* shows you how to meet a kid's problem with a warm heart and a light touch and provides an endless supply of ideas that will help him or her thrive in school.

The practical strategies I describe require a measure of trust, an investment of effort, and often some challenge on the part of you and your child. Growth is not always easy, but it can often be magical. I write from the perspective of an award-winning classroom teacher, school principal, and the "Teacher Says," education columnist for the *Washington Post*. I have investigated topics as if they were breaking news, interviewed experts, and vetted these ideas with a veteran educator's eye.

To keep your work lean and concentrated, I eliminate educational jargon and abstract theories because they do not connect on a gut level and kids rarely gain traction with them. When an idea rings true, it fuels your commitment to follow through until you and your Ruby or your Sam are both swept off in that magnificent learning momentum.

Like my "Teacher Says" columns in the *Washington Post*, each chapter begins with a verbal snapshot of a fictitious kid with a problem. Hogan mistakes kindergarten for a professional wrestling ring. Middle school Sally writes only two-word sentences which make her sound like Tarzan, and James's high school grades unfortunately don't reflect his percentage of coolness achieved.

Though you've probably heard that you shouldn't compare one kid to another, my "kids" prove that there's always something to be gained when you do. *Teacher Says* will help you ignite that spark in a kid's eye and blast off into learning—you're in for quite a ride.

PART ONE

Three Things to Think about Every School Year with Kids of All Ages

Making Every School Year Successful

Alex swears he won't stuff erasers up his nose in reading group this year. Ollie pledges, hand on heart, that his handwriting won't look like hairballs. Another school year gets off to a promising start.

Alex and Ollie aren't the only ones who need to pledge they'll change their behavior, habits, and thinking to make each school year brighter than the last. Parents, grandparents, aunts, uncles, teachers, principals, school bus drivers, mentors, and tutors need to take the pledge, too. In fact, anyone who cares about a child in school should renovate, revamp, and revise their thinking at the start of every school year. All it takes is a brave heart and an open mind.

The following suggestions help adults and kids of all ages make every school year better, and healthier.

Twelve Adult Attitude and Action Adjustments

1. Be a teacher. If you are involved in any way in Alex's and Ollie's growing up, you are a teacher to them whether you've had formal training or not. Be proud of it. And stay with it until they are at least forty years old. Caring, conscientious, and ever-teaching adults are the most powerful change-makers in a kid's life.

2. Be the boss. You can be a friend and still be a kind source of authority to Alex and Ollie. Boundaries are benign parameters that make kids feel safe and secure to do the difficult growing they all have to do. Don't be afraid to set limits, stick to them, and smile. Whining, pleading, and negotiating with kids undermine your role and cause them to lose respect for you. Be as good as your word.

3. Be a caped crusader. Be on the lookout for injustice, unkindness, prejudice, or poor manners that thread through the daily lives of you and your kids. Rectify what you can on the spot. At the very least, discuss incidents later in private, but don't give wrongheaded ideas—like ignoring someone who obviously needs help—a chance to grow in Alex and Ollie.

4. Give yourself a time-out. Borrow this age-old disciplinary method and use it to give yourself a breather when life with kids puts a strain on your good nature. It can be as simple as closing the bathroom door and taking ten deep breaths or making a show of leaving the room when behavior or noise becomes more than any self-respecting adult should have to bear. You deserve a break every day.

5. Learn how to calm yourself. Continue that deep breathing; take martial arts, yoga, exercise classes, or long walks. There's a lot to be gained by finding your center point and learning to stay there. Practicing your methods in front of your kids every day teaches them that knowing how to calm yourself is critical to living healthfully and successfully in the world.

6. Be mannerly. Simple good manners aren't simple at all but powerful lessons that reinforce for kids the importance of human kindness and consideration. Hold the door open for the people behind you, listen more, don't interrupt others, and write thank-you notes. By your example and your instruction, you'll teach Alex and Ollie to do it, too.

7. Leave neatness trails. Even if you never considered yourself a neat or organized person, pick up after yourself when a kid is near or watching. This could form a good habit. Leaving a clear, clean space behind you demonstrates thoughtfulness, reinforces order, and models efficiency. Kids need all those things for daily living and for facing the constant challenges of school.

8. Be a stuff editor. Don't let miniature plastic bear collections, magazines, newspapers, old clothes, plastic containers, books, or assorted stuff take over your life. Sort, discard, or donate your excess items regularly. Set aside special times, seasonally, to keep stuff from distracting and disrupting your life and the lives of the kids you love. The lesson is, don't let your possessions own you.

9. Speak a foreign language. Research shows that all language skills improve when kids under ten years old become familiar with a language other than their own. So do not stop speaking your native language or an adopted second language just because Alex and Ollie attend English-speaking schools. Learn and speak and give them directions in a new foreign language. *Venga!*

10. Be a storyteller. Tell stories or jokes about yourself as a kid, about your grandmother, or about the lady in the supermarket today who surfed fifteen feet on squashed grapes and came to a safe stop in the arms of the produce manager. Spontaneous oral presentations highlight the rhythm and beat of language, make vocabulary come alive, reveal the theater in daily life, and fire the imagination—all of which translate directly to Alex and Ollie's reading and writing skills.

11. Think out loud. Talking out loud as you ponder a new problem provides a timesaving and simple way to teach Alex and Ollie how to analyze a challenge, consider alternatives, select a course of action, and solve the problem at hand. Do this for your own problems and offer your out loud strategies whenever thorny issues face them. If not for you, how many opportunities will they have to witness the inner thinking of an adult, especially of an adult that you want them to emulate?

12. Raise the bar. If you challenge yourself, it's easier to challenge Alex. Tell him, for example, that this year you're keeping the same study hours he does so that you can learn Italian. Ramp up his Spanish grade by offering to test him on his verbs if he'll test you on yours. Next year, try Chinese.

Eighteen Adjustments to Make with Kids

1. Seek better, not redundant, school supplies. Rather than stocking up on more of the same markers, pens, and pencils, each year consider "therapeutic" or more "ergonomic" school supplies. Is there a chair, table, lamp, pencil, or other kind of backpack that has a more efficient and comfortable design? Buy brighter lights for Ollie's desk or a slant board to ease Alex's eyes during reading. If Alex's handwriting, as he approaches fourth grade, still looks like something the cat ate yesterday, get him a mechanical pencil to force a lighter touch. Think smart tools.

2. Keep a log. If your child has academic, behavioral, or social problems throughout the school year, document them. Note test grades, especially. To avoid unnecessary paperwork, use your personal appointment book to record events as they occur. Running commentary has three benefits: It reveals behavior patterns and might reveal a link to something as unexpected as a lack of sunshine. It charts the course of and often reveals reasons for an academic shift. It provides invaluable documentation for teacher, counselor, therapist, or physician conferences. Refer to notes in last year's appointment book to anticipate the timing of recurrent challenges in the coming year. This practice helps you to be proactive, right on schedule.

3. Make predictions and set goals. When Alex can forecast future action logically, it means he can recall details, select key ideas, and sort them in a reasonable order. Forecasting is not only essential to planning, but it is also an important comprehension and note-taking skill, so use it regularly when you and Alex strategize about the new school year. If he thinks math will be a breeze this year, ask him why. Is it because he finally got a calculator that will allow him to download data in class and graph it later at home? Ask him to make forecasts about academic subjects, extracurricular activities, and social events. Jot his predictions in your appointment book, then critique and revise them together in January and June.

4. Plan like corporations do. Decide which areas need focus and discuss measurable ways to achieve goals. For example, have Ollie work with an English tutor for six weeks, and then evaluate his progress. Action steps and time frames allow kids and parents and major corporations to compare actual, measurable outcomes to planned ones and then revise future plans more realistically. Give Ollie his own erasable wall calendar to track his progress through his designated activities, time frames, reviews, and to set new goals.

5. Set a study time and nail it down. Establish study time for kids, no matter their ages. Elementary-aged kids typically need 30–60 minutes per night. Middle schoolers need 60–90 minutes, and high school students, two hours. Demonstrate that study hours are a priority by maintaining them despite thunderstorms, babysitters, and unexpected guests. Enlist the support of other family members, too.

6. Stake it out. Together, pick a study spot that's all Alex's own, even if it's a corner of the dining-room table. Kids in primary grades like visible access or shouting distance to parents, so pick a nearby spot for studying your Italian. Though older kids often prefer a secluded space for doing homework, their computers should be located in a quiet but common area to allow for regular parental monitoring. Don't be shy about dropping by for a look.

7. Be a homework detective. Being a homework detective means knowing what is required of Alex each day. This puts you in an excellent position to evaluate his planning, organizational skills, and study habits, Teacher monitoring and intervention during the elementary school years helps most kids maintain a productive organizational structure. However, because the changing cast of teachers and increased demands of middle and high school can disrupt the study methods of even the best students, you'll need to stay vigilant for clues during those years, too.

8. Don't help if they don't need it. Unnecessary aid creates dependency and stifles a sense of responsibility for their own work. Ask for a short demonstration to gauge Ollie's ability before you slide up a chair and hunker down. Play dumb like a fox and watch instead. If Ollie can maintain a productive pace for even as short a period as five minutes, he is demonstrating confidence, so go off and study your Italian. Don't succumb to the temptation of doing Ollie's work for him. You've already been in elementary school.

9. Monitor understanding. If Ollie has a problem with a concept covered in a homework assignment, this often becomes evident in the first five minutes, too. If you try teaching it yourself, you will likely be challenged by the words, "that's not the way we learned it in school." Avoid adding confusion to the homework equation by immediately writing a note or sending an e-mail to the teacher. Do this whether Ollie is in elementary, middle, or high school. Ask the teacher to review the concept with him and give him a second chance to complete the assignment. Most teachers will be happy to oblige, as long as it doesn't happen too often.

10. Watch for three strikes. If difficulty with a concept or in a certain subject occurs during three homework sessions in a row, this might signal a misfit of task and skill or merely a lack of listening in class. This is the right time to conference by e-mail, phone, or visit with the teacher.

11. Don't let problems persist. Don't let problems drag on from one year to the next. Don't forget that sometimes even the biggest problems have simple solutions. Look for them first. Each year, take stock of recurrent issues before school starts and again in the middle of each quarter.

• *In elementary school:* Focus on persistent problems in phonics, spelling, reading, and handwriting, which along with math are the core skills of the early grades. Track Alex's progress by tuning in to some common, everyday activities. Listen to how he reads cereal boxes, relates stories, writes thank-you notes, or divides up grapes for a snack to share with his sister and his best friend. Is he still miscalling the short *e* sound? Or is he having comprehension problems because he still doesn't stop at periods when he reads? Does he have trouble dividing by three? Inform his teacher of persistent patterns by note or e-mail before school starts. Then follow it up with a phone call or schedule a conference. Ask for suggestions for helping him at home. Consider giving them both a hand and getting him a private tutor. Core skill problems unresolved in the early grades drag like a ball and chain straight through high school.

- *In middle school:* Focus on friends because they matter most to those delightful but hormone-hammered kids in grades six through eight. When friendships and social situations are calm, middle schoolers turn their heads toward academics. Make lists of social conquests last year and establish a four-week strategy for handling back-to-school friendship flare-ups. Don't bother building long-term plans; short-term strategies are better suited to the constantly changing friendships and social upheavals that characterize middle school.

- *In high school:* Keep coursework balanced and matched to his capacity. While satisfying their requirements for graduation, don't let kids enroll in so many difficult courses in one semester as to imperil grades and increase stress to unhealthy levels. Encourage inconsistent achievers to take the hardest courses in summer school. If physics is on the schedule this year, choose an elective that provides a hands-on creative outlet, like pottery. Help Alex choose courses all through high school that keep both sides of his brain stimulated and satisfied. Give him chances to demonstrate his broad-range talents, and open the door to new career options or academic interests.

12. Constantly consider new alternatives. When kids have personal or academic problems, always keep your eyes and ears open for new solutions. Use quilting to teach geometry, for example. Or for a change of perspective and fresh ideas, look to cultures other than your own. Check out people like Michio Kushi, an expert in the Japanese macrobiotic diet, for some startling ideas about how to raise calm and healthy kids.

13. Teach kids to be diet detectives. Draw Ollie's attention to the fact that he runs up the wall and across the ceiling every time he eats too much chocolate. Then show him, with a simple elimination diet, how to detect and then avoid food culprits that could be contributing to his inability to focus, hyperactivity, or allergies.

14. Put the computer in a central location. If Ollie is prone to non-productive online chatting and distracting Internet browsing during homework times, don't put the computer in Ollie's room, especially if he's in middle or high school. Place it in the family room or in a large hallway where you can just happen by, regularly. Though there might be opposition to this proposition, know that it unequivocally puts you in the best position to derail potentially dangerous online or game-playing habits and helps Ollie use the computer more productively.

15. Use TV as a learning tool. For kids of all ages, limit TV-viewing time during the school week to one favorite show per night, and then use it as a tool to improve reading and writing skills. During commercials, talk about plots and characters. Play thickheaded about details or the sequence of events. Ask Alex to predict how the story will end. To improve his persuasive writing skills, watch a home-shopping show together, and analyze the methods they use to sell cheesy watches or tacky shoes.

16. Read every day. Add 15–30 minutes for reading to nightly study hours and weekends. If reading is a sore spot, don't hesitate to offer to partner read. This means taking turns reading alternate pages, paragraphs, or sentences. Don't let beginning or reluctant readers struggle with words. Tell Alex the word and get on with the reading. Make notes for his teacher about repeated phonics, pronunciation, or pacing problems. Watch middle school kids' comprehension problems or difficulty focusing on the page, tracking a line of words, or sweeping their eyes across a line of words. If Alex is in high school, read to him from a book or the newspaper while he's lounging on the sofa or eating breakfast. Keep the daily habit of reading before his eyes and in his ears, no matter his age.

17. Don't be a stranger. Become a familiar face at school, even if Ollie is in middle or high school. At the elementary level, volunteer your talents at least once a month in the classroom, such as chaperoning trips or painting the scenery for the class play. In middle and high school, become a part of the parents' organization, or offer to chaperone school trips or dances. Offer to demonstrate your skills when kids are studying career options. Help the newspaper staff by giving interviews or providing experts for news articles. Find creative ways to become a familiar face at school. If you can't come by, then call more often. Building a good relationship with students, teachers, and staff on a good day puts you in a much better position when Ollie has a bad one.

18. Teach kids to take risks. This does not mean doing things that will endanger health or safety. This means encouraging Alex and Ollie to step out of comfortable old habits and move into new adventures. Whether it's trying a mechanical pencil or experiencing life without chocolate or taking on a new school project, carefully guided forays into the unknown expand the mind, amass knowledge, and raise self-confidence levels, something all kids and adults need. Kids are willing to take on more challenges if they have the freedom to fail as well as the opportunity to succeed. Given a safe, supportive environment, Alex and Ollie will learn that defying their own limitations is an exhilarating and rewarding thing.

Keeping Kids Healthy during the School Year

Another sure-fire way to make the school year better is to teach Alex and Ollie how to battle with germs, not with each other. The following bacteria-fighting tips particularly help primary graders understand how infection spreads and provide some simple but effective ways to avoid becoming sick. They will make the whole family feel better.

A GERM-REVEALING ACTIVITY

- *Show Junior that germs are spread by touching.* Hand-to-nose transfer is the most common way to get a cold. To bring the lesson home in a real and visual way, you will need a small amount of flour poured into a plastic bag and some old magazines. This makes a minor mess, so do it in the kitchen, wearing old clothes. Have Junior wet his hands, then dip them lightly in the flour. Dip yours, too. Next, purposely ignoring your flour-coated hands, open the magazines and find advertisements for cold, flu, and pain medication. Discuss typical symptoms like fever, shivering, aches, coughs, and sneezing. Now reveal the flour mystery—tell him that the flour on his hands represents germs. Track where the flour has spread. Is any on his nose, mouth, or ears? Or on yours? Talk about how it got there and what would happen if the flour were really germs and he put his hands in his mouth.

- *Show Junior how to wash germs away.* Rhinovirus, the nasty culprit that causes the common cold, can survive for hours on objects and surfaces like pencils, books, tables, and playground equipment, so teach Junior to wash his hands often throughout his day. While your hands are still covered with flour from the above activity, spray them with cooking oil spray. Then move over to the sink together and wash your hands. Count aloud to time how long it takes to get all the flour and oil off your hands. (It should ideally take a count of 15–20.) Remind him to wash his cuticles and the backs of his hands. Tell Junior that since real germs hang tough on the hands, too, he should use the same count to kill them whenever he washes his hands at home, school, the movies, a restaurant, or a friend's house.

• *Show Junior that germs are spread by coughing and sneezing.* You will need a spray bottle with a strong spray and some black construction paper. Tell him how fast germs spread—sneezes travel at 75–100 miles per hour and coughs at 300 miles per hour! Then demonstrate. Fill a bottle with water (the "germs"), and have Junior hold it next to his mouth, nozzle pointing forward, away from his head. Now, hold up a piece of construction paper about six inches from the spray bottle, and have Junior spray water onto the paper. Are there any "germs" on the paper? Step backwards at one foot intervals to gauge the power of each spray. Ask Junior what would happen if the water were really germs and the paper your face. What might happen if you swallowed some? Review how touching, coughing, and sneezing spread germs that make people sick.

GERM-HALTING TIPS FOR PRIMARY GRADERS

• *Show Junior how to catch the culprits.* Show Junior how to use his elbow to catch his cough or sneeze if a tissue is nowhere to be found. Since he can't easily touch anyone with his elbow, he's less likely to spread germs.

• *Show Junior the bathroom is not a playground.* Teach him that this is a place for important, private business. Show him how to properly and hygienically use urinals and toilets. And how to wash hands and properly dispose of towels at the end of every trip to a rest room.

• *Show Junior how to touch and go.* Encourage Junior to use his knuckle or his elbow to press an elevator button or the push bar on a door. Or use his hip, his bottom, or his sneaker, especially when he's just spent twenty seconds washing the germs off his hands.

- *Show consideration for others.* Out of respect for his teachers, tutors, and classmates, keep Junior at home when he has a cold or other upper respiratory or sinus infection that causes excessive coughing, sneezing, or dripping. When he is well enough to go back to school, place small tissue packets and disposable wipes in his pockets, lunch box, and backpack, and remind him to keep his hands to himself.

2

Finding the Best School for Your Child

Everybody's got an opinion about where you should send Wadsworth to school. Dominic down at the deli is convinced the local elementary school is the best place for him. But your mother still believes it was the worst thing she ever did to you.

To find a new school for your child, remember one cardinal rule. It has to be the best fit for him, not Dominic, his grandmother, or his uncle Freddie. "For a school to have the best success with a child, it must be flexible enough to meet the child at his or her own developmental level," says educational diagnostician and school placement counselor Patricia Lemer of Developmental Delay Resources in Pittsburgh, Pennsylvania. "Find schools that are consistent with your child's learning style and acceptable to your educational philosophy," she says.

For Kids of All Ages

Whether or not you choose to involve Wadsworth directly in the school-selection process, at the very least talk to him about the biggest fear most kids have about going to a new school: making friends. Though worrisome to preschoolers and elementary-aged kids, it can cause panic in middle and high schoolers. Don't let it fester. Only after he feels confident that he has some strategies for making new friends can he consider other important aspects of his new school.

Prior to attending a new school, try some of the following ideas to help preschoolers through high schoolers initiate and sustain friendships.

PRESCHOOL TO GRADE FIVE

Even preschoolers have made a friend or two, so start by discussing together the birth and development of some of Wadsworth's current friendships. How did he meet Harry? Talk about the happy accident, shared interests, or love of dogs that brought them together. Then talk about what made the friendship grow. Do this for each important friendship, then help him determine how he might transfer those friend-making tools to his new schoolmates. Talk also about the symbols that might signal a new friend. Does that boy next to him have on a sweatshirt with Wadsworth's favorite baseball team on it? When it comes to an important social skill like making friends, reviewing, strategizing, and planning give your kids the best chance of success.

MIDDLE AND HIGH SCHOOL

In middle and high school, friendships are always paramount, often tenuous, and periodically hurtful. Focus first then on how Wadsworth dealt successfully with past social skirmishes. Reidentify the past problem, clarify the circumstances surrounding it, and then discuss which solution attempts worked best. Did some well-timed, well-aimed retorts cure a bully? Did the timely intervention of a friendly adult ease the situation? Then review Wadsworth's role in resolving the problem. Did his negotiating skills win him a new friend? Enumerating Wadsworth's past social skills and successes will give him the confidence he needs to make friends in the future.

Involving Kids in the School Selection Process

Then, use your own judgment about how much to involve your son, Wadsworth, in the school-selection process. Remember, however, that the more he's involved, the greater his stake in the final decision. And the older the student, the greater his involvement should be.

Selecting schools to visit is the next critical step in the process of finding a new school. Limit the number of visits and entrance tests for kids of all ages to four, advises Patricia Lemer. "You don't want kids to get overloaded and exhausted by visits and tests," she says. "You can visit more yourself and narrow it down for Wadsworth to go to three to five. If he has to go to more than that, you haven't done your homework. You want one sure thing, two probablies, and one long shot," she says. Lemer cautions against picking a school by reputation alone.

Request information about schools by mail or learn about them by searching public or private school websites. Many schools offer brochures, videos, open house events, student visiting days, or family referral networks. Try to visit your selected schools while they are in session. But first, do your homework.

Previsit Homework

The following questions cover a broad range of critical elements to consider when developing your concept of the perfect school for Wadsworth. Review them and make notes and take them along on your visits to help you focus on your goals while you are immersed in the sensory soup of a school.

1. **Will your child be safe?**
2. **What are your educational priorities?**
3. **What is the school's population?**
4. **What is the ratio of teachers to students?**
5. **How accessible are teachers and administrators to students and parents?**
6. **What makes this school unique?**
7. **Which state or private organization accredits or oversees the instruction and curriculum in this school?**
8. **What provisions are made for gifted or special-needs students?**
9. **What are the fees for tuition, books, supplies, labs, or school activities?**
10. **How heavily does the school rely on parent funding for academics, supplies, and extracurricular programs?**
11. **Is the school close to home, or will commuting be a daily grind?**
12. **Does the school provide transportation or coordinate carpools?**
13. **What will transportation cost?**
14. **Is there before- and after-school care?**
15. **Can you afford this school?**

Keep the answers to those questions in mind as you go off to visit your selection of schools. Then use the questions below to guide your observations as you visit each one. Copy these lists and take them along.

Appearance of the School

1. What methods, like visitor passes or school security guards, are in place to make kids feel physically secure?
2. Are the classrooms, hallways, common areas, and bathrooms clean?
3. Is the general noise level constructive or disruptive?

The Classrooms

1. Is class size manageable?
2. Are students participating?
3. Are brains in motion creatively, or do students seem constrained?
4. Can teachers gently and easily regain whole class focus?
5. Do teachers accommodate a variety of learning styles?
6. Do teachers accommodate students with special needs?
7. Do younger students get adequate play and wiggle time during the day?
8. Do older ones get adequate time to move between classes?

Note that many private schools assign students to host visiting students and families. When arranging visits to public schools, make a special request to be introduced to students. Parent introductions can be facilitated by Parent-Teacher Organizations. As you and Wadsworth observe a school or classroom in action, keep the following ideas in mind.

Interpersonal Relationships

1. Are students in the school happy?
2. Do they love going to this school?
3. Do they make and keep friends there?
4. Do kids respect and enjoy their teachers?
5. Do teachers look happy, engaged, and enthusiastic?

6. **Do they treat kids with dignity, respect, and caring?**
7. **Are kids held accountable for their actions?**
8. **Are teachers and administrators visible to and supportive of students?**

Parent-Teacher Organizations

1. **Are parents encouraged to participate in a variety of ways?**
2. **What parent organizations, such as a PTA, exist?**
3. **How active are they?**
4. **What is the relationship between the PTA and the school?**
5. **What recurrent issues does the PTA focus on?**
6. **Does the PTA consistently provide parents with ways to get involved in school activities?**

Many public schools provide testing results and curriculum on state or school district websites. All public schools are ranked by the US Department of Education. Many private schools are accredited by the National Association of Independent Schools (NAIS) and undergo a regular and rigorous evaluation process. All schools should willingly provide rank and testing information if available. If they don't, find another school.

Testing and Programs

1. **How does the school rank according to federal or state indexes?**
2. **Is it accredited by reliable independent evaluators like NAIS?**
3. **What are current test results for the school population?**
4. **Has the school received awards or recognition for excellence?**
5. **Are there exams for admission or for special programs like magnet schools?**
6. **What are graduation requirements?**
7. **Are there advanced placement or International Baccalaureate programs?**

8. What programs and activities recognize individual achievement?
9. Which ones promote individual creativity or effort?
10. Are there programs for students with special needs?
11. Will these programs enhance or disrupt their school day?
12. What is the ratio of computers to students?
13. Is the school's media center/library comprehensive, accessible, and obviously well used? Is staff accessible and helpful?
14. Are art, music programs, and physical education activities a part of the weekly schedule?
15. Are there any performing arts or vocational programs?
16. Are bilingual programs available?
17. At what grade levels are foreign language courses and cross-cultural programs provided?
18. What is the homework policy?
19. Is there a homework hotline?
20. What kind of community service projects is the school involved in?

Evaluation Processes

1. How does the school report student progress? Grades? Do teachers provide anecdotal reports?
2. Are teacher conferences scheduled regularly and available on request?
3. What is the school's "early warning system" for academic problems? Do teachers issue a pink slip or a "letter of concern?"
4. Are tutoring staff or resources available through the school?
5. Is there any cost to you for this?

Pay close attention to fees and expenses at both public and private schools while visiting, to avoid unexpected and unbudgeted expense later on.

Fees and Expenses

1. **What will school cost for an entire year?**
2. **Are there extra fees for books, labs, and gym classes? (Ask even in public schools.)**
3. **Are extracurricular activities and sports teams available?**
4. **Are there any related costs to you?**
5. **Who provides transportation to and from games and other events?**
6. **Are there any costs for this to you?**

Knowing what school normally "feeds" into another is important to insure that the level of Wadsworth's education will be consistent and lay the track you want for him toward college or a future vocation. The broader the picture you have of the community feeding into the school, the better you can determine if this school will support your educational goals and ideals. Ask these questions of a principal, admissions officer, or guidance counselor when you visit a school.

The Feeder System

1. **What schools do students typically attend before and after this one?**
2. **What other schools feed into this one?**
3. **What percentage of students graduate?**
4. **What is the school's reputation among colleges?**
5. **What percentage of students attend colleges?**
6. **Which colleges?**

Visiting Public Schools

Kids who are resilient, comfortable in social situations, and at least somewhat confident about their academic skills often thrive in public schools. The large class size and school population combined with the intense pace could be a nightmare, however, if Wadsworth is fearful and insecure.

Public schools don't have scheduled visiting periods or days as do private schools. Most accommodate prospective families throughout the school year. Students are often invited to sit in if classes are in session, and meetings can be arranged with teachers and school administrators. Call the school principal's office to set an appointment.

Explore special education programs if Wadsworth has physical, mental, emotional, behavioral, or learning disabilities. A federal law, known as the Individuals with Disabilities Act of 1975, requires that public schools provide this service free for families who qualify. To determine if you can receive services, apply to your school first. In what is often a long and drawn-out process, the student and parents as well as classroom teachers, administrators, guidance counselors, and school psychiatrists meet together to identify and evaluate the student's needs and develop an individual educational plan (IEP). Once this process is complete, students are provided with a range of support systems, called "accommodations," like special programs, classes, or even personal instructional aides. IEP's are reviewed and revised at the school's or parent's request. Many families are now seeking the aid of a private educational diagnostician or an education advocate to support them through this complicated process. If you feel you'll need special services for Wadsworth in a public school, don't hesitate to alert the prospective school. They will provide you with contacts in the special education department who can brief you on testing and admissions requirements.

Magnets, Charters, and Vouchers

Investigate these options if your school district provides them, especially if your current public school is below standard.

Magnet schools. Seek this option if your late-elementary through high school-aged child is academically talented or demonstrates deep interest in a specific field of study like science or the arts. Magnet schools are popular and fill up quickly, and wait-lists are not uncommon. Ask your superintendent's office about qualifications and entrance requirements for the magnet program of your choice. If testing is required, note that it is usually administered *the year before* students are admitted to these programs, so plan ahead.

Charter schools. According to the Center for Education Reform in Washington, DC, charter schools are independent public schools, designed and operated by educators, parents, community leaders, or educational entrepreneurs. The curriculum typically reflects the philosophies of the founding group. Charter schools are sponsored by designated local or state educational organizations. Like all public schools, they are free because they receive funding from the district and the state according to the number of students attending. For more information, go to *www.edreform.com*.

Vouchers systems. School "vouchers" redirect the flow of education funding from school districts directly to individual families. This allows families to select the public, private, or religious schools of their choice and have all or part of the tuition paid. Though a new and controversial school choice option, the Supreme Court ruled in June 2002 that the state of Ohio's program does not infringe on the constitutional separation of church and state. A wide variety of voucher systems can be found in states like Minnesota, Iowa, Illinois, Pennsylvania, Florida, and Arizona, and vouchers are a hot political issue in many more. Check the availability or status

of voucher programs by calling the office of your state's superintendent of education. See resources.

Visiting Private Schools

Private schools, also called independent schools, pride themselves
on providing a quality education, small class sizes, and low student-
teacher ratios. However, unlike public schools, which are federally mandated to accommodate kids with all types of needs, don't
automatically expect that all private schools will accommodate
students with special needs. Ask what, if any, supportive programs
they can provide for Wadsworth. Survey 1200 schools nationwide
on the website of The National Association of Independent Schools
at: *www.nais.org*.

Start private school visits the year before you want to enroll
your child. Most schools host open house events in October and
November to highlight programs and provide tours for prospective families. They also typically have admissions personnel who
handle the entry process.

Many private schools charge application fees, which range
from $25 to $100 or more. Most require entrance testing, though
some allow applicants to be tested privately using a psychoeducational battery like the Wechsler Intelligence Scale for Children
(WISC). An increasing number of private schools require that
prospective students for grades 5–11 pass the Secondary School
Admissions Test (SSAT). Find out more about this test at *www.
ssat.org*. Ask about testing fees and test locations for each private
school you visit.

Independent school tuitions can range from as low as $120 a
month for a two-day-a-week private preschool to $4,000 a month
for a private, live-in, therapeutic school for middle and high
school students with severe emotional, social, or psychiatric disorders or substance abuse issues. Yearly tuition in Catholic arch-

diocesan schools can be lower than $2500 per year. Financial aid programs are available in many private schools. Ask about them up front. If you think you might qualify, apply when you fill out your initial application. Know, however, that grants are limited and favor current students.

Vouchers, where available, in combination with established financial aid programs can make the high tuition costs of private schooling more affordable than ever for families at any income level. Check with your state's department of education to see if vouchers are available in your area. See resources.

Single-Sex Schools

An all-boys high school with a strong baseball team might be a great fit if Wadsworth is a hotshot shortstop. A single-sex school might be a viable option for adolescents who are overly distracted or intimidated by the opposite sex. This option is available in independent schools, religion-based schools, and more recently some public schools. For more information, contact the International Coalition of Boys' Schools at 1-216-831-2200 or the National Coalition of Girls' Schools at *www.ncgs.org*.

Homeschooling

Homeschooling is a major undertaking for any family. If you intend to help Wadsworth stay on the median academic pace with his peers nationwide, you should view it as the equivalent of committing yourself to a full-time job. However, teaching Wadsworth at home might be an option if he's recently been put on medication with powerful side effects or if his school doesn't provide programs that support your family's spiritual or moral beliefs. Homeschooling is legal in all fifty states, but many states set restrictions. Some states merely require parents to notify the local school district of their intent to homeschool their child or children. Some states reserve the right to review your proposed curriculum. Since restrictions so widely vary, contact the homeschool office or superintendent's office in your school district. For information and resources on homeschooling, go to *www.eric.ed.gov/archives/homesc2.html*.

Using School Placement Counselors

If the school hunting process sounds like a monster headache, contact a professional. As the popularity and wider accessibility to private schooling grows, prospective parents are increasingly turning to school placement counselors or independent school counselors (ISCs). Through family interviews and student evaluations, they help families select the schools best suited to their children's talents and needs. Some also provide school entrance testing or act as authorized testing centers for groups of private schools. ISCs are certified by the Independent Educational Consultants Association (ICEA). Those with the most experience hold the title, Certified Educational Planner.

The good thing about using an ISC is that they have personal knowledge about the schools they recommend, often spending 25 percent or more of their professional time visiting and developing relationships with schools locally and even nationwide. Many ISCs will orchestrate the application process for the targeted schools. A well-established ISC is usually known by the private schools in the area, and the recommendation of a respected ISC might well aid your efforts to win a coveted spot for Wadsworth.

The bad news, however, is that like private school education, ICS services can be costly. They receive payment from clients, not schools. Their fees can range from as low as $75 to conduct standardized testing to over $2500 for placement in a therapeutic program.

ICEA offers a referral service for thirty-eight states, but few in the Midwest. If one is not available in your area, ask your local school to recommend someone who does private psychological and educational testing. Many do school placement, too. Then, shop around. Conduct phone interviews until you click with one and suspect Wadsworth will, too. You know you've found a good one if, during that first family interview, he or she directs all or most questions to Wadsworth. It means he or she is governed by the undeniable truth that you can't find a perfect school for a child until you know the kid. Contact the Independent Educational Consultants Association at *www.educationalconsulting.org*.

About Switching Schools

What drives a change from one school can be as simple as a transition from elementary to middle school or as serious as a personal safety issue. Sometimes family moves have to be made in a hurry. Employees of large, multinational corporations are often transferred unexpectedly and have to relocate their families on short notice. Likewise, military families must be ready to move quickly when reassignments are made.

Sometimes the child outgrows the school. A lack of academic challenge, insufficient support for special needs, prolonged teasing or bullying situations, or detrimental friendships often make parents and kids seek a new school environment. And rightfully so.

Sometimes the school no longer fits the child, especially if its standards are low. Are there consistently low school test scores and attendance rates? Or too few supplies, unusually easy tests, and little or no homework? Is too much time spent in the classroom and around the school disciplining students instead of teaching them? Are students advanced a grade or do they pass courses despite below-level performance? If your school is showing all or most of these symptoms, it may be time for a move.

Moving around the USA

If your family is moving to another part of the US because of a business transfer within a large corporation or business, contact the human resources department within the company. They will be able to provide you with real estate contacts who can help you coordinate your housing needs with school needs for Wadsworth. Real estate agencies often have detailed information and brochures about area schools. Hedge your bets by contacting the state's Board of Education about schools in your new location, too. During trips to look at housing, walk through the neighborhood and talk to families about local schools. Real estate agents can often provide contacts for you. If everyone in the neighborhood favors the private schools over the public schools, consider this added expense in your housing decisions. The National Center for Education Statistics of the US Department of Education provides a convenient method for researching public schools in your new area, called "Search for Public Schools" at *http://nces.ed.gov/ccd/schoolsearch/*.

Moving out of the USA

If Wadsworth needs a new school because you have been transferred out of the country, consider contacting an international relocation counselor. Most major corporations provide recommendations. Or seek out an international school in your new city. Some of these schools will even permit Wadsworth to use his own textbooks until he learns the local language. Check out School Match at *www.schoolmatch.com* for public or private elementary and secondary schools, international schools, American community schools, boarding schools, or US Department of Defense dependent schools.

Military Moves

Military families or civilian personnel working for the government overseas have schools provided with their transfers. Check out the Department of Defense Education Activity at *www.odedodea.edu/index.htm* for regulations, school information, and contact people worldwide.

Just like any important purchase you make, wise school shopping yields the best results. Make this monumental task manageable by narrowing your options to schools that provide transportation or are within an easy drive from your house. Talk to neighbors, friends, retired teachers, salespeople, and physicians about schools they like. When you call a school that sounds interesting, ask if they can recommend a family who would be willing to share their experiences with you. Then meet them for tea and chat and perhaps make a friend on the inside before you arrive.

3

Form an Alliance with the Teacher

Ollie's behavior sends most teachers from calm to roiling in nine seconds flat. But not Mrs. Kahlmankuhl. She loves Ollie and he loves her. He even allows her to teach him division.

When the bond between kids and teachers is strong and warm, the learning channels blast wide open. It can inspire a math-anxious fourth grader to spout fractions or a moody teen to read poetry. However, when this precious interaction gets fractured, strained, or tense, a kid's learning can slow to a grinding halt.

You can begin to understand the dynamic by listening to how Ollie talks about his teacher. At the elementary level, kids feel a great sense of ownership about their primary or homeroom teacher. They'll frequently provide unsolicited accounts of the teacher's clothes, mannerisms, favorite expressions, or ways of disciplining. Expect this interaction to follow the natural flow of any close interpersonal relationship. Periodic grumbling is natural. Sometimes it's not the teacher's fault, but a change in Ollie's feelings of vulnerability if he's been ill, upset by a home situation, or confounded by a friend. Sometimes the teacher really is at fault. Only carefully listening will reveal important patterns and help you discern your role in this critical relationship.

The following exercises focus on ways kids and parents can form a strong and lasting alliance with any teacher. Use these ideas year after year with the grade levels indicated below.

What Kids Can Do

PRESCHOOL THROUGH GRADE THREE

• *Advise Ollie to listen to how the teacher says his name.* How did his teacher sound when she said, "Ollie," today? Was it soft and sweet? Then, ask him what he did to make her sound that way. Students as early as preschool recognize the difference in tone between approval and disapproval. Then ask if there was a time when her voice sounded differently. Did she ever say, "Ollie!" in a curt, short way? What was he doing when she sounded like that? Help him see the link between his actions and his teacher's reactions. Make a game of it by having him count the ways she says his name during the day. Aim for one more soft, sweet "Ollie" each day.

• *Advise and encourage Ollie to use all his skills.* Teach kids to expand their role in the classroom by using as many of their talents as possible. If Ollie is a detail guy, he might elect to coordinate book clubs or class projects. If he has great spatial skills, he can help his classmates design and plan large posters or displays. If Ollie is a skilled puzzle solver, suggest he use his talents to write mystery stories to share with his class. Teachers adore assistants, no matter their ages.

GRADES FOUR AND FIVE

• *Give Ollie tips on how to monitor his reactions in class.* Adopt a teacher-pleasing behavior technique from driver's education classes. Student drivers are taught to count to three *after* the light turns green before proceeding ahead. Teach kids to wait a count of three seconds before blurting out answers or making disruptive moves. Kids might like to count in their heads or on their fingers or take a deep breath before responding to directions, to invitations to participate, or to transitions between subjects. Deliberately delaying impulses gives kids of all ages more time to exercise self-control.

MIDDLE SCHOOL

- *Show Ollie how to get the homework particulars right.* Teachers are crazy about homework being completed and submitted on time. If Ollie is in middle school and his work has been inconsistent, role-play the night before how a specific teacher will react if work is not submitted or is incomplete. Will she be patient because she knows this kind of assignment gives Ollie trouble? Will his teacher frown because this is missing assignment number three? (Most teachers will forgive one or two, but three starts looking like a pattern.) Brainstorm alternative solutions like getting an extension so he can get the help he needs or asking his teacher for a homework partner. Since adolescents still have a hard time seeing other solutions, don't hesitate to enumerate options for them.

MIDDLE AND HIGH SCHOOL

- *Teach Ollie how to be a better friend.* Teachers are indebted to kids who aren't afraid to extend themselves to someone who's new or confused or someone who helps the class negotiate sticky social situations. To help middle and high school kids learn how to become better friends, have them consider what kind of friend they are. Have Ollie make two columns on a piece of paper and list his positive and negative friendships skills. Which positive skills could he use at school? Which negative characteristic could he change to help his whole class? What good things could happen tomorrow if he changed one of those negative characteristics today? Assign a time, like one week, to institute a change in a negative characteristic. Then, discuss how that change affected a particular friendship.

What Parents Can Do

- *Be an appreciator.* Parents can form stronger bonds with teachers, first by appreciating the monumental task they face. They are responsible for knowing and conveying vast, ever-changing subject areas, raising test scores, working with always-diminishing budgets, and maintaining a safe school environment. They must also tailor lessons and activities to an ever-widening range of student learning styles, behaviors, learning disorders, socioeconomic levels, ethnic backgrounds, and native languages. And "teachers must be there for the children no matter how blue they may be. Parents appreciating all that a teacher must know, do, and be will help cement a strong child-teacher and parent relationship, a union more important than any mega-corporate merger," says psychologist Richard Bromfield of Hamilton, Massachusetts.

- *Submit your own assignments on time.* Teachers esteem those parents who respond immediately to emergency forms, back-to-school letters, permission slips, or appeals for trip chaperones. If you can't get the glue stick Ollie needs in time for his science project, send a note and explain why. Then make a friend by buying some extra ones for classmates who can't afford them.

• *Let your kids do their own assignments.* There is nothing more transparent nor defeating to teachers than homework that was obviously done by a 35-year-old executive, not her nine-year-old child. Doing homework for kids reinforces the notion that it's okay to take credit for someone else's work. And perpetuating the practice often creates resentment or even apathy. Monitor study hours, offer advice and comfort, relay problem areas to teachers as quickly as they occur, but keep your hands off that pencil. If you can't refrain from helping, ask the teacher to recommend ways that won't negate her instruction or thwart Ollie's academic growth. Teachers are eternally grateful to parents who let them do the teaching.

• *Respect school protocol.* Don't do anything to jeopardize your rapport with the person who is your point guard if Ollie has serious learning, developmental, or behavioral needs. The fastest way to torpedo this budding relationship is to take a complaint to the principal before you've met with the teacher. Proper protocol is teacher first. The classroom or homeroom teacher is the one who gathers and coordinates the team of guidance counselors, school psychologists, or school administrators who will create and coordinate Ollie's individual educational plan. Even if it means waiting longer than you'd like for a conference, give the teacher the right to respond before involving school administrators. Use the time you have to document problems and collect samples of Ollie's work. Let a teacher lead the way, and you've gained a comrade.

• *Respect conference etiquette.* Before your leap into your long-awaited agenda, wait for the teacher's input on Ollie's strong and weak areas. Use the same three-count wait suggested above to formulate your answers and provide information and suggestions. Showing good conference manners demonstrates your respect for a teacher's knowledge and experience. Teachers deeply appreciate that.

- *Sit on the right side of the desk.* Don't switch sides of the desk. During conferences, don't try to out teach the teacher. Reading the latest book on science teaching methods will never give you the depth of experience a teacher has had. Offer to share the book instead.

- *Bring food.* Rather than trying to shoehorn a conference into those hectic first weeks of school, drop off some nourishing snacks for the class. Or relieve everyone's stress during days of performance or standardized testing by bringing a bag of apples or bagels or chocolate chip cookies.

- *Be a team player.* Inform Ollie's teacher immediately if there is a situation at home that might impact his behavior or performance at school. In addition to serious problems like a death in the family or an impending separation or divorce, inform teachers about family problems like an older sibling with disruptive behavior problems, the death of a pet, home renovations, or a long business trip out of town.

- *Be a spontaneous helper.* Offer to help, off the cuff. Kids whose parents are actively involved in their education have the best chance of succeeding, so get in there. As your time and energy allow, join parent groups and volunteer to help in the classroom, even if Ollie is in middle or high school. Better yet, offer some unscheduled help. If you find yourself with a few free hours in the coming week, send the teacher an e-mail or voice mail asking if she needs help on Tuesday copying papers, calling trip chaperones, compiling book orders, or setting up for the science fair. Or suggest that while he's grading papers, you play phonics, math, spelling, or vocabulary bingo with the class. You'll be welcomed whenever you help, but you'll make a friend when you offer to off the cuff.

- *Be frank and sincere.* When nothing you or Ollie have tried seems to improve his relationship with his teacher, be frank and sincere about it. But before you admit defeat to Ollie, set up a teacher conference and discuss the issue adult to adult. Sometimes bad chemistry is merely a periodic and mysterious clashing of molecules between two people. In that case, consider bringing in a school counselor or therapist to meet with Ollie, his teacher, and you. In some instances, an objective voice can patch things up so everyone can move along. If the clash can't be resolved in one meeting, meet weekly until it smoothes out. If all else fails, talk with the teacher and the school administrators about getting Ollie switched to another class. Though this is never an easy thing to do, there are times when the best solution is just to give everyone involved a fresh playing field.

- *Make the best of a difficult situation.* Keep your negative comments and feelings to yourself. Only more hard feelings are to be gained by sharing negative opinions about a teacher with your kid. Your words can forever color Ollie's attitude toward and prevent the possibility of any positive turn in the relationship taking place. Kids forgive quickly and forget even faster when an unexpected kindness occurs in a formerly strained relationship. You see this happening with his friends all the time. Allow Ollie and his teacher the chance for reconciliation they both deserve.

Just as importantly, avoid trading war stories with other parents about teachers Ollie has had. Take with a grain of salt any opinions you hear from other parents about upcoming teachers. No one can predict the chemical reaction of two unique personalities. It could be a happier blending than anyone thought possible. Give it a chance.

Tucked in your memory there's probably a teacher you loved— a person who, with a bright smile and a warm word, touched your young heart and opened your mind to learning. It's that magical relationship that can make a reading-repelled sixth grader enjoy Shakespeare or a math-panicked freshman breeze through algebra. When friendships between families and teachers are born, their influence on learning lasts a lifetime whether or not you ever lay eyes on each other again. Do your part to make them happen.

PART TWO

Kindergarten:
Wrestling with Learning
and Behavior

4

How to Discipline When Kids Are Defiant or Loud and Teach Them Self-Control

Pushing his way to the front of the line, Hogan takes down his best friend, Jesse, the hamster cage, and three quarts of orange poster paint. Hogan's body is in kindergarten, but his heart is in professional wrestling.

Kindergarten is a happy, chattering place. Trying new things is exhilarating to the kids, and risk taking is the norm. It's also prime time for Hogan to push his behavior to the limits. Encouraging a little exploration is healthy, but when his actions or words become defiant or his tone becomes loud and rude, it's time to intervene.

The Typical Five-Year-Old

To sort normal behavior from defiant and loud, first, brief yourself on what is normal behavior for five-year-olds. Kids this age take life pretty much at face value. They make judgments based on what they see, not on logical analysis or projection. They often focus on only one aspect and completely overlook other important facts. They can't think through steps and reverse direction, returning to the starting point. In other words, though Hogan sees the orange poster paint splashed all over the hamster cage, he might, quite naturally, have trouble reconstructing how it got there.

Defiant and loud behavior takes many forms; however, the following characteristics are typical. Copy the following boxed items and use them as a guide as you observe him, particularly in large group situations. Then compare notes with his classroom teachers, his art, music, and physical education teachers, and the school secretary and principal.

Then, launch your campaign to help him learn better behavior and self-control by observing him in a group situation at school, with a group of friends at home, or with his cousins at a family event. To get a true sampling of whether poor behavior is characteristic or just a spate of bad days, observe him on four to six separate occasions. Avoid being obvious, if possible.

---------- **IS HOGAN DEFIANT AND LOUD?** ----------

If you answer "yes" to most of the following questions, your child is defiant and loud:

Does he have a never-ending source of reasons why he should always go first?

Does he understand what "no" means?

Does it take him thirty seconds to stop beyond the time he's asked to?

Does he have trouble understanding boundaries and limitations?

Does he always negotiate the rules?

Does he always push rules to the limit without breaking them?

Can his voice usually be heard above the rest of the group?

Does he shout out answers as he raises his hand to respond?

Does he use a raised voice to make his point?

Does he raise his voice when he loses his patience? Or when he has to take turns?

Does he think he's the teacher and boss his classmates?

What Kind of Limits Do You Have?

If you've determined that Hogan's behavior is defiant and loud, it's time to examine your own limits. Just how much challenging behavior are you willing to put up with? Are your limits firm or soft?

Soft limits blur boundaries, make everything negotiable, and constantly redefine the rules. This makes some kids manipulative and others insecure. And most importantly, soft limits neglect the crucial need a five-year-old has for someone he depends on to bring logic and order to the visual kaleidoscope he is still learning to interpret.

Firm limits address the developmental needs of a five-year-old—they show him how to get there and how to get back. By giving him a choice, they reinforce his pivotal role in his own behavior from an early age. They also underscore the notion that good discipline doesn't come from the outside: it is knowing how, when, and where to control yourself. He'll learn this lesson best if you use each behavior challenge as a teaching/learning opportunity.

Test Your Limits

Test your limits with the following checklist, based on the work of psychologist Robert J. McKenzie in *Setting Limits in the Classroom*.

-------------------- **TEST YOUR LIMITS** --------------------

If you answer "yes" to most of the following questions, your limits are soft:

Are you constantly repeating yourself?
Do you make long disciplinary speeches?
Do all your requests begin with "I wish", "I hope", "You should"?
Do they end with "Okay?" or "Is that all right with you?"
Does "no" mean anything but no?

Do you try to reason with a five-year-old?

Do you make deals?

Do you get into pitched disagreements?

Do you beg for favors?

Do you make empty threats?

If you answer "yes" to most of the following questions, your limits are firm:

Do your requests spell it out in no uncertain terms?

Do you keep your voice down?

Do you focus on a specific behavior?

Do you restate the rules?

Are your rules fair?

Do you give the child a choice?

Do you spell out the consequences?

Are you as good as your word?

Discipline Styles

Now that you know your limits, learn your discipline style. Four popular styles are explained below: The Boss, The Give and Take, The Good Buddy, and The Uninvolved. Sample situations and suggested techniques help you see how they might be applied. All these discipline styles are equally good when used appropriately. Do not limit yourself to one disciplinary style. Experiment with them all so that you become fluent and can apply them spontaneously.

Use them alternately as the situation dictates, but not before you've taken a few moments to stand back and evaluate what is going on. Sometimes the best intervention is none at all. However, if Hogan's behavior remains unresponsive to your teaching, get advice from his teacher, the school psychologist, or his physician. Each can help you sort out whether what you're experiencing is natural kindergarten shenanigans or signals of a behavior dysfunction, like attention deficit hyperactivity disorder (ADHD).

THE BOSS

This style is characterized by direct, frequent intervention and the setting of firm, fair rules. Be creative in how you establish your leading role.

- *Refocus on you.* Turn the spotlight back on you. If you suspect Hogan's behavior is just an attention-grabbing device, pull the spotlight back on you. Burst into song, do a soft-shoe around the kitchen, or turn to your cat and describe in detail the kind of behavior Hogan is displaying. Though Hogan might think you've finally lost your mind, you've effectively switched the attention back to you. Now you can reset the course.

- *Repeat, repeat, repeat!* When Hogan is being defiant, make like a CD with a scratch on it and repeat yourself. Stand in front of him in a nonthreatening way (no glaring or pointing), look him in the eye, and give him a command like "Hogan, please stop bellowing so we can talk to each other." Repeat this until he calms down. Later, tell him how many times you had to repeat yourself, and make a plan to keep whittling that number down.

GIVE AND TAKE

This approach gives Hogan a clear message, a few choices, and consequences that will teach him something. It often gives him the means to discipline himself, though adults reserve the right to intervene.

- *Offer rewards.* When Hogan is wrestling with the cat instead of getting his things ready for school, offer to become his wrestling coach. Tell him you'll give him pointers on his holds for five minutes if he takes the next ten to get his backpack and papers ready for school. Deal out something he loves to reinforce his good behavior.

- *Open up his ears.* If Hogan constantly interrupts while you are talking to someone else, give him one chance to stop, using a silent palm-up stop signal. If that doesn't work, motion him over to you and give him an ear massage. Do not interrupt your conversation. While you're talking, massage both his ears simultaneously, gently starting at the top and moving around to the lobes, and then repeat it several times. Sometimes just the attention will quiet him down. Later, have him practice it on himself. Explain that this special massage opens his ears so he can hear important signals about how to behave. Suggest he do this whenever you get on the phone. When he forgets, massage the message into him.

- *Help him learn cause and effect.* When Hogan is being loud or bossy, give him a choice. Say, for example, "You are supposed to be working on your coloring for school. Would you like to finish it quietly, or would you rather have a time-out?" Cause and effect discipline is especially effective when the consequences are immediate.

- *Provide jobs for high-activity kids.* When Hogan's behavior is getting out of hand, give him a job to do, preferably one that will make him sweat a little. If you live in an apartment, give him the job of taking out the trash and dumping it down the trash chute. You get a job done, and he gets a math and science lesson if you both estimate and then count just how long it takes for his old sneaker, a feather, or last night's chicken bones to hit bottom.

GOOD BUDDY

Central to the Good Buddy style is the belief that sometimes, more than discipline, kids like Hogan need an understanding friend. Good Buddy disciplining means providing emotional tools and games that promote self-discipline.

- *Teach your child diplomacy.* When kids hurt each other's feelings, "teach them to use inside thoughts and outside thoughts," says Lisa McPhearson Robinson, a licensed clinical social worker from Bethesda, Maryland. "Outside" thoughts are voiced thoughts that could compliment or help someone. "Inside" thoughts are thoughts best left inside because they might hurt a person's feelings. Role-play situations or read stories that illustrate the terms. Encourage kids to observe faces for responses that silently signal the effect of their words. When an inside thought accidentally pops outside, teach them to seek a pardon with the words, "I'm sorry."

- *Get your child moving.* Exercise is a gentle way to help kids whose misbehavior results from a short attention span or ADHD. Show Hogan some simple yoga stretches or the easy calf-stretching or shoulder-loosening exercises that joggers do to warm up. Teach him an exercise based on the ancient Chinese martial art called "chi gong." He takes a deep breath and raises his arms slowly straight up over his head. He then exhales slowly, bringing his arms all the way down until his fingers touch his toes. He should repeat this slowly three times. Teach Hogan to rely on his breath and his muscles to help him focus whenever a stressful situation threatens to shatter his attention.

Uninvolved

The Uninvolved style recognizes that sometimes classroom antics aren't entirely Hogan's fault. Occasionally, it's the toys, supplies, and equipment that make matters worse. Uninvolved disciplining provides structures that silently reinforce rules or creatively reengineer the way things are used.

- *Design for easy clean up.* When kids won't clean up or take care of their toys or equipment, look to the toys and equipment. Is there a better way they could be stored or used? Italian educator Maria Montessori was one of the first to set up classrooms so that proper use of supplies was engineered into the design. Taped circles on the floor show students just where to sweep in left-to-right circles with their brooms. Small towels or rugs delineate individual work areas for math or reading games. Julia Child, the famous chef, made utensil outlines on the Peg-board in her kitchen to show where every item should be placed. Yogurt containers of all sizes, for example, can be tacked to a corkboard or Peg-board and filled with an ever-changing array of supplies Hogan needs to complete his hobbies or schoolwork. The Uninvolved discipline style relies on structures and organizational systems, not words, to reinforce good behavior.

Though learning a variety of discipline styles might sound like lots of work, you gain a wealth of options for dealing with the everyday tussling matches in Hogan's young life. With lots of practice opportunities, which he will happily provide, your disciplining confidence will soon grow. Adapt your methods to fit each situation and the growing needs of your child, and then apply them wisely and surely. And perhaps a path that began at a kindergarten wrestling match will one day lead him to a governor's mansion.

5

How to Tell If Your Child Has an Attention Disorder and What to Do about It

Sam's kindergarten report card says that if he weren't inattentive, hyperactive, and impulsive, he would be Plato.

Do you know the warning signs of an attention deficit disorder? Though sitting still, paying attention, and controlling impulses are hard for all kids sometimes, when they disrupt schoolwork, home life or friendships, they might be signaling a disorder called attention deficit/hyperactivity disorder (ADHD). It affects 3 to 5 percent of all school-aged kids, says CHADD, a national organization that supports children and adults with attention deficit/hyperactivity disorder (*www.chadd.org*).

Hyperactivity was first documented in 1902. Today, though the cause of ADHD is still unknown, and there is no single test to diagnose it, criteria for determining it are very clearly spelled out by the American Psychiatric Association. Using those guidelines, professionals like school psychologists, social workers, or neurologists take careful histories from parents, teachers, and sometimes even kids themselves. Medical exams, including hearing and vision tests, also help determine whether other conditions are causing symptoms that look like ADHD. Developing a detailed picture of a child's academic, social, and emotional functioning and developmental level helps determine whether the disorder exists or rules out other causes for it.

There are three types of ADHD. The first is characterized by symptoms that involve mostly "inattentive" behavior, the second by those that involve mostly "hyperactive-kinesthetic" behaviors, and a third "combined" type in which kids' symptoms span characteristics of both primary types.

The "Six Rule" for Determining ADHD

Six is a key number to remember when considering whether Sam might have an attention disorder. Kids around the age of *six* who display at least *six* of the nine characteristics in either type consistently over a *six*-month period might have ADHD. These behaviors must be causing difficulty in at least two or more areas of the child's life, like school life or home life or friendships.

Does your child fit the six rule for the "inattentive" type of ADHD? Characteristic behaviors are:

Fails to give close attention to details or makes careless mistakes

Has difficulty sustaining attention

Does not appear to listen

Struggles to follow through on instructions

Has difficulty with organization

Avoids or dislikes tasks requiring sustained mental effort

Loses things

Is easily distracted

Is forgetful in daily activities

Does your child fit the six rule for ADHD of the "hyperactive-kinesthetic" type? Characteristic behaviors are:

Fidgets with hands or feet or squirms in chair

Has difficulty remaining seated

Runs about or climbs excessively

Difficulty engaging in activities quietly

Acts as if driven by a motor

Talks excessively

Blurts out answers before questions have been completed

Difficulty waiting or taking turns

Interrupts or intrudes on others

Behavior Strategies

While you're debating whether to have a formal evaluation or awaiting the results of one, implement some behavior strategies that will bolster Sam's attention skills right now. The National Institute of Mental Health's research shows that kids with attention deficits improve when behavior interventions become a routine part of their day. They work, too, for kids who have only periods of inattention. The following ideas are targeted for grades kindergarten through two:

Get tutoring. To ensure that Sam's skills don't lag behind his behavior, get a tutor. Find someone energetic and bright who connects with him and feels positive about him. A tutor provides an unbiased, objective, professional perspective that will help you see how Sam processes and functions when his focus is funneled by a one-to-one relationship. He or she can also help a fledgling student like Sam identify his learning style and favorite methods for studying, like singing his spelling words. Tutoring keeps his skills progressing while you investigate what's interrupting his attention.

Lower the stimulation. Does his daily schedule look like a corporate president's? Overstimulation can fragment his attention. Carve out some completely unstructured time for him. Let his own natural energy, curiosity, and creativity inspire inventive ways to fill his time. When was the last time he dug a hole to China in the backyard?

Build a behavior team. Gather a behavior management team consisting of all the important adults in Sam's life. Enlist his teacher first. Schedule a conference that includes Sam. Let the teacher know in advance that your objective is to coordinate a behavior plan that links home and school. Encourage team members to help you incorporate the following strategies into Sam's life.

Draw the line. For Sam's benefit, assert your authority out loud. Say, "You are not in charge here. I am," coaches Gary Spivack, child psychiatrist with Columbia Associates in Arlington, Virginia. When Sam forgets, teachers, parents, grandparents, aunts, uncles, and even babysitters need to make their roles clear, nicely, firmly, and repeatedly until he understands. Kindergarten and first grade kids like Sam play best when they know who is making the rules. Be the boss.

Define your terms when giving him directions. If you've ever watched five- and six-year-olds playing a game in a group, you know that they set rigid rules, then vigorously maintain and defend them. Take advantage of this natural tendency to explain, for example, what "Be good!" means in various situations. Does it mean not watching TV for more than thirty minutes when the babysitter comes? Does it mean walking quietly down the hallways and not shoving the person ahead of you in line at the water fountain? You are speaking his language when you s-p-e-l-l out the rules.

Uncover Sam's most disruptive behaviors. Explain to him what his body is doing so he can hear it. "Sam, you are using your fists to punch the pencil sharpener." Isolating the behaviors provides focus. Verbally connecting his body to his behavior helps him understand that self-control takes not only eyes and brains, but bones and muscles.

Make yourself clear. Give him clear, practical reasons why he can't head-butt his sister. Say, "You can't hit your sister like that because you will hurt her," advises Spivack. Drive home the idea that certain actions have consequences.

Make it a game. Choose some nonverbal cues to signal Sam about his behavior. If he likes football, try using referee signals. Just as he is about to karate chop his best friend, touch the back of your knee (clipping). If he takes your cue and stops, reward him with a soft high five and a gain of five yards. If he doesn't stop, give him a five-yard penalty. Child behavior management experts suggest tracking incidents on a paper chart for a five- to eight-day period. Remember that keeping your signals subtle and his scores private makes it seem like good fun and takes the negative spotlight off Sam.

Build in the perks. Tally up Sam's yardage at the end of the day. To reinforce the team effort, yardage gained at school can be worth rewards at home and vice versa. You and Sam might decide that a 15-point gain is a winning behavior day.

Change the angle. At school, ask the teacher if Sam can change positions to do his work, especially if the assignment is challenging. Most elementary classrooms have separate areas for quiet reading or working on art projects. Can he stand up at his table or desk to complete a math worksheet? Sit on a stool to listen to a story? Lie on the rug to read a book?

At home, when he's having an attention-challenged day, let him do his math sheet perched on the kitchen counter or study his spelling words while riding his bike around the garage. Just like adults who get up from their chair to pace and think, Sam's concentration will be refreshed when demanding work is viewed from a brand-new angle.

Let him do some muscle work. Sensory integration therapists believe that kids who have overstimulated or understimulated sensory systems can become hyperactive or inattentive. Carrying objects that give "sustained deep muscle stimulation is calming to kids who have trouble knowing where their body is in space," says Colette Silver of Chevy Chase, Maryland, an occupational therapist who specializes in sensory integration.

Make sure that the objects kids carry are not so big that they "get them out of breath or are a big deal. Use things they can carry for a while like a backpack or dictionary," says Silver, noting that it is more calming if they can carry something half as heavy twice as far.

Give Sam a lunch box with a full thermos to carry to school each day. Encourage him to tote his school supplies in a pack on his back or a bag on his shoulder instead of using a small wheeled backpack. Suggest to the teacher that Sam get the classroom job of handing out and replacing science books or upending student chairs on the desktops at the end of the day so the school support staff can clean the floors.

Make teacher conferences routine. Parents and teachers should get together regularly to critique and amend their behavior game plan. Set a schedule, no longer than a month, to meet throughout the school year. When time is tight, use voice mail or e-mail.

Lastly, make some behavioral changes of your own that will help Sam. Make an effort to become a regular fixture at school. You hear things immediately if you happen to be somewhere in the school helping out. And immediately is the perfect time to amend Sam's behavior plan.

Behavior intervention programs are a no-wait way to support Sam's attention skills. So bring on the team. A coordinated behavior campaign conducted by caring adults can make a constructive difference in the life of a cantankerous six-year-old. Try a new angle or speak in sports metaphors to help Sam get a firm grip on his attention. Then sit back and smile as he reaches each and every goal.

6

How to Bolster Budding Language Skills

Writing letters and learning phonics makes Claudia cranky. She recently grumbled, "I hope I won't have to read too many books once I get to first grade."

When handwriting, phonics drills, and endless workbook pages yield little more than aggravation for kindergarten kids like Claudia who are learning to read, try something foreign. A foreign language, that is, to bolster her budding language skills in English. You can do it even if you don't *habla español*.

Learn a Foreign Language

Learning a second language in kindergarten or first grade isn't a foreign thing. As a matter of fact, in terms of brain growth, it's prime time. Pediatric neurologist Harry Chugani, Director of the Children's PET Center at the Children's Hospital of Michigan in Detroit, believes that the time to learn foreign languages is in preschool and elementary school when the chemistry of the brain is charged for it. Using PET (positron emission tomography) scans to measure brain activity, Chugani found an increase in glucose in the brains of kids between the ages of four and ten. This "brain spurt" signals high activity and receptivity. "When we postpone learning foreign language until high school, we aren't paying attention to biological phenomenon," he says.

When kids compare a foreign language to their own, they begin to understand the nature of language itself. As far back as 1961, studies found that English-speaking students who received instruction in a foreign language showed gains in tests of English grammar, reading, and even math.

More recently, a 1994 study of 100 third-grade students in the Pittsburg, Kansas, public schools, showed significant gains in students' language and math on the Metropolitan Achievement Test after receiving only half-hour Spanish lessons three times weekly during the course of one semester.

"Learning a foreign language increases creativity and cognitive skills. Benefits from early language instruction include improved overall school performance and superior problem-solving skills. The more children learn about a foreign language, the more they understand about their own language," says Nancy Rhodes, Director of Foreign Language Education at the Center for Applied Linguistics in Washington, DC. Most importantly, "foreign language is for all children of any ability," she says. Even kids who get cranky over phonics.

Learning a foreign language early also builds a bridge between cultures. "At an early age, cultural differences are viewed as different and interesting, not right or wrong," says Harriet Barnett, an educational consultant for the American Council on the Teaching of Foreign Languages. "This early exposure to other ways of speaking and doing things is most effective when children are young and their minds are open," she says.

Several major types of elementary school foreign language programs, summarized below, have emerged in public and private schools. They vary widely, however, from school to school. If none exists in your school, use the resources that follow for help in establishing a program.

FOREIGN LANGUAGE IN THE ELEMENTARY SCHOOL (FLES) PROGRAMS

This is the type of language program most frequently offered at the elementary level. Taught as an individual subject like math or science, classes are typically held three to five times weekly for 20–30 minutes. FLES programs focus on listening, speaking, reading, and writing as well as the culture of the country. As noted above, students who participated in this type of program for two years showed gains in English language skills.

FOREIGN LANGUAGE EXPLORATORY PROGRAMS (FLEX)

Taught in a shorter time frame than FLES programs, this type of program provides an introduction to one or more foreign languages but doesn't teach for fluency. FLEX programs give kids exposure to and experiences related to another culture and provide a good basis for learning a foreign language in a long-term program. Kids will not attain fluency in this type of program.

IMMERSION PROGRAMS

English-speaking kids spend all or part of the school day learning their basic subjects in a foreign language. In these programs, the language is the medium for instruction rather than a subject itself.

In "partial immersion" programs, time spent in a foreign language is 50 percent of the day throughout the elementary grades. In the partial-immersion program in Fairfax County Schools in northern Virginia—one of the largest in the United States with three thousand students in thirteen schools—kindergarten through sixth grade students spend half of their school day learning math, science, and health in Japanese, French, German, or Spanish. The rest of the curriculum is taught in English. Students with six years in the program have the fluency of a five- or six-year-old in that foreign language. Studies reveal that students perform equally well in testing with the bonus of learning another language.

In "full immersion" programs, time spent in a foreign language is 100 percent a day in the early grades with English phased in anywhere from second grade to fifth grade. However, optimum fluency results when use of English doesn't exceed 20 percent a day.

TEACHING A FOREIGN LANGUAGE AT HOME

Rather than a school-based program, you can introduce Claudia to a foreign language at home. It might be easier than you think, particularly if you pick a language that holds special meaning for your family. If, however, she shows an interest in learning a totally new foreign language, that's prime time for learning a new language together. And for finding a book she won't mind reading once she gets to first grade!

Start by taking yourself to the library or your neighborhood bookstore to look for books, cassettes, videos, or CDs, or on the Internet to help you teach a foreign language to kids like Claudia, aged 4–8. The following are excellent examples of many on the market:

1. *Learn Italian Together: An Activity Kit for Kids and Grown-Ups, Ages 4–8* by Marie-Claire Antoine, published by Living Language. Package containing an activity book, cassette, and learning stickers. A teacher's guide is also available.

2. *Berlitz for Travelers.* Cassette series recommended by FLEX teachers for helping teachers and parents learn proper pronunciation. Berlitz Multimedia Publishing.

3. *Picture Word Book.* Versions in English, French, Hebrew, German, Italian, and Spanish. Dover Publications, Inc.

4. *All-in-One Language Fun!* CD-ROM for ages 3–12 which uses native speakers and colorful graphics but no reading, writing, or spelling. Syracuse Language Systems at 800-797-5264.

5. *Romance Language Resource Page.* University of Chicago program using native speakers to teach samplings of French, Italian, Portuguese, and Spanish at *www.humanities.uchicago.edu/ humanities.*

When you work on a foreign language with kindergarten students like Claudia, use a popular foreign language instructional method called Total Physical Response (TPR). Its multisensory approach responds well to the needs of a broad range of learning styles and differences.

In the TPR method, listening is what promotes language acquisition, and it must precede speaking. In other words, you do the speaking and she does the listening, at first. But don't let the phonics of a new language make you cranky either. Show Claudia that listening, mimicking, and practicing soothes even the wildest and strangest new letter combinations. Let her respond at her own pace.

Rely on familiar objects and experiences in your work together. Incorporate short lessons (10–20 minutes) into her normal routine several times a week. For example, play language games when you're driving together to the supermarket or at bedtime.

Foreign Language Activities,
Grades Four through Eight

To prepare for the activities below, find and use examples from your selected books, cassettes, videos, CDs and Internet resources.

- *Listen to a song sung in another language.* The cadence and rhythm of music are echoed in language, and native singers melodiously model proper pronunciation. Play a song several times as she helps you make lunch or feed the dog. After several days you will probably be singing the chorus together. Find an excellent selection of Arabic songs in the music CD entitled, *Cairo to Casablanca: An Arabic Musical Odyssey*, published by Putumayo World Music in 1998.

- *Count aloud the proper amount of string beans for dinner, in Swahili.* The Swahili numbers and pronunciations from zero to ten are *sifuri* (see-foo-ree), *moja* (mo-jah), *mbili* (m-bee-lee), *tatu* (tah-too), *nne* (nay), *tano* (tah-no), *sita* (see-tah), *saba* (sah-bah), *nane* (nah-nay), *tisa* (tee-sah), and *kumi* (koo-mee). When she's comfortable, she might join you in counting how many mateless socks there are in the laundry basket.

- *Play pick-up-sticks in Spanish.* This game not only introduces a foreign language but helps Claudia strengthen fine motor coordination for handwriting, using scissors, and pinching her little brother. As she jiggles a stick or retrieves it successfully, say the color aloud, in Spanish. Some Spanish color names and pronunciations are red: *rojo* (ro-ho); blue: *azul* (ah-sool); green: *verde* (vair-day); white: *blanco* (blahn-koh); black: *negro* (neg-roh); yellow: *amarillo* (ah-ma-ree-yo); orange: *naranja* (na-ran-ha); purple: *morado* (moh-ra-doh); and pink: *rosado* (ro-sah-dough).

- *To aid her memory of new vocabulary words, get her physically involved in the new language.* Point to the pizza in front of her and say, "Pizza," and then point to her mouth and make chewing motions and say, *"Mangia!"* As she chews on a big, gooey piece, say *"mangia* pizza!" meaning "You eat pizza!" in Italian. At the grocery store, put an apple in her hands and say in Italian, *"Mela"* (maylah). Then, print a label that says, "I sit" in Italian: *siedo* (see-yay-dough). Holding the *"siedo"* sign against your chest, sit in a chair and slowly say, *"Siedo in la sedia."* Make a label that says, "I jump" in Italian: *salto* (saal-toe). Then jump up and down. Make one for run, catch, and pinch, and do the actions as you say the words. Getting her body involved increases retention by helping her associate the muscle movements with the words.

- *Use a recent close-up photo of her or a family member to show Claudia the parts of her face in a foreign language.* In Italian, some facial features are eye: *occhio* (okk-yo); nose: *nasso* (nah-so); mouth: *bocca* (boh-ka); and chin: *mento* (men-toe).

- *Eat lunch in a Japanese restaurant and order some foods in Japanese.* Be sure to let your server in on your language lesson. Many are only too happy to become teachers, too. Many common food words were adapted from English. Soup: *supu;* chop: *choppu;* sauce: *sosa;* salad: *sarada;* lemon: *remon;* and dessert; *dezato.*

- *Shop at a Chinese grocery store.* The sights, conversation, and colorful letters on the signage will give Claudia a sensory introduction to a delicious part of Chinese culture: the food. Discover new vegetables together like a long, brown root we call burdock but the Chinese call *"gobo* (go-bo)." A trip down the dessert aisle will show her that Chinese kids love sweets, too, especially fat steamed buns called *"mántóu* (man toh)."

• *If possible, take Claudia on a trip to a non-English-speaking country.* Let her see that another language isn't a foreign thing at all, merely the unique sounds people use to communicate to each other their feelings, needs, and desires. Teach her a few words she can use to greet hotel or restaurant staff.

RESOURCES FOR GROUPS

If your school does not offer foreign language programs in the early grades, take heart and take the lead!

Parent groups who can garner community interest and support for starting elementary language programs in their schools can get guidance and start-up details from the following resources:

1. Resources on Foreign Language Learning in Grades K-8. The Nanduti website sponsored by the Center for Applied Linguistics and the Brown University Regional Educational Lab at *www.cal.org/earlylang*

2. The National Network for Early Language Learning at the Center for Applied Linguistics in Washington, DC. E-mail *nnell@cal.org*, or phone 202-362-0700.

3. The FLES Institute in Baltimore, Maryland, by fax at 301-230-2652.

4. The American Council on the Teaching of Foreign Languages at *www.actfl.org*

Learning a foreign language is an age-appropriate, sensory-rich endeavor that paves the way to stronger language skills even for preschoolers. There is also no better time than right now to engage Claudia in lessons that will deepen her understanding and respect for other cultures. And keep her happily working on phonics and reading far beyond first grade. *Andiamo!*

Another Way to Bolster Budding Language Skills—
Hire a Tutor with a Golden Edge

When poor attitude or reluctance to read threatens to nip your kindergarten or first-grade student's reading skills in the bud, consider a reading-trained, senior-aged tutor. Senior tutoring is tutoring with a golden edge because:

1. Most tutors are retired and have available time.

2. They provide the nurturing grandparent factor.

3. They have stricter standards of behavior and expect the child to act accordingly.

4. They are motivated by the experience of working one-on-one with young students.

5. They become an advocate for the child.

6. Many senior-tutoring programs are free of charge.

It works! An annual survey by the Older Adult Service and Information System (OASIS) of their twenty-one city, nationwide tutoring program as well as a three-year study of senior-tutored first graders in Cambridge, Massachusetts, found that students in such programs gained in the following ways:

1. Improved attitudes toward reading and language arts

2. Increased class participation

3. Greater willingness to read aloud

4. Heightened self-esteem

5. Longer attention span

6. Better verbal skills

7. More completed homework assignments

8. Higher test scores

9. Improved attendance

10. Kids learned to like books

Many senior-tutoring programs are not only free of charge, but they are also personal and convenient. OASIS tutors provide one-to-one, forty-five minute sessions once weekly in the student's school. Investigate intergenerational tutoring programs at your local school, faith-based organization, civic group, or senior organization, or use the resources below.

RESOURCES

OASIS Intergenerational Tutoring Program, Nationwide Locations: (314) 862-2933 or *www.oasisnet.org*. Ask city program coordinators about local referrals.

Generations United: a resource for one hundred intergenerational tutoring programs nationwide at *www.gu.org*. Search by US Postal Service state codes like PA, CA, or NJ.

PART THREE

Grades One through Three: Getting a Handle on School

7

What to Do When Kids Are Disorganized

In the first six weeks of school, Charlie lost four library books, forgot eleven math assignments, and has an odor coming from his backpack that makes you think of Limburger cheese.

Just like math, reading, and writing, organization consists of a subset of skills that must be taught. Though some kids are neat by nature, most need guidance, supplies, and systems to help them efficiently organize their papers, places, tasks, and time.

Organizational Skills for Grades One through Three

Teaching organizational skills to kids in first through third grade is a good match for their developing cognitive, motor, and sensory skills. It also pivots on order, which they love. As anyone who's ever taught first grade knows, they are sticklers about rules, schedules, and routines, which are core elements in all organizational systems.

But if you think you can be disorganized and teach organization, think again. Six- to eight-year-olds process information in a logical way, especially when it is presented to them in a concrete, visible form. In other words, if Charlie sees that you don't make your bed, he won't make his. So the first step is to make your bed each day.

Being conscious of muscle and motor development also helps you match organizational activities and systems to growing abilities. Girls at this age have more developed small motor coordination than boys, which makes it easier for them to make precise movements, especially with their hands. So filing systems, pigeonholes in desks, or small-drawered cabinets would be appropriate and comfortable for girls this age. Boys are slightly behind in small motor development at this age, but ahead in the large muscle skills requiring force and power. So incorporating lifting, moving, rearranging, reaching, and pulling actions into Charlie's organizational plan would be right up his alley.

But no matter whether you are helping a boy or girl, every organizational plan should be guided by two unchanging principles: it relieves stress in kids' lives and involves them at each step. Does Charlie have a tough time getting himself together on school mornings? Does he get upset because he invariably leaves his homework on the desk right next to the clean soccer uniform for his game today? Teaching him organizational skills helps reduce the stress he suffers from not having the assignments and supplies he needs for a successful day.

The greater the stake Charlie has in the organizational systems you create together, the more effective and long-lasting the effects will be. Sit down together and make a plan of action that suits his developmental level and his needs. Organization gives kids the handholds they need to successfully move through their stuff, their places, and their time—not only in their classrooms and homes but in how they study and complete homework assignments, too.

The following suggestions, plans, and projects are targeted to kids in grades one through three.

REINFORCE THE UNDERLYING SKILLS

Logic, order, and sequence are at the root of organizing, so focus on those as you work with Charlie. Simple household activities like setting the table not only reinforce these skills but give him practice in assembling supplies and preparing a place for a specific activity, two essential organizational skills for completing homework and studying for tests. Eating utensils, incidentally, are placed in the same order as reading and writing, from left to right. Current etiquette dictates the following placement, moving from left to right: napkin, salad fork, dinner fork, and then the plate, knife, and spoon.

Design-conscious kids might enjoy folding cloth or paper napkins in unique shapes as seen in restaurants or at formal occasions. To complete the shape correctly, directions must be followed precisely and in the order presented. This process mirrors the same skills needed for completing class work, assignments, or tests. *Folding Napkins* by Gay Merrill Gross has clear diagrams easy for early readers to follow. If not into napkins, Charlie might enjoy instead the Japanese art of paper folding called *origami. Easy Origami* by Dokuohtei Nakano includes some excellent designs and text, which third graders can read independently.

BACK-TO-SCHOOL ORGANIZING

Take inventory. Before you go racing out to buy new school clothes, take inventory of what Charlie already has. Visual proof is hard to deny and it might save you money. On Charlie's bed, assemble his "school" clothes like uniforms or shirts with collars and the pants, belts, and shoes that he'll need to wear for special events. Stack up everyday clothes like t-shirts, socks, underwear, sweatpants, vests, sweaters, jackets, coats, and sneakers. Then, count them and have Charlie record the totals on a piece of paper. Then, together, appraise his supply. Does he really need new t-shirts when he already has fifteen perfectly good ones? Go through the same process with school supplies like notebook paper, pencils, erasers, construction paper, and so on. Now you can make a more realistic shopping list.

Call your school. Next, call your school or check out their website to see if grade-level school supply lists are available. Teachers often provide lists for their classes. It's better to find out before you buy one that the enormous neon blue notebook he so desperately wants is banned because it won't fit in his desk at school.

Make a school budget. This simple exercise will teach Charlie the rudiments of personal finance like spending within his means, prioritizing, wage earning, and making decisions about how to allocate his money. Though you don't have to be specific about your school spending budget, Charlie needs to know that there is a set limit to what you will spend. Begin by listing the clothes and supplies he needs as he saw from the piles you made together above. Next, brainstorm the gizmos and gadgets he's positive he'll need to get good grades this year. Prioritize this list and select the top one to purchase now. The rest of the list he can purchase from his allowance or with the money he gets from walking the neighbor's dog.

Make a school-morning routine. If Charlie has trouble getting out of the house on school mornings, make a plan that lays out the steps in plain sight. Because they are such a big part of first-grade classrooms, large posters with big letters are familiar vehicles for conveying information. Use one to make a chronological list of steps that need to be completed each morning. As he completes each phase, have him do a karate kick and an energy shout to signal you that he's moving through his list. Or help him develop his small motor coordination by keeping a wad of plastic putty in a jar near the list so he can pull off a wad and affix it next to tooth-brushing when he's finished with his teeth. He can remove them when he returns home each afternoon. Sticker-happy kids will gladly and easily use them to mark each step completed.

PAPER MANAGEMENT

Get on top of the paper pipeline at school. Many schools reserve a day each week for sending newsletters to parents. Find out if and when your school does and ask Charlie for it when he comes home from school that afternoon. To give primary graders a feel for long-term assignments, some schools provide weekly home-work books which outline spelling, handwriting, or reading assignments for each night. This is an excellent way to keep track of his paperwork and also a fine place for making notes about his work to his teacher.

Get plastic boxes in different colors for all Charlie's pertinent papers. Place them in a convenient spot where he can unload his backpack each day after school. Label boxes for completed school and homework, Spanish classes, piano lessons, parent informa-tion, and sports schedules. Pitching papers into the right box gives him a chance to perfect his eye-hand coordination. And to make sure the paper lands in the right box, he must skim the page, a crucial reading and organizational tool. On Fridays, make it a habit to clear the boxes out to make room for the next week. Then have Charlie exercise his muscles to carry the load out to the trash. Along with his boxes, this is also a logical place for a coat hook, boot rack, and box for sports equipment.

Make Charlie's place for school supplies inviolable and logical. That home could be in his desk in his room or a drawer of the kitchen hutch near the table where he does his homework. Better yet, ask Charlie where he thinks his glue sticks, paper, markers, paper clips, rubber bands, and scissors could be safely stored. Make it a rule that if things don't make it back to his special place, you are not responsible for locating them. He is.

Do not keep every paper. Establish a routine each week to edit and pitch unnecessary papers like graded homework papers, old assignment sheets, and outdated reminders. Or do it each night when Charlie comes home from school. Keep samples of good work and tests for teacher, tutor, or counselor conferences. If Charlie can't bear to part with anything, do your paper edits when he is not around.

SPACE MANAGEMENT

Charlie's trouble with stuff might be that he has too much of it. If something hasn't been used for a year, it probably won't be used again. Trouble is, kids, like adults, develop emotional attachments to their belongings. To gain control over the encroaching load, take one weekend day each season to do some seasonal edits. Tell Charlie it's to make space for the things each new time of year brings.

Once a year, do a major edit. Even primary graders can help you with the process described in detail below.

You'll need four large cardboard boxes, tape, marking pens, a pad, and a pencil. Before you begin the editing process, label the four boxes: give it, store it, toss it, keep it. The "keep it" box might be clear plastic with a hinged lid for easy viewing and accessing later. When you're finished, help Charlie haul the boxes to the garage, his room, or the trash as determined by their labels.

Use the following questions to walk him through the editing process:

1. Is this valuable if it's broken?

2. Is this valuable if you haven't used it since preschool?

3. Is this valuable if you don't remember how to use it?

4. Is this valuable if you can't remember whether it's yours or your sister's?

5. If this is important to you, why is it buried in the bottom?

6. When was the last time you played with this?

7. Do you think you might be too old for this now?

8. Can we donate it to kids who don't have one?

TASK MANAGEMENT

Especially when organizing kids' time, setting time limits is just as important as defining what is to be accomplished within the given time.

Take fifteen minutes at the start of each day or new project to detail and prioritize the tasks. Previewing plans, actions, and areas that need special attention gives Charlie, and you, a chance to head off problems and prepare the best start to each new day or assignment. Don't forget to schedule some free time in each day.

Make plans visual and auditory. Jot plan notes on an erasable board in a high traffic area at home. Then review them aloud as you walk him or drive him to school each day. Don't hesitate to repeat yourself. When he finishes your sentences, it means he's heard you.

Define the parameters. First graders, especially, need directions spelled out and not just when they're misbehaving. To check that he understands the parameters of a given situation, ask him to explain what it means, for example, to be "ready for school each morning." Spelling it out avoids trouble-brewing assumptions.

Make a rule in your house that the pile on the floor belongs to who-ever made it. Don't thank Charlie for helping you when he cleans up after himself. Instead, tell him it's just another sign of the big first grader he is now.

Last but not least, if organized is one thing that you will never be, hire someone to help you get Charlie on the right track. Professional organizers will come to your home, conduct careful interviews, and design systems that will help Charlie, and you, become more effi-cient and productive. Many specialize in working with children. Most charge an hourly fee and work a minimum number of hours, typically three. Some organizers will schedule "maintenance" calls several months later to evaluate and amend their plans. The Na-tional Association of Professional Organizers (NAPO) provides nationwide referrals. Call NAPO Information and Referral Hot-line at 512-206-0151 or e-mail *napo@assnmgmt.com*.

Teaching Charlie how to get organized might start with mak-ing your bed, but it doesn't end there. The logic, sequence, and order essential to arranging his spaces, stuff, tasks, and time are found in the most common household activities. As you do dishes, iron a shirt for school, or follow a recipe for his favorite peanut butter cookies, walk him through the logical, orderly, sequential stages of each operation. And in easy and time-saving ways, you'll forge organizational skills that will take him far and forever be-yond a sock- and cheese-scented backpack.

8

How to Prepare for Standardized Tests

Test-taking has the same effect on Nathan that a potent potion once had on a bright young doctor—he grows hair and fangs and howls like a werewolf all night long.

Don't let testing make a beast of Nathan. Whether it's a needle-toting nurse poking his soft flesh or a standardized group test at school, testing can rattle a kid's nerves, no matter his age. Helping students prepare for formal evaluations goes beyond making sure they memorize facts or get a good night's sleep before test day. To help your son turn back into the bright and bouncing third grader you love, establish a pre-testing environment that will give him the mental, emotional, and physical support he needs to do his best whenever he's tested.

If Nathan is a third grader in public school, he will have a group standardized test this year. He will likely only take an individual battery of tests if you or his teachers suspect problems like a developmental or learning delay or an attention deficit disorder. Use the following to familiarize yourself with the two major kinds of standardized tests. Within each section find suggestions for establishing a supportive pre-testing environment. Lastly, find tips for defanging any testing situation.

Group Standardized Testing

Unlike teacher-made tests, standardized tests have precise procedures for administering, timing, and scoring. Under the federal
No Child Left Behind Act of 2001, standardized testing is not required until grade three, when most kids are expected to know
how to read. This federal act mandates annual testing in reading
and math of kids in grades three through eight. However, many
school districts also administer standardized tests to grades one
and two.

As a third grader in a public school, Nathan will have a grade-
level battery of standardized tests in reading, math, language,
spelling, science, and social studies. Standardized tests given at
school are typically "norm-referenced." This means his scores are
compared to the average performance of a large reference group,
or "norm group," of students of similar ages and varying abilities,
as in a typical third grade. Scores are based on one hundred points
and fifty is considered average.

A "battery" of tests is a group of carefully selected tests administered to a specific population. Two examples are the Metropolitan Achievement Test (MAT) and the California Test of Basic
Skills. In many elementary schools, these tests are often scheduled
over the period of one week. Developers of the MAT recommend
that not more than two subtests be administered in one half-day
session; however, teachers are encouraged to test according to the
comfort level of each class. The MAT contains five subtests of
35–40 minutes each and timing is adhered to strictly. Though
timing was developed to accommodate varied work pace, public
schools will make special testing arrangements for students with
diagnosed learning disabilities. See the box below for determining
what Nathan's scores mean.

--------------- **WHAT THE SCORES MEAN** ---------------

Most standardized tests translate scores in the following different ways:

A *raw score* is the actual number of questions Nathan answered correctly. This is the basis for scoring the entire test.

A *percentile rank* is the percent of people in the norm group whose scores were above or below a given score. For example, if Nathan's math score was at the 63rd percentile, 62 percent of the students scored lower than he did and 26 percent scored higher.

A *standard score* tells you how he scored compared to the numerical average of the test, which is called "the mean." If the mean of the test is five, a standard score of seven means his score is well above average.

A *stanine* is a grading scale divided into nine segments which represent nine levels of performance. Nine is the highest level. A score in the fifth stanine is considered average.

A *grade-level or grade-equivalent score* compares his score to a grade level. A score of 5.4 means he's functioning at the fifth grade, fourth month level.

SUPPORTING GROUP TESTING

Long Before Testing Happens

Note the test dates. If testing dates are not posted on your school calendar or website, call your school and mark the dates on your calendar at home. Avoid making doctor's appointments for Nathan or scheduling vacations or business trips on those days, or the day before. Your absence on these critical days could have negative results.

Ask his teachers who will be administering the test, and ask about testing room conditions and what subjects will be tested. Find out when and what kind of preparation sessions are planned. Ask for suggestions about how you can help Nathan at home. Keep your schedule clear for these prep sessions, too.

Keep his score. Create a baseball-style card to illustrate how this test will become part of the growing data on his performance at school. And just like it does for a baseball player, it will keep track of his "stats" without putting the onus on a specific test. Since many third graders are already familiar with computer graphics programs, Nathan will probably be able to design a card with a little help from you. When the test results come in, log them on his card.

Keep it light. Don't make worried eyes and fearsome noises before any test. Rather, show Nathan by your calm attitude that testing is a natural part of life. Remind him that his grandmother and grandfather had tests in school, too. Tell him the best thing he can do is listen carefully to instructions and read directions twice.

Learn about the content areas and skills required for group standardized testing done in schools. Log onto *www.kidtest.com/ sequencebenefits.html*. The Kidtest Benchmarked Sequence, a standardized test, provides easy-to-follow details.

After You Get the Results

Don't jump to any hairy conclusions; get help instead. Some schools time parent conferences to coincide with the delivery of standardized test results. If not, schedule one yourself. Teachers will review scores, explain the types of questions asked on a particular test, and discuss in detail how Nathan compares to the norm group. This is also the perfect time to ask how he's doing compared to his own class. Ask the teacher, too, how she thinks Nathan did on this test, compared to his own ability and/or his typical performance in class.

Ask questions until you feel satisfied that you understand the content and the results of this test. When it comes to interpreting test scores, there's no such thing as a dumb question. Then, ask some more.

Don't put too much weight on any one test. Remember that all tests are only snapshots of Nathan's academic progress. Use each test instead as an indicator of his strengths and weaknesses and as a prime opportunity to make plans for shoring up any weak areas. Don't let any one of his standardized tests carry too much weight regarding Nathan's overall abilities.

Individual Testing

There might be times in Nathan's academic career when you will want in-depth details on his potential, how he processes what he learns, and how he actually performs in a variety of academic and cognitive areas. It could be that he's experiencing academic failure or that an emotional or psychological issue is impacting his school performance. Two examples of tests that would yield that information on Nathan are the Wechsler Intelligence Scale for Children (WISC) and the Woodcock Johnson Psychoeducational Battery.

Public schools recommend comprehensive individual testing when they suspect a student has a learning delay, developmental disorder, or attention deficit. This is the type of testing that always precedes placement in special education programs.

Parents can initiate formal individual testing as well, either privately or through Nathan's school. Such testing can only be conducted by a licensed testing professional like a psychiatrist, psychologist, or a testing-certified educational diagnostician.

Though thoughts of this type of testing can be intimidating to parents, it provides a wealth of information about how Nathan is functioning now and how he is likely to perform in the future. Though the process might be nerve-wracking for you, Nathan will probably enjoy it. It involves a wide range of interesting activities and lots of individual attention. What kid doesn't love that?

How the Testing Process Works

A complete testing session consists of a family interview, testing, post-testing parent consultation, and other appropriate meetings. Prepare for the process by collecting former test results and work samples to help you build a complete picture of Nathan's performance. Some testers also want to know medical history, so make notes about allergies, vaccinations, or recent medical test results.

After the personal history is established, the tester will select a series of tests to address and answer specific questions about Nathan's ability. Prepare him for one to three hours of testing time. In most cases, you will not be invited to sit in on the testing.

Expect a written evaluation in addition to your post-test consultation. Most testers also provide follow-up recommendations and activities. For an additional fee, your tester will meet with appropriate school personnel to discuss test results or accompany you to a conference.

Private testing is expensive, however, often as high as $1500. Normally there is a set price for the testing, and additional consultations are charged at an hourly rate.

There might be a chance, however, that you won't have to pay for individual testing. If Nathan is in a public elementary school, the school will pay if his teachers, or you, feel that testing might uncover suspected academic, emotional, or psychological barriers to his school success. Know, however, that a school-based individual testing process can take many months.

Before testing is considered, the school will form a group that is known as a "child study team" or "pupil personnel team," consisting of the school principal, the classroom teacher, the school psychologist, the school counselor, the parents, or others concerned with Nathan's academic progress. In a series of group meetings, they will share observations, evaluations, and opinions about the need for testing. If testing is indicated, the school psychologist or someone appointed by the school will conduct the testing. The child study team meets again to share test results and plan a course of action called an "individual educational plan" or IEP. IEPs are designed to be flexible and are periodically reviewed and amended as Nathan's needs change.

A Sample Individual Standardized Test

A test frequently administered by private and school testing professionals for third graders like Nathan is the Weschler Intelligence Scale for Children (WISC). This test is normally administered by a psychologist.

The latest edition is called the WISC-III. It is intended for students aged six-and-a-half to sixteen-and-a-half and takes 60–75 minutes to administer. It contains a series of verbal subtests in information, similarities, arithmetic, vocabulary, comprehension, and immediate memory through a test called "digit span." Performance subtests include picture completion, coding, picture arrangement, block design, and object assembly. Look to individual WISC-III subtests for readings on Nathan's perceptual organization, verbal comprehension, and freedom from distractibility.

The WISC-III yields Nathan's intelligence quotient, or IQ, in three separate scores: verbal IQ, performance IQ, and full-scale IQ. The full-scale is a combination of the first two scores. IQ scores above 130 are considered very superior and might qualify him for accelerated programs at his public school. A score of

90–109 is considered average. Scores of 80–89 are considered low average. Students at this level may qualify for remedial or academic support programs in public schools.

Supporting Individual Testing

Before the Test

Get names. If you are testing privately, ask for referrals from Nathan's pediatrician, health care provider, or school psychologist. Then conduct phone interviews to see who you feel would inspire your test-averse kid to want to do his best on a test.

Shop around. Don't hesitate to compare services, prices, and willingness to dialogue by phone, mail, or e-mail. Ask if the tester will explain the test results not just to you, but to Nathan, too. Make a wise and informed choice for your child.

Talk to Nathan about this testing before it happens. Tell him that you are looking for more than numbers. Explain that this type of testing is to show you how he individually thinks and learns. Tell him that you've found a person to test him that you think he will like very much. Assure him that you or his tester will discuss the test results with him. Including him in the complete process reinforces the fact that he is the most potent part of this equation.

Speak up. In the initial meeting with your selected tester, explain exactly what you need to know about how Nathan performs. If you are concerned about his math functioning skills, for example, be sure to ask the tester to examine not just Nathan's numerical skills, but also his quantitative judgment ability—can he predict and plan his time well? Inform the tester that you are also interested in knowing about Nathan's sense of direction and spatial skills.

After You Get the Results

Get a second opinion. If you disagree or feel confused about the tester's explanation of Nathan's results, get a second opinion. Set a conference date and discuss them with his doctor, teacher, tutor, school principal, counselor, or school psychologist. Another excellent opinion giver might be an old favorite like his kindergarten teacher.

After the test, explain to Nathan what you learned from it. Plan on twenty minutes for a general review of his results and time to answer his specific questions. Don't bore third graders with minute details. Enter his scores on the "baseball card" you made together. Remind him once that one test doesn't make a kid's reputation.

Make a game plan. Discuss, with Nathan, any changes that you and his tester feel will improve his academic performance. Elicit suggestions from him about ways to make his learning environment easier and more productive.

Tips for Taking All Kinds of Tests

Prepare Nathan for the unexpected. If his airborne sneaker fractures his grandmother's antique tureen the night before the test, expect it to show up in his scores. In the weeks before testing, brainstorm possible scenarios like the flu or car troubles. Plan for emergencies before they happen.

Serve brain food. In the weeks before testing, serve Nathan meals high in protein like a 3- to 4-ounce serving of eggs, fish, tofu, chicken, or yogurt. Tyrosine in proteins forms neurotransmitters in the brain. Neurotransmitters are electrically charged chemical messengers critical to alertness, quick thinking, and fast reactions; they increase attention span and help the brain perform calculations.

Get a tutor. Due to the range of information most tests cover, it's impossible to study for these types of tests. Some kids feel more confident taking tests, however, if they work one-to-one with someone ahead of time to review content areas, reinforce weak skills, and review the mechanics of test taking.

Share test results with his teachers or any person in an important guidance position in his life, like his doctor, his nanny, or his tutor. The more information they have, the more efficiently they can do their job.

Don't hesitate to ask his teachers for special consideration if his testing shows that he needs more time for doing math problems or if he works better standing, not sitting, at his desk. If testing reveals many unanswered test questions at the end of each test, investigate the possibility of an untimed test.

Testing is never easy whether it's a needle poke in the arm or a week-long session with a bunch of roaring third-grade buddies. You will be comforted if you remember two things:

First, formal testing doesn't measure Nathan's ability to make plans, his enthusiasm, sense of humor, nor his ready wit. It does not measure his independent nature, his persistence, independence, devotion, motivation and engaging personality. Most importantly, it does not reflect parental support and encouragement.

Lastly, the howling testing beast in Nathan can be calmed and tamed when, together, you learn some tricks for making the best of every testing situation.

9

The Right Way to Help with Homework

For science class, Olivia had a month to make something creative us-
ing recyclables. She spent her time watching TV while her dad built a
life-size prototype of the NASA space shuttle for her using egg crates,
bubble wrap, and Chinese take-out boxes.

If Olivia's in first, second, or third grade, don't do her dirty work night after night. Give her the homework support she needs without enrolling yourself in the primary grades again. When you find your place in the homework equation, she'll find hers.

This balance is critical when the tasks assigned have due dates far in the future. Despite her moaning and writhing to the contrary, long-term assignments aren't impossible missions, especially if Olivia is performing at or above grade level in the second half of third grade. They are perfectly matched to her developing skills. With the rudiments of reading, spelling, handwriting, and composition now behind them, most third graders are ready to work on a project that demands the use of all these skills.

Handling Big Assignments

Long-term assignments teach the ability to maintain a lengthy and ever-developing thought process and complete appropriate tasks within an assigned time. Even first graders get a feel for extended tasks with homework books that cover a week's worth of assignments. Kindergarten kids get their first taste by taking home the class teddy bear on Friday and telling the class, on Monday, how the bear spent his weekend.

How much homework help is too much? If you find yourself complaining too often and too loudly about the time and nature of Olivia's homework assignments, chances are you're doing more than your share. If her teacher can see your sticky hands all over her assignments, and most teachers can see this while standing on one foot with both eyes closed, know you've broken the balance. If Olivia becomes disinterested or cantankerous about her nightly work, or she can't sort her ideas from her dad's ideas from her mom's ideas, you've stepped way over the line. "If parents and kids and teachers think it is too much, it probably is," says Mona S. Wineburg, Director of Teacher Education at American University in Washington, DC. Parents, however, do have a pivotal role in homework for students in grades one through three.

The Adult Role in Homework

Act as point man. Don't make it obvious, but hover nearby when Olivia does her homework. If she likes working at the kitchen table, for example, sit at the other end and write bills or work at your computer. This puts you in a prime position to watch how she paces herself, how she plans her work, and what kinds of problems make her restless and edgy. Note that if she can accurately explain her task and engage with her work comfortably for a short period of time, about ten minutes, she doesn't need help.

Be proactive. To update her teacher about negative homework patterns you see forming and especially before the next long-term assignment, schedule a conference. "Teachers are less apt to be defensive when parents address problems as they're forming or before they happen," says Wineburg.

Come clean. Parents get better homework grades from teachers when they admit they were the ones who made that refrigerator box elephant with the Clorox bottle legs. Admit it, and then be specific about which tasks you felt Olivia was incapable of doing. If, for example, you drew the state of Ohio on poster paper because hers was the size of a postage stamp, admit it, and then discuss ways to teach Olivia size and proportion. If you put the teacher in the teaching position, you've won an advocate for your child, and you.

Set a good example. Obviously, you don't want to send the message to Olivia that it's okay to take credit for work performed by others (namely, you). Subtle patterns about honesty and accountability are being shaped here.

Homework-Balancing Strategies

The following strategies for long-term assignments will help you balance your role in the homework equation. For students in grades three and above, try the following:

Assign jobs. Ask the teacher to divide project tasks into "parent actions and child actions," says Wineburg. For example, parents might be responsible for library runs or saving egg crates and Olivia for reading, typing, and drawing. Specific directions from the teacher equalize the homework equation when you can point to the assignment sheet and say, "Sorry, sweetie, typing is not one of my jobs."

Use examples. When she hasn't a clue what to make out of recyclables, give her examples she can identify with. This is especially important for third graders who "don't think in the abstract," says Robert Pianta, Professor of Education at the University of Virginia's Curry School of Education, in Charlottesville, Virginia. Link plastic soda bottle rings around her wrist and ask her to identify her favorite type of jewelry. Hold up an empty gallon can of olive oil and ask, "Doesn't this look like daddy's head?" Or make a snaky line of soup cans on the floor and ask her what reptile it resembles. Don't spoon-feed ideas like mashed peas. Instead, give her visual and sensory examples to help her make her own creative links between what she knows and what could be.

Keep the target in sight. Pianta suggests three easy questions to coax Olivia through long-term assignments. Use them especially for students in grades three through six. What is the target we're trying to hit here? What are the steps to get to the target? When do we need to do them? "This trains them in important tasks of targeting, evaluating, discussing and scheduling," he says. If she can't put ideas in words, have her draw them. Avoid saying, "Why don't you try this?" says Wineburg. Repeat target questions whenever she loses her way. Or you lose yours.

Know how long it should take. When homework assignments are correctly gauged to Olivia's age and developing skills, they should take a corresponding amount of time to complete. If she's too slow or too fast for a third grader—taking forty minutes instead of twenty or completing an assignment in under ten minutes—talk to her teacher about adjusting her nightly assignments to better fit her abilities. According to the US Department of Education, most teachers agree on the following age-matched nightly homework periods:

First through third grade: 20 minutes
Fourth through sixth grade: 20–40 minutes
Seventh grade and above: 2–2½ hours per night

See how the teacher does it. Though this online book is written for teachers, *Helping Your Students with Homework* by Nancy Paulu provides some excellent "behind the scenes" tips on how parents or tutors can help with homework without doing all the work. Log on at *www.ed.gov/pubs/HelpingStudents/title.html.*

Fit the space to the kid. Often overlooked but crucial to effective work production is the space where Olivia completes her assignments for school. The better suited to her size, age, and needs the area is, the more comfortable and productive she will be. Consider her furniture first of all. If she likes working at the kitchen table, use a footstool and booster seat to give her the ideal ninety-degree angle for her back and knees. Better yet, get a table and chair scaled for her size. Then consider her lighting. Ceiling light provides wide-space illumination for large projects, but smaller lights placed on either side of her worktable are essential for close work and allow her to focus without strain on her eyes. Arrange supplies in easy-to-find locations close to her work area.

Consider noise factors. Though some kids can work effectively with the TV, vacuum cleaner, and a baby brother all blaring at once, most kids concentrate better on assignments when the noise volume is low. During homework periods, turn down, turn off, or remove the noisemakers to another room.

Set study hours. Show Olivia that academic work is an important priority in your house by establishing a study hour each night. Forty-five to sixty minutes would be a comfortable period for a third grader. Set it to accommodate her energy and hunger levels and after-school activity schedule. In addition to her twenty-minute homework time, add time for reading books, listening to books on tape, or reading aloud to her. Practice keyboarding or Internet search skills. Play games with multiplication facts or practice cursive writing. Setting a study time each night, even for kindergarten students, ingrains good study habits at an early age.

Promote independence. During study hour, don't do all her academic activities together. Make like a teacher and give her an assignment with a time limit. If she's struggling with cursive writing, for example, after ascertaining that she knows how to make a small *a* properly, ask her to make twenty-five of them. Tell her you'll check back in five minutes. Then evaluate her work by making small stars or circling her best attempts. When she's ready, move on to the next letter, then on to short words. Extend the assignment time gradually each night. Or set a regular schedule for her study hour, one that she can maintain even when she's under the care of a babysitter. She might do her twenty-minute homework assignment first, then spend twenty minutes practicing handwriting. The last twenty minutes can be spent silently reading her new library book. Breaking work time into small parcels optimizes concentration, and a variety of tasks helps sustain interest in schoolwork. Putting a clock, with hands, not digital, on the wall in her bedroom encourages self-management and reinforces time-telling skills.

Ask first. Don't assume that Olivia needs, wants, or welcomes your help on every assignment. Even when you see her struggling, ask first if she wants assistance or if she's got this one under control. There's nothing more personally fulfilling, even to an eight-year-old, than successfully completing some "hard work" all by herself. Giving her the benefit of the doubt demonstrates your faith in her ability.

Assess her work. Use some simple household activities to get a handle on how Olivia processes information, reads, writes, spells, and comprehends. Then share it with her teacher at your next conference. For example, note how she listens to directions and follows them in sequence. Can she locate the orange juice, get a glass from the cabinet, pour it without spilling it, and serve it to her brother, and then do the same thing for herself? By third grade, three-step directions should be getting easier to do. If you leave her a note reminding her to put her library book in her backpack tomorrow, can she read the note and successfully complete the task? Can she leave you a legible and well-spelled note all by herself? To check comprehension ability, observe her telephone manners. Can she properly answer the phone, identify herself, listen accurately, understand a message, and convey it to you, whether you are at home or not? Even seemingly simple chores are teeming with skills, so use them to learn volumes, every day, about how your child learns.

If one year in third grade wasn't enough when you were eight years old, then pull up a chair and do Olivia's homework for her. Or do only those adult jobs that balance the homework equation, like designating a special project area where long-term assignments can develop undisturbed. Steadily pitch a target question or two. And when you feel the homework balance shifting in the wrong direction, use your eyes and your common sense. Step back and ask yourself an honest question. Could a typical eight-year-old turn paper towel tubes and gallon spring water bottles into a three-person igloo with a wraparound porch?

10

How to Choose Toys and Games That Help Kids Integrate Their Senses for Learning

Sawyer's like a porcupine with ingrown quills. He's crabby and twitchy and blares like a megaphone. He pushes and shoves his class-mates till they scatter far and wide. Sawyer's sensory circuits are overloaded and about to blow.

A faulty sensory system might be discombobulating how Sawyer behaves and learns. More than just hearing, seeing, touching, tasting, and smelling, the human sensory system also includes critical functioning skills like balance and movement, and coordination and muscle tone as well as attention and behavior. He might have what occupational therapists trained in sensory integration call a "sensory integration (SI) dysfunction," though the term varies. It can also be called a sensory integrative dysfunction or a sensory processing dysfunction.

Sensory Integration Dysfunction

"Children with SI dysfunction don't modulate information well and may be oversensitive or undersensitive to touch or movement," says Lynn A. Balzer-Martin, a Chevy Chase, Maryland, occupational therapist with extensive training in sensory integration. "They may have a problem in the central nervous system with modulating how they respond to sensory stimulation," explains Carol Stock Kranowitz, author of *The Out-of-Sync Child: Recognizing and Coping with Sensory Integration Dysfunction.*

DOES SAWYER HAVE SI DYSFUNCTION?

To conduct a quick appraisal to see if Sawyer's behavior might have sensory roots, scan the typical symptoms in the box below. Be on the alert for reactions to sensory stimulation that seem extreme—too low or too high—or for repeated behaviors that interfere with learning. If you see him too clearly, too often, and with too many of these symptoms, consider having him evaluated for an SI dysfunction. Because many of these behaviors are also characteristic of an attention deficit disorder, seek a professional assessment by an occupational therapist trained in sensory integration techniques to help you sort it through.

A Tangled Sense of Touch

Bellows and bleats at the slightest scrape, bump, pinch, or push.
Or at the other extreme, barely responds to scrapes, bangs, or falls.
Hates messy projects like making papier-mâché or finger painting.
Loves making a big mess whenever he works.

None Too Light on His Feet

Bangs his toes, bumps his head, falls, or trips regularly.
Avoids fast moves, games, or sports.
Gets spooked by heights.
Gets dizzy, seasick, or carsick.

Ebb and Flow

Slouches and drags; posture and gait appear loose as a goose.
Or, at the other extreme, holds himself stiff like a robot.
Grabs the toothpaste so hard it spouts like a geyser.
Can't get a good grip to open the peanut butter jar.

Can't Adjust the Volume

Reacts excessively to loud noises.
Can hear the slightest sound, like grass growing one hundred yards away.
Or, at the other extreme, yells or shouts instead of speaking in normal tones.
Needs oral directions repeated till you're blue in the face.

Can't See the Forest for the Trees

Squints and squirms uncomfortably in bright lights.
Has trouble seeing the difference between colors and shapes.
Can't keep his eyes on track while reading.
Can't adjust his focus from near to far and back for copying.
Has poor grades or a low self-concept.

On the Scent

Has a sense of smell like a bloodhound.
Or, at the other extreme, couldn't smell it if you held it under his nose.

Ants in His Pants

Is twitchy, itchy, fidgety, or constantly tapping his foot.

Is easily distracted.

Impulsive, can't calm or control himself.

Has difficulty making transitions from one activity to another.

Can't find his way out of a paper bag, or even find the bag.

SI THERAPY

Sensory integration theory and practice was pioneered by the late A. Jean Ayers, an occupational therapist and trained clinical psychologist in Torrance, California. SI therapists believe that an inefficient sensory system can contribute to behavioral and learning problems. They say that for sophisticated academic skills like concentration and handwriting to develop successfully, kids with poorly integrated sensory systems need help in learning how to comfortably and accurately incorporate the fundamental information they get from their auditory, visual, and tactile senses as well as sensations transmitted through lifting, pulling, or vigorous movement.

Trained SI therapists use family interviews, standardized tests, structured observations of a child's posture, balance, coordination, and eye movements to make recommendations for treatment. Therapeutic sessions include sensory and movement-based activities. The amount of time spent with each child "depends on the age and severity of the problem, particularly since younger children make faster progress," says Balzer-Martin.

In addition to games and activities, SI therapists also use toys to help kids more effectively organize their sensory information. However, all kids, not just those with sensory system irregularities, benefit from toys and games that help integrate all their senses. "A brain that is nourished with many sensations operates well, and when our brain operates smoothly so do we," Kranowitz notes.

Sensory Toys, Games, and Activities

The following sensory toys, games, and activities work well with kids in grades one through three:

SEEING

- *Brightly colored, looping, drinking straws.* Using straws to suck in liquid sets in motion "a synchronicity of muscles that enhances both visual and language functioning," says Patricia Lemer, Executive Director of Developmental Delay Resources in Bethesda, Maryland. "Think how your eyes naturally focus when you use a straw. It's impossible not to focus. What happens is the eyes converge when you suck and diverge when you blow. Sucking and blowing strengthens the lips as well as the eye muscles. That's why articulation improves, because you work the oral motor skills, too," she explains.

- *Finger puppets or hand puppets.* Playing shadow games on the wall with puppets strengthens hand muscles and reinforces visual strength and focus. Putting finger or hand puppets in each hand enhances bilateral coordination. Encourage Sawyer to create gestures to accompany dialogues or stories between the two characters in his hands. Show him how to stretch his hands or fingers to imitate surprise or cup them to show a character crouching and jumping. Make a character agreeable by moving his fingers up and down. Teach him to show how disagreeable one can be by twisting his wrists or fingers back and forth.

TOUCHING

- *Modeling clay or small gel-filled athletic balls.* "Tactile integration has a big impact on a child's ability to learn at school," says Carol Stock Kranowitz. It also has a big impact on how Sawyer plays and interacts with friends. Bury a nickel inside a ball of modeling clay or play dough and have Sawyer exercise his hand muscles by digging it out. Give him a hand-sized sponge or gel-filled ball to squeeze each time he spells his spelling words or counts by tens. Art materials, science equipment, musical instruments, sports equipment, and writing materials all require well-coordinated hands-on use. And the sense of touch also increases visual memory. "By touching and manipulating objects, a child stores memories of their characteristics and relationships to one another," Kranowitz says.

- *Peg-Boards and geoboards.* Peg-Boards stimulate tactile and visual sense, too. As do geoboards in which kids place small, brightly colored shapes into larger formations. Geoboards are also a boon to kids who need practice discriminating between colors and shapes. The ability to discriminate between letters and numbers is critical to reading, spelling, math, and handwriting.

HEARING

- *Flutes and recorders.* Certain musical instruments like these have frequencies that can help kids regulate or modulate their senses so they can focus. Teach Sawyer tunes that run up and down the scale to exercise his fingers, or add a chorus that repeats a muscle-movement pattern. Teach him to play a simple Mozart tune, and you've added a calming element.

- *Hammers and nails.* When Sawyer wants to help with building projects, give him a hammer. For younger kids, use a soft wood and large-headed nails, and firmly set the nail in place before they begin. Hammering is an excellent activity for integrating hand movements and dexterity with visual steering. This vital set of skills is also critical to manipulating a mouse or a joystick while reading from a computer screen.

- *Whistles.* Rather than waste your breath telling Sawyer to take deep breaths to calm himself, give him a whistle. Or if you're desperate for quiet, give him a bottle of bubble-blowing solution. SI therapists believe that deep breathing is calming and helps kids "organize" their senses. Because it's impossible to make a sustained noise or blow big bubbles when you're slouched over, these activities also promote good posture. Good posture expands the lungs, rests the back, and relaxes the shoulders and makes Sawyer more comfortable in his own skin. A calm mind and a comfortable body help all kids concentrate better at home and at school.

SMELLING

- *Scented pens, markers, and lotions.* "What your nose smells can change your mood and sometimes help you remember things," says Diana Henry, a Phoenix-based occupational therapist specializing in sensory integration. Henry recommends finding scents that kids enjoy to help them settle down. For calming, she recommends vanilla, banana, and coconut scents. Rub Sawyer with coconut lotion after his shower or give him a cup of decaffeinated vanilla tea or hot cocoa. For keeping him alert, she recommends pine, citrus, or peppermint. When he has to draw a map of Kansas for his social studies homework, give him a lemon-scented marker to create his masterpiece. "Be aware of individual sensory needs," she cautions. "Some children with allergies or other respiratory difficulties may be uncomfortable with any smell. Commercial perfumes should be avoided," she adds.

TASTING

- *Popcorn, pretzels, and pickles.* Diana A. Henry calls these "mouth tools" and says "They provide oral stimulation that increases focus." Foods that are crunchy, chewy, salty, sweet, sour, or spicy or ones that can be sucked, bitten, pulled, or licked all provide good sensory feedback. "Any adult who has ever chewed a pencil or sipped a cup of tea while working also knows that mouth tools can also relieve tension." However, when buying food gifts for Sawyer, Henry cautions that buyers should be aware of food allergies.

LARGE MUSCLE MOVEMENT

- *Jump ropes.* Jumping rope stimulates the sensory system by involving the large muscles. It helps kids focus their movement and improve their overall balance and coordination. Carol Stock Kranowitz believes the large muscles come first in sensory integration. "We usually can't get to the fine muscles unless the large muscles are working properly," she says. Structured jumping games or counting while jumping teaches rhythm, another important skill for efficient movement. Alternating feet while jumping will help Sawyer effectively and simultaneously use both sides of his body. Calling out "right foot" or "left foot" while he jumps reinforces directionality, which could, in turn, reduce reversals in writing his numbers and letters.

SMALL MUSCLE MOVEMENT

- *Flour sifters.* This common kitchen utensil can help kids integrate small muscle movement. Start with the kind with the turn handle, and then move to the one that requires more hand and arm strength, the squeeze-handle type. Strong hand muscles are essential for pencil control for handwriting, drawing, cutting with scissors, and opening uncooperative tubes of poster paint.

- *Pick-up-sticks.* This is an excellent game for building concentration and focus. It also reinforces the proper pencil gripping position and mirrors the muscle moves and strategies needed for smooth and legible handwriting. This game also reinforces eye-hand coordination. Use larger sticks with younger kids. As Sawyer's technique improves, gradually decrease the thickness of the sticks.

- *Dice.* The hand-cupping position for shaking and tossing a pair of dice will strengthen the palmar arches of Sawyer's hand, which are needed for neatly squeezing toothpaste from a tube and not creating those messes he despises.

If you suspect that Sawyer's inability to interpret sensory information is interfering with his daily functioning, investigate it. And in the meantime, buy games and toys that nourish his senses and are appropriate to his personal challenges. Get beyond fluffy and cute to toys that will help him focus and learn and behave better. Then maybe one day the only quills around Sawyer will be the ones he uses for penning fancy correspondence to his large and growing circle of friends.

RESOURCES

The Ayers Clinic at *www.sensoryint.com* provides excellent background information on the disorder and common symptoms.

Tool Chest: For Parents by Diana A. Henry, OT, "Over-the-counter" sensory integration activities that can be tailored to a child's individual needs. Details at *www.ateachabout.com* or by calling 888-371-1204.

"A Teachabout." Diana A. Henry's specially equipped mobile home classroom brings sensory integration classes and workshops to schools and groups nationwide. Details at *www.ateachabout.com*.

What to Do When Physical Movement Gets in the Way of Learning

Jerry Lee's awkward at throwing and clumsy at catching. He avoids sports, playground games, and most outdoor activities. His handwriting is horrendous. And if he's not banging his toes, he's cracking his head. It seems like Jerry Lee's body is beyond his control.

Jerry Lee's problems might come from not moving enough at the right time in his development. Kids with normal intellectual ability and no other neurological disorders may still have difficulties with academic tasks like handwriting, physical education classes, and organizational skills, or with sports, playground activities, or social interaction. The most common denominator is slower movement time regardless of how a task is taught.

Movement therapists believe that certain movements form the foundation for later academic skill. Cross-body movements, like skipping or crawling, train the brain to use each of its halves in harmony. Creativity, for example, is a product of both parts of the brain: the left hemisphere provides technique and detail, and the right side of the brain provides flow and emotion. In language, the left side of the brain gives us the right words and proper sentence structure, while the right side gives us images, emotions, and dialogues.

"Moving is problem solving with the body," explains Joye

Newman, a perceptual motor therapist in Bethesda, Maryland. Perceptual motor development is the relationship between Jerry Lee's ability to process what he takes in through his senses and his corresponding movements.

Signs of Perceptual Motor Difficulty

Perceptual motor problems can make Jerry Lee appear awkward, clumsy, or slow in developing eye-hand coordination. He can't get his arms and legs organized for movement games and activities, so he avoids sports and playground equipment. Perceptual motor problems can make some kids move too slowly or cause others to be revved up and always on the go. They can also show up in letter and number reversals or problems with reading. In short, perceptual motor problems can cause "cognitive and academic stress," says Newman.

Though warning signs were first recognized in the early 1900s, kids with movement skills problems got little therapeutic attention because the consensus was that they'd outgrow it. However, strong evidence and research studies to the contrary show that these kinds of problems don't decrease with age and that they can lead to academic, behavioral, physical, and social interaction problems. It is estimated that 5 to 6 percent of the world's kids have what the American Psychiatric Association designated in 1994 as developmental coordination disorder.

Causes of Perceptual Motor Difficulty

Though the causes for perceptual motor difficulties have not been clearly established, some movement therapists believe that a lack of movement, like crawling, at appropriate developmental stages can cause movement problems later on.

It also might be caused by stress. "If kids have been traumatized in a learning situation and feel embarrassment and fear, then adrenaline pumps, creating a fight or flight situation and kids get stuck there; they don't feel safe and secure enough to move ahead," says Kathleen Carroll, a Specialized Kinesiologist from Washington, DC.

How Is Jerry Lee Moving?

The first question to ask yourself as you watch your primary grader moving around and about is, "How does his motor development compare with other kids his age?" says Joye Newman. Are his movements smooth and fluid or choppy and stiff? Does he use his whole body efficiently to help him move—like using his arms as levers to help him jump? Or does he bounce a ball with one hand while the other arm pumps furiously?

To get a thorough gauge of his movement skills, "observe him over the course of a month in different situations," Newman advises. "Keep in mind that something that looks like a problem in a six-year-old may just be slower development, while the same issue in a nine-year-old is indicative of a problem," she notes.

Moving in the Right Direction

If something in the way he moves sends up a red flag in your mind, engage him in some simple whole-body activities. Be sure to include movements Jerry Lee did easily as a younger child, like hopping. See suggested activities for kids aged 6–8 at the end of the chapter.

Or consider a professional evaluation with a movement therapist. At The Kids Moving Company in Bethesda, Maryland, Newman and her staff of therapists provide individual perceptual motor therapy to people ranging in age from two to sixty years. "Kids who don't move as well as they could need more movement. We need to teach them how to use their bodies to get from here to there," says Newman.

They also provide enrichment classes for kids aged 2½ to 8 years, which move them along the motor development continuum in age-appropriate stages. Students engage in activities to promote language development, social skill development, and self-confidence, while encouraging the development of specific skills including balance, eye-hand coordination, body and spatial awareness, and rhythm. Under supervision, they use full-sized and minitrampolines, tunnels, mats, balance beams, climbing equipment, hoops, and jump ropes, "all of which encourage creative and challenging movement," says Newman.

Overlapping Disorders

Because there is much overlap between perceptual motor problems and other disorders like attention deficit/hyperactivity disorder (ADHD), sensory integration dysfunction, or vision-related learning problems, seek a professional to sort through them. Therapists who observe kids as they perform normal daily activities can usually determine whether Jerry Lee is just inattentive during a task involving movement or he has actual difficulty learning and performing certain tasks.

Help in diagnosing or working on underlying physical function skills is available from perceptual motor therapists, psychologists, pediatricians, neurologists, family physicians, physical therapists, and occupational therapists who specialize in sensory integration.

Get Moving at Home

Engaging kids, even those with no movement issues, in activities that cover a wide range of physical skills will help them develop more confidence in both sports and academics. Have Jerry Lee try swimming, horseback riding, martial arts, board games, and musical instruments. For kids with small motor difficulties, look for movement activities that will increase grip and pinching strength as well as muscle tone in hands and arms and provide practice coordinating arm, wrist, and finger movements. Ball games, tennis, Ping-Pong, and eating with chopsticks are all excellent small muscle exercises.

The following activities help primary grade kids get their whole bodies moving in the right direction:

Freeze! (1-minute activity.) Use this method to help Jerry practice his stopping skills and balance, while you get a little peace and quiet once in a while, for goodness sake. When Jerry Lee is about to crash into a wall again, call out, "Freeze!" Do this whenever he's riled up and wild, or you have a noise-induced headache, or you need his attention in a hurry. Have him silently hold the position for 5–10 seconds and then release the freeze by calling out, "Unfreeze." As soon as he starts moving again, call out, "Freeze on one foot!" Change the freeze commands to practice his kicking, pitching, or catching positions.

Cook it up. (3-minute activity.) Do exercises together that mimic foods cooking. How does bacon look as it cooks in the frying pan? How about popcorn in an air popper? Water boiling? Burgers being flipped on the grill? Or pizza dough being flipped in the air? Can he imitate what happens when someone shakes a can of soda and then opens it up? All these moves force him to link his thoughts with his body and give him a better sense of where his body is in space. As his proprioception increases, he will be able to maneuver smoothly around the corner of the dining room table without banging his hip.

Make alphabet people. (5-to-10-minute activity.) Have Jerry Lee make the letters of the alphabet using his whole body. How will he make a capital A? Decide in advance of movement whether he will make capital or small letters, and then sit back and call out the letter for him to make. Do not do it for him. However, if he gets frustrated or stuck, stand next to him, not in front of him, and show him move by move how you would construct this letter. Encourage him to modify your form. Call and construct individual letters in the order of a word: c, a, t. When he's perfected each letter, have him slowly spell out the word with his body. And you've linked his movement to phonics, spelling, and reading. If his handwriting is sloppy, have him make the letters with his fingers to strengthen the small muscles.

Walk crabby. (5-to-10-minute activity.) Check Jerry Lee's ability to plan his motor movements by playing a game where he imitates the gait of different animals. Can he walk like a crab? Wiggle like a snake? Sleep like a flamingo? Walk like a one-thousand-pound gorilla? Tiptoe like a three-ounce bird? This gives him practice in planning his moves, the same motor-planning skill he needs for playing sports, dancing, or figuring out how to fit under the sofa or through the dog's door.

Do the swim. (5-to-10-minute activity.) Make like dancers mimicking swimming moves. This will help Jerry Lee exercise and strengthen his upper body muscles. Put on a favorite record and move with Jerry Lee. Can he do ten regular strokes? Change them to sidestrokes. How about a backstroke or a breaststroke?

Do the hula. (10-to-20-minute activity.) Can Jerry Lee keep a hula hoop moving on his hips? Build spine mobility and torso muscles by doing the hula together, or try belly dancing. Put on some disco music and do "The Bump" together to help him organize his muscle moves so that you can bump your hips together in time to the music. Do the tango together to help him lengthen and regulate his stride.

Do you wanna dance? (15-to-30-minute activity.) To exercise large muscles, work on coordination and build muscle memory, dance together. To encourage personal growth, pick non-partner dances like the Hokey Pokey, the Electric Slide, the Macarena, or even the Charleston. Find dance instructors in each generation of your family and friends.

Do you wanna feather? (30-minute activity.) Once he's feeling more comfortable with his body, invent and invite him to play games with a small group of comfortable people. This is where you add handheld objects like balls, balloons, scarves, feathers, or beanbags to add eye-hand coordination to the muscle-moving mix. Put on some music, form a circle, and pass a feather around in time to the beat. Invent interesting positions to pass the feather to the next person, like over your shoulder or under your leg. Then move your circle round and round as you pass the feather. Change tactics whenever the feather makes a complete circle.

Movement therapists believe that it's never too late to start moving. If you suspect Jerry Lee has movement difficulty or a developmental coordination disorder, get the professional input you need to set him off in the right direction. And keep your primary grader moving! Start slowly, and as he masters one movement, add progressively more complicated muscle work in the games and activities you share. This process helps a child learn how to think, organize, form, regroup, and find the correct way to move his body—the same thinking skills he needs at school for handwriting, spelling, writing a composition, taking tests, and correctly answering questions in class. So what are you waiting for? Grab your kid and your red shoes and dance, dance, dance.

12

How to Improve Visual Skills
for Better Reading

Patty loses her place when she reads and mispronounces the word monkey *three times on the same page. She always says reading makes her sick to her stomach and then pitches the book on the floor. Patty is a bright little girl but she hates to read.*

Primary grade kids who are otherwise academically bright can still have big trouble with reading. Some specialists believe the culprit is vision. "There's a lot more to vision than just acuity," says optometrist Anne Barber of Puyallup, Washington.

---- BASIC VISION ABILITIES NEEDED FOR SCHOOL ----

1. To see clearly and comfortably at 10–13 inches.
2. To see clearly and comfortably beyond arm's length.
3. To use both eyes together.
4. To aim the eyes accurately, move them smoothly across the page, and shift them quickly and accurately from one object to another—like in reading a book.
5. To keep eyes accurately focused at the proper distance to see clearly and change focus quickly—like in copying from a blackboard, a computer screen, or a book.

6. **To be aware of things located to the side while looking straight ahead—the stronger the peripheral vision, the faster the reader.**

7. **To use hands and eyes together—like in handwriting, using scissors, or bouncing a ball.**

Vision Is More Than Eyeballs

According to the American Optometric Association (AOA), vision is a process that involves not just sight, but fixation and eye-movement abilities, eye focusing (accommodation), eye aiming (convergence), eye-hand coordination, visual perception, visual-motor integration, and visualization. Any one or several of these vision issues could be a problem for Patty. Fortunately, there are things you and Patty can do to help.

Specially trained optometrists, called behavioral optometrists, conceive of vision as a total mind-body process and draw a link between vision-related learning problems and Patty's behavior. Washington, DC, optometrist Amiel W. Francke believes the following can all be related to vision problems: chronic fatigue; poor ability at ball games, reading, or math; chronic skin problems; susceptibility to colds and infections; bumping into things; need for abnormal quantities of sleep; and poor handwriting.

The Optometric Extension Program (OEP), an education and research foundation in Santa Ana, California, finds the incidence of vision problems in the classroom increasing. It found that in the average classroom, about 25 percent of kids have some degree of nearsightedness. "And the percentage is going up every year," says Anne Barber. "We also believe that 80 percent of myopia is stress-induced, not genetic," she adds. OEP literature abounds with experiments in which myopia (nearsightedness) has been induced.

Why are things getting so fuzzy? "Television and computers. Kids sitting in front of these things for extended periods of time don't get a chance to develop their vision for distance," Barber explains. According to Parents Active for Vision Education (PAVE), a nonprofit, information-sharing group of experienced parents in vision training, the average kid watches 6,240 hours of television before first grade.

--------- **DOES PATTY HAVE A VISION-RELATED** ---------
LEARNING PROBLEM?

Is Patty experiencing the following symptoms frequently while reading or doing close-work tasks? They might signal a vision-related learning problem.

1. Loses her place while reading
2. Avoids close work
3. Holds reading material closer than normal
4. Tends to rub her eyes
5. Has headaches
6. Turns or tilts her head to use one eye only
7. Makes frequent reversals when reading or writing
8. Uses finger to maintain place when reading
9. Omits or confuses small words when reading
10. Consistently performs below potential

To avoid confusing a vision-related learning disorder with other learning disorders like attention deficit/hyperactivity disorder or dyslexia, the American Optometric Association recommends having Patty's vision tested every two years.

Vision Therapy

Diagnosis begins with an evaluation by a behavioral optometrist. Harry Wachs, a Washington, DC, optometrist and Director of the Vision and Conceptual Development Center, begins with a student evaluation that's both visual and developmental. Parent attendance is required. Wach's evaluations last 60–90 minutes and involve a kaleidoscope of activities most kids enjoy, like doing puzzles, playing games, and playing with a ball.

In addition to an evaluation, behavioral optometrists give traditional eye exams and prescribe therapeutic eyeglasses. They also provide vision therapy that, they say, can eliminate vision-related problems and enhance visual performance. "If vision is learned, I can help a child relearn and retrain visual skills," says Anne Barber.

Vision therapy (also called visual therapy, vision training, or orthoptics) is not just exercising the eyes. Supervised by trained vision-care professionals, this program of exercises and procedures is tailored to Patty's individual needs. Sessions typically last 30–60 minutes and are held one to three times weekly. Often, specialized equipment is used, like therapeutic lenses, prisms, filters, eye patches, electronic targets with timing mechanisms, computer software, and balance boards.

However, it is not academic tutoring. "It is a treatment to improve visual efficiency and visual processing allowing the individual to be more responsive to educational instruction," says optometrist Stephen Miller of the AOA in St. Louis, Missouri. In fact, the optometrists often recommend academic tutoring during or after vision training. "Vision therapy does not directly treat learning disabilities," says Miller.

Does vision therapy work? That depends on whom you ask. The College of Optometrists in Vision Development (COVD) in St. Louis, Missouri, publishes an extensive document filled with research and clinical studies that prove that vision therapy can modify visual function and that treatment can bring lasting improvement. Copies are available at *www.covd.org* or by calling the COVD at 888-COVD770.

Be advised, however, that comprehensive vision therapy is vigorously discounted by many ophthalmologists. They contend that learning-related visual difficulties are not eyeball or eye-muscle problems but processing problems and might, instead, recommend psychoeducational testing or tutoring for Patty. Duck the controversy and investigate all learning-related vision theories and practices for yourself, and for Patty. Incorporate some of the suggestions below for supporting the visual strength of kids in the primary grades.

Supporting Good Vision

Get Patty tested. There's no disagreement that the first step to maintaining good vision is regular eye exams for Patty with the ophthalmologist or optometrist of your choice. Behavioral optometrists believe it's never too early to begin. "Parents can have their kids' eyes examined as early as six months of age," says Anne Barber. Schedule regular visits every two years. More frequently if conditions warrant it or health risks exist.

Feed her eye nutrients. Carrots aren't the only things good for Patty's eyes. The following nutrients and foods are eye wise, too:

Vitamin A: carrots, fish, poultry, egg yolks
Vitamin B1, 2, and 12: whole grains, nuts, eggs
Vitamin C: citrus fruits and watercress
Vitamin D and Calcium: sunlight, dairy products, tofu, tempeh
Vitamin E: green leafy vegetables
Chromium: corn oil, meat, whole grains, sweet vegetables and fruits, brewer's yeast

Play vision games. The following suggestions for primary grade students are provided by OEP:

1. For increasing peripheral vision: Pull up to a stoplight and ask Patty, without turning her head, to identify the color of the car next to you. In the classroom, have one group of kids pretend to be playing a sport and have Patty describe it "from the corner of her eye."

2. For helping Patty practice and perfect her eye shifts when reading (called saccades): In a large-print book, have her read only the first letter and then the last letter on a page, and so on through the book.

3. To enhance eye-hand coordination: Spread Cheerios cereal out on a table and have Patty pick up the Cheerios, one at a time, with a toothpick, a wooden skewer, or a plastic pick-up-stick. Then have her pick up two at a time until they are all gone. Kids in the upper elementary grades and above can color in all the letter *o*'s they can find in a newspaper paragraph. Or they can poke holes through them with a pencil.

4. To enhance visualization skills: Have Patty pretend she's up in a helicopter looking down on her day. Ask her to describe her "bird's eye view" including colors, flavors, textures, and smells.

The following activities are provided by Donna Wendleberg, Executive Director of Achievers Unlimited of Wisconsin, a group of educators who work with behavioral optometrists to diagnose and train kids and adults with learning disabilities. Use them with primary grade students.

1. **Build focusing skills.** Give Patty jigsaw puzzles, which require her to focus on only one area at a time. This is especially good if Patty has trouble sorting through details and selecting pertinent ones.

2. **Build visual stamina.** Try the following to help Patty build stamina, which she needs to be able to read comfortably for a sustained period of time:

   - Bounce a basketball ten times, first with one hand, then the other. Gradually decrease the size of the ball and increase the number of times dribbled. Patty's "goal by fourth grade should be to dribble a 1-inch Super Ball one hundred times with her dominant hand, then alternate hands," says Wendleburg.

   - Blow out candles to encourage deep breathing, which also builds visual stamina. Have Patty pretend she's blowing out one hundred candles on a birthday cake. Repeat three times and make a wish that it's her own cake someday.

   - Toss a look. Have Patty pick out a faraway object like the tree outside your kitchen window, and a close object, like her thumb, and "toss" her eyes back and forth between the two objects. Repeat 3–5 times. "This builds up visual stamina by shifting the vision from far to tight," says Wendleburg. This also strengthens her ability to copy correctly work from the blackboard to her paper.

3. **Help Patty think, track, and focus.** Listen to books on tape. After listening to a story for five minutes, stop the tape. Ask Patty, "What are they wearing, what does the room look like," says Wendleburg. Repeat periodically until the story ends.

It is challenging enough for kids to learn to read when they have good vision. Overcoming vision issues at the same time can be daunting. Do all the eye-wise things you can do for Patty to transform reading from a repeated and unhappy grind to the breathtaking source of enlightenment, adventure, and joy it can be. Here's looking at you, kid.

RESOURCES

Achievers Unlimited of Wisconsin *www.achieverswisconsin.org*

American Optometric Association *www.aoanet.org*

Optometric Extension Program *www.oep.org*

Parents Active for Vision Education *www.pave-eye.com*

PART FOUR

Grades Four and Five:
Grappling with the
Ropes of School

13

How to Mend Rocky Relationships

Stan fed Mrs. Kohrpussel's pet mouse to the science class snake. When he lied about it, his reputation among the fourth graders went just like Whiskers, straight down the tube. Now, Stan would rather eat live mice himself than face fifth grade.

When Stan's social skills or his reputation needs resuscitating, consider the landscape. Part of his problem could well be fourth grade, which some teachers consider a preview to the hormonal throes of sixth.

Fourth and Fifth Grade Landscape

With primary reading and writing skills now in place, learning moves to a more sophisticated and demanding level. Decimal points, once calmly separating dollars from cents, suddenly become moving targets. And so do friendships. In fourth grade, conformity rules, feelings get hurt, names get called, and allegiances shift in the blink of an eye. These increased academic demands, coupled with hormone-fueled sensitivities, force emotions inward, to probe deep down in new and often depressing places. Fourth graders are learning that the real world is not always easy to digest. Fortunately, parents and teachers are still powerful and positive influences.

Academics, emotions, and changes in established routines put a strain on a kid's social skills. Moving to another city and attending a new school, a teacher going on maternity leave in the middle of the school year, or the school undergoing construction can all play havoc on relationships and friendships even with kids who have strong people skills. Completely natural changes, like moving from elementary school to middle school, can put kids in an emotional tangle that ricochets off teachers, families, friends, and classmates.

When transitions loom large, the grade-level landscape is rocky, start your engine for change. Before the hormone-hammering years of middle school begin, give Stan the tools he needs to weather social storms and establish long-lasting friendships.

Use the strategies below to teach fourth and fifth graders insight and give them an internal radar system. Then, find the perfect type of story to share that will give him practice in identifying the obvious and subtle clues that lead to solving puzzles or mysteries. The same skills needed for sorting through the always challenging and intriguing episodes he'll encounter in living and learning with other people. A journal or a cartoon strip can lead him to a better understanding of himself and a more objective view of his actions in social situations. You can help him develop a team of allies to support his newly sprouting social skills. These methods will help you and your kids establish responsive and flexible ideas that will make the social world of fourth and fifth grade a whole lot easier for everyone to digest.

Teach Stan Insight

Because fourth graders are still guided more by emotions than reason, you will need an accurate sequence of events to help Stan see the connection between actions, reactions, and consequences in any sticky social situation. Call, e-mail, or visit his teacher and take notes about the incident with the mouse and the snake.

Once you have the facts in hand, sit down with Stan and help him see what's inside himself that could be contributing to his current social standings in fourth grade. Tell him that you will teach him something called "insight" and that it comes from asking yourself some tough questions and accepting some honest answers. Offer to be his guide till he knows the ropes himself. Then, retreat together to a quiet place where you can work peacefully and without distraction. Designate this his special place for thinking through troublesome issues and for making positive plans.

Start by asking Stan whom he considers his best friend in class. Don't assume you know the answer to this question. Then, have him list the characteristics about this person that make him or her a good friend. Is his friend fun? Kind? Generous? How does Stan measure up in each category? Use this conversation as the basis for your work together and as a reference point when new problems arise.

Use the questions below to guide your dialogue with fourth and fifth graders whose friendships or relationships are jammed up. To acknowledge Stan's growing need for social interaction outside the family, give him a copy of these questions so he can use them later on by himself.

------- **GUIDE FRIENDSHIPS FROM HERE TO THERE** -------

Is there a cycle here that I want to break?

How can I go about breaking it?

Which ideas are getting in my way?

Which habits are getting in my way?

What behaviors are getting in my way?

What is one thing I can change about myself to help break this
   cycle?

What other people might be able to help me with this?
What would be the perfect outcome in this situation?
What two steps can I take to make it happen?

After brainstorming these issues with Stan, rehearse his "two steps to make it happen." To help him become more flexible, responsive, and resourceful in his people skills, play the contrary person. What if Mrs. Kohrpussel doesn't want him to buy her a new mouse? Then, help him revise and amend his approaches to deal with unexpected situations and unpredictable teachers, classmates, cousins, or neighbors. For insurance, have him develop at least one good backup plan.

Demystify Social Situations

To give Stan an entertaining and objective way to practice sorting through emotions for facts and clues to solving puzzles, find entertaining, age- and ability-appropriate mystery books to read together. Start the process with books that will have him cutting out and reconstructing the picture puzzles in *You Be the Detective* by Marvin Miller. Then move on to two- to three-page mysteries like *Baffling Puzzles* by Jim Sukach or *Great Book of Puzzles* by Falcon Travis. As Stan's instincts and clue-finding skills improve, move next to short story mysteries in the eighteen-book series called *Clue* by A. E. Parker. Then, try some excellent full-length mystery books for fourth and fifth graders written by John Bellairs, like *Mansion in the Mist* or *The House with the Clock in Its Walls*. Strong readers might like *Artemis Fowl* by Eoin Colfer, which incorporates symbols to decode and track through the entire story.

In addition to hunting for obvious and subtle clues in the story, select a perplexing character and discuss his or her reasons and motivations for acting in a certain way. What does Stan think the character might have been thinking by not telling anyone about the murder he witnessed? Then steer him to look not just at the clues, people, objects, and events provided, but at how the setting or environment of the story might indicate a reason or a solution. How does the haunted house influence the miserable old man in the story?

Journaling and Cartooning through Social Situations

To record the valuable strategies from these brainstorming sessions and the behavior clues he learns from reading mystery stories, have Stan document his experiences by writing in a journal or drawing cartoon strips. After some initial guidance, most fourth and fifth graders can work independently on these activities. However, don't hesitate to guide them along when they get stuck or invite your help.

JOURNALING

If Stan doesn't mind writing, give him a journal to record his thoughts and feelings about fourth grade and his plans for fifth. "Sit him down and come up with what he would like the school year to be like, academically, behaviorally, socially," says Rod Baber, a licensed clinical social worker in Alexandria, Virginia. Encourage Stan to focus his writing on the good examples he sees around him. "What other kids would he like to be like? How do they get the results he wants?" asks Baber. Help Stan keep his writing and his mind on his goal by periodically asking, "What image would you like people to associate with you by the end of this year?" coaches Baber.

Don't limit Stan to a small leather journal with a lock. Offer him a spiral notebook, a blank book, or a three-ring binder for dividing up important notes, drawings, or photos. If he doesn't love writing, supply him with a small recorder and cassette tapes to tape his private dialogues or a video player to record his private thoughts. Be sure to tell him you respect his privacy and won't read or listen to his musings, unless he cares to share them with you.

CARTOONING

If Stan would rather draw than write, teach him to use a comic strip to find his way through a thorny social situation. Carol Gray, Director of the Gray Center for Social Learning and Understanding in Jenison, Michigan, creates simple, personalized comic strips with students to help them practice social skills. Formulated originally for kids with autistic spectrum disorders, their use is expanding to general education students, including preschoolers. "Comic Strip Conversations slow down and visually display an interaction so kids can 'see' and gain a sense of control and competence in conversation. It's drawing and talking," explains Gray, author of a book called *Comic Strip Conversations*.

To help Stan make his own, you'll need drawing paper and crayons or colored markers. To focus on the action, draw characters, settings, and objects in black. Carol Gray reserves color for only writing dialogue; for example, teasing statements are written in red. "In this way a student gradually learns to use colors to represent the emotional content of statements, thoughts, and feelings," says Gray. She recommends the following colors though she allows students to select their own meaningful ones.

COMIC STRIP CONVERSATIONAL COLORS

Green: good ideas, happy, friendly
Red: bad ideas, teasing, anger, unfriendly
Blue: sad, uncomfortable

Purple: proud
Yellow: frightened
Brown: comfortable, cozy
Black: facts, things that we know
Orange: questions
A combination of the colors: confused

Use the following steps to guide Stan as he draws. If he'd rather not draw, tell him you'll be the hand, and he can be the mind that guides it.

1. *Set the scene.* Identify the social environment with a simple "location" symbol in the upper left-hand corner of the page. For a playground, for example, he might sketch a swing or some climbing bars.

2. *Concentrate on the characters.* Identify the individuals, and then draw stick figures to represent people. Draw a speech bubble coming from each mouth.

3. *Fill in Stan's words first.* What did he say that day? What color are his words? Before writing, have him look at the color chart and identify his feelings. Was he feeling friendly (green)? Uncomfortable (blue)? The best way to get Stan's take on the situation is to let him script the dialogue. Seeing the situation first through his perspective puts you in a better position to provide missing or incorrect information.

4. *Now write his thoughts.* Have Stan make a dotted thought bubble above the head of his personal stick figure. What was he thinking when he said those words? Was he frightened (yellow) that they wouldn't want him to play? Select the color and fill in his thoughts. Don't let on that you notice a difference between what Stan said and what he thought.

5. *Now write words and thoughts for each other character.* Remind Stan that he can't fill words in until they're assigned a color.

6. *Now teach Stan to make guesses about what others were thinking, an asset in any social situation.* What does he think the other kids were thinking? If at first he picks green for a red emotion, give him time to self-correct. If he doesn't, then step in. "Suggest trying another color, like red instead," says Gray. At this stage, "when you identify the correct choice for kids, you bring logic to the situation and they recognize it," she says.

7. *If Stan is still attentive, have him sketch another cartoon strip incorporating new logic and suggestions for future situations.* According to Gray, "nine times out of ten, children will come up with a very good new response they can use in that situation." Keep a journal of Stan's colorful conversations for reminders or later revisions.

Use Comic Strip Conversations to reinforce personal social skills, group skills, classroom rules, or responsibilities at home. Middle and high schoolers might even improve their reading comprehension by illustrating the words, thoughts, and actions of a cast of characters in a book.

Partnering through Social Situations

Lastly, help Stan create alliances and partnerships at school to support his campaign for changing his social patterns. Meet with his teacher to sort out the facts whenever an incident makes Stan's social situation hard to swallow. Take Stan, if he can handle it. Be brief and honest about any incidents and enlist his or her support in Stan's campaign to improve his social skills or recoup a tarnished reputation. His teacher might be the type who takes pride in helping kids make 180-degree turns in the right direction.

Don't stop with teachers. Have Stan share his plan for change in his own words with other school personnel who will only be too happy to lend their support, like the principal, the school secretary, the bus driver, and the school custodian. Inform coaches, tutors, neighbors, and friends that Stan is on a new road and needs all the guideposts they can provide. The more alliances and partnerships he forms along the way, the better his chances of making his turnaround permanent.

Teach Stan to look up, down, and all around, and into the eyes of the people around him for clues that will help him increase his people skills and build friendships. Social relations can be tangled situations for kids, no matter their age, grade, or learning differences. Developing strong skills based on personal insight takes practice, especially for kids with developmental or learning delays. Journals, engaging mysteries, and simple comic strips can clear the emotional clouds that muddle social episodes for Stan, and for you. Though one transition might tarnish a kid's reputation or put the crunch on his people skills, use the next one, like the one coming in September, to show Stan that though it's too late for Whiskers the pet mouse to improve, it's never too late for him.

14

How to Help Fourth and Fifth Graders Get Organized

All you need to do to find out what Jack and Jill have been up to is follow the clutter trail. Though these twins are double the fun, they are also double the mess.

Learning how to organize time, work, possessions, and spaces is important for all kids, but for some it makes the critical difference between successful performance and a mess in fourth and fifth grade. It also paves a smoother way to middle school.

When Disorganization Makes a Difference

It makes a difference when schoolwork slides. If Jack's grades in school are suffering because he loses his homework, can't find his books, forgets his papers, or fails spelling quizzes because the words were buried somewhere in his lost notebook, then learning practical and dependable ways to keep himself organized will get him back on track.

It makes a difference if kids are visual learners. If Jill frequently says, "Let me see it," when learning something new, chances are her favorite learning style is visual, not auditory or kinesthetic. She is probably sensitive to color and has an eye for details. She's probably the patient in the dentist's office who straightens pictures on the wall. However, because she's a visual learner, messy things and untidy places create an annoying distraction that makes her uncomfortable and less productive. Organizational skills for Jill will be a comforting relief.

It makes a difference if kids have ADHD. Kids with attention disorders typically exhibit wide variation in the amount of time they can concentrate and focus on a task. Periodically, they are hyperfocused and can work at a task for a surprisingly long period of time. At other times, focus time is infinitesimal and every minor distraction fractures it. Well-developed organizational systems are critical for Jacks with ADHD when their attention lights here and there but stays nowhere.

The famous Italian psychiatrist and educator, Maria Montessori, knew that one of the most powerful ways to help very young children develop initiative and independent learning skills was to show them how to organize their time, work, and spaces efficiently. In her preschool classrooms in Italy, as early as 1906, materials and supplies were arranged not to distract kids from the learning process, but to facilitate it. In Montessori classes worldwide today, students not only take an active role in choosing their daily learning activities, they select and gather their own materials and supplies. And most importantly, they return them all to their original places. In Montessori classrooms, putting things away is an organizational skill engineered into every learning activity.

Organizing is a skill that you can teach your kids, like sledding or riding a bike. Fortunately, you do not have to be an organized person to teach a kid how to be one. To get Jack and Jill interested in organizational activities, however, it's essential to tap into their individual styles, personalities, and needs. "Get on their wavelength, see how they process and create ways to work from there," advises Ann W. Saunders of Baltimore, Maryland, a licensed clinical social worker turned professional organizer. Start your organizing campaign wherever there is stress or a mess or both.

The following ideas help fourth and fifth graders make plans, organize and sort supplies, and make better, safer use of their space.

Organizing Time

Make family plans. Weekly family planning sessions help Jack and Jill make organizing their time a natural thing. "Planning teaches kids to think ahead of time," says Saunders. Decide first when you will meet as a family to make plans for each coming week. Sunday nights? Or Fridays in the car on the way to Grandma's house?

Make fun plans. "Plan what nourishes you and your family first," Saunders advises. What nights will you have dinner together, go to the movies, or listen to music? Plan Jack's time for practicing soccer kicks or Jill's for making computer greeting cards. Planning for downtime teaches kids how to balance work and play.

Make work plans. Consider the time and supplies needed to complete tasks, appointments, and schoolwork. What does Jack need tomorrow for his job raking the neighbor's leaves? When will Mom and Jill make a practice run to the new orthodontist's office? What supplies are needed for Jill's math project due Friday? Tap your kids' past experience in similar situations and have them make predictions based on known factors. Set your schedules accordingly.

Track and balance the plans. Post a large erasable calendar in a central location to keep track of plans. Have the kids chose a favorite color marker, and then routinely fill in their projects, practices, games, and events in their color of choice. Use a third color for family or pet plans. With only a quick glance, color-coding makes plans obvious. It also provides a color-ific warning signal when work plans and downtime plans are way out of balance. Make it a family rule that if kids independently add activities to the family calendar, they are tentative until confirmed by you or during the next family planning session. Advise them to consider travel time when they make plans. Can Dad realistically get from a dance rehearsal to a soccer game in time for the start?

Factor in emergencies. Line up emergency backup people before the school year starts. Then make auxiliary plans if those people are unexpectedly unavailable. Plan the order in which they should be called for help. The person who is called first should be the one who is most often available, like Grandma. If Jill is stranded at the mall in the snow and Mom is trapped at the dentist's, Jill should know to call Grandma first and, if she can't come, call Uncle Jim next, then Aunt Jane. Use a luggage label attached to a backpack to write emergency contact information, or write it on a 3x5 card, and then cover it with clear tape and pin it inside the backpack.

The skills kids acquire during family planning sessions have a direct effect on their ability to figure out personal challenges. Make fourth and fifth graders even more self-reliant with the following ideas:

Organizing Work

Make hand maps. Teach kids how to use "hand maps" to plot their plans for writing compositions, homework projects, and long assignments. Hand maps provide a visual tool to reinforce logical, orderly thinking about schoolwork, events, and activities, even vacations or summer camp. Using paper and pencil, have Jack trace the outline of his own hand with fingers spread. In the space made by his palm, he writes the title of the prospective project, event, or activity. Using the finger spaces, he then writes five things needed to complete his project. Encourage him to prioritize the work by numbering the five finger spaces. Use two hand maps for large projects.

Organizing Things

Give it, pitch it, want it, store it. When toys, shoes, clothes, sports equipment, CDs, videos, games, hair clips, or stuffed animals are tumbling your kids into a mess, show them how to efficiently "edit" and prioritize all their things. This advances the plan in Chapter 7 for primary graders to fit the more sophisticated skills of fourth and fifth graders. Though Jack and Jill will need guidance to set up and use this system the first time, they can easily implement it later all on their own. Plan routine editing times, like April for winter belongings and August to make way for school.

Set up a work area near the spot where the junk has spread deep and wide. To sustain Jack and Jill's interest during the process, take breaks in the action at least every thirty minutes. The junk will wait happily for your return. You will need four or five cardboard boxes, marking pens, masking tape, a notepad, and a pencil.

1. *Decide on four or five destination points for all the stuff.* Are there things that you should donate to charity? Gloves, hats, and scarves that need to be stored for winter? Which things can be handed down to younger siblings or cousins?

2. *Label each box: give it, pitch it, want it, store it.* Use colored marking pens to print the title in large letters on each box. If you are having a garage sale in the near future, get a fifth box and label it "sell it."

3. *Now, write the corresponding name of each box on a separate piece of notepad paper.* Assign one person to write down each item's destination. This solves fretful wondering and frantic hunting later on.

4. *Now assign the other jobs.* One person fills the boxes, another tapes the filled ones closed with masking tape, and another stores them in their new locations. After the break, switch jobs.

5. *To move the process along, prompt Jack and Jill to ask themselves questions that help them work through the emotions of letting things go.* Ask them the following questions until they automatically do them, and try not to spend more than thirty seconds on each item:

------ **QUESTIONS FOR JACK AND JILL TO SORT BY** ------

Do I need this? Why?
If it's important, why is it buried in the bottom of the closet?
How valuable is this if I've forgotten all about it?
How valuable is this if it's broken?
How valuable is this if I can't remember how to use it?
How valuable is this if I can't remember what it's for?
Would this be better for someone younger?
Would this be better for a family member who's never had one?
Am I bored with this now?
Could I get good money if I sold this now?
Is it still in good enough shape to donate?

Organizing Spaces

Engineer the space. Teach kids how to "creatively engineer" their spaces. This method circumvents jabbed fingers and banged knees by making places safer and more efficient for kids to use them. To help Jack remember the safest place for his bike, make a tape outline or "silhouette" of it on the floor of the garage. Make silhouettes on Peg-Boards for scissors, hammers, or other tools that require careful use. Then, use S-shaped hooks to attach the tools to the Peg-Board wall in Jack's bedroom or Jill's hobby area. By carefully "framing" objects in such a way, they become more important and therefore command more respect.

Make color the theme. If you organize things in engaging and colorful ways, kids will gravitate toward them. If Jill is passionate about purple, use that as her organizing theme. Use it for marking her events on the family calendar. Pick purple storage boxes, hanging files for her rolling file cart, and ribbon to go around the basket that holds all her art supplies. Let her favorite color become a silent reminder that order makes life more efficient and productive.

Make color trails. Help Jack establish a meaningful way to visually track school materials and supplies. Assign a specific color for each subject and use it for all things that relate to it. For example, cover his math book with green paper, use green manila file folders to separate tests and quizzes at home, and select a green divider for holding homework in the math section of his notebook. Let green point the way to his math.

Pave a Neat Path to Middle School

Attending middle school means moving to different classrooms and encountering different teachers for each subject. For some kids, this is a paperwork nightmare. They also will likely be assigned hallway lockers for storing books, which can become another rat's nest of disorganization for some kids. Implement these two ideas toward the end of fifth grade to smooth the way to middle school.

Make homework folders. If a large notebook sectioned by subjects will overwhelm Jack, use individual pocket folders for homework assignments, one for each subject. Maintain his color code here, too. On the left side of the folder, he might place a small notebook for recording math assignments or math assignments sheets. On the right side, he might place completed work. He can carry this back and forth to school each day. Clean it out weekly, keeping only study guides and other long-term instructions.

Prepare for the lock. Most middle schools provide individual hallway lockers for kids' books and supplies, which are locked with key or combination locks. If Jack will use a combination lock, practice setting, locking, and opening one during the summer before he moves into sixth grade. This sidesteps a classic start-of-school stress factor.

Set up the locker. Visit his middle school the summer before he starts sixth grade to examine and measure the typical locker Jack will be assigned in the fall. Does it have hooks for hanging his coat and gym supplies? Are there any shelves for books? Brainstorm how he will arrange his locker for quickly grabbing and running between classes. Consider purchasing one of the small, ready-made closet dividers that are sized to fit school lockers. The door of his locker might be an ideal place to attach a small corkboard or mirror. Buy things that can be easily removed at the end of the school year.

Teaching organizational skills to fourth and fifth graders provides them with anchor points that will help them progress more successfully through the academic, social, and emotional upheavals coming all too soon in middle school. Though schedule charting, hand mapping, and color tracking are external elements, they create an internal awareness of and sensitivity to times, places, and possessions. This doubles Jack and Jill's effectiveness, no matter the paths they choose to forge.

15

How to Help Kids Improve
Their Science Skills

Newton's in the kitchen putting crayons in the blender. He's invent-
ing a new color. Success, he believes, hinges on adding just the right
amount of bright red, oil-based house paint.

"You don't have to be a rocket scientist to think like one," says research astronomer and former astronaut George "Pinky" Nelson.
Nelson was the first director of Project 2061, a nationwide science
education reform initiative of the American Association for the
Advancement of Science (AAAS). Mindful of all the scientific and
technological changes kids will witness before the return of Halley's
Comet in the year 2061, Project 2061 aims to help all kids become
"science literate." This takes not only knowledge and skills in
math, science, and technology, but essential "habits of mind."

Shake Off Old Attitudes

The first step to helping Newton develop a "habit of mind" for
science is to dump some of your old attitudes, like thinking science is too hard or that you can only do well if you have the "aptitude" for it. Solar physicist Don Michels agrees. He believes
American kids have heard those kind of negative comments en-

tirely too long, not only from parents and teachers but from classmates and friends. "By the time we're in sixth grade, we've already heard how hard physics is," says Michels, project scientist for the coronal imaging experiments on the SOHO solar satellite. "If you're told something is hard often enough, you'll believe it," says Michels. "Actually there is a great deal of science that is very easily explained. In fact, physics is fun. Billiards and sailboats are physics, even the colors of your shirt or of the leaves on the trees. It's all physics," he explains.

"The mistake we make with kids is calling it 'science,'" says Gerry Wheeler, Executive Director of the National Science Teachers Association (NSTA). "It's really just bringing nature into the home. It's ice cubes and string telephones and wiggly worms," says Wheeler, a nuclear physicist and former physics professor.

In other words, make science learning a natural and comfortable experience in Newton's life. The following ideas and activities will help develop a scientific habit of mind for most fourth and fifth graders.

Know the Ingredients

Familiarize yourself with the topics Newton should know something about in order to be successful in science by the end of fifth grade. The following section provides a science curriculum snapshot, based on Project 2061's "Benchmarks for Science Literacy." Find the clearest information about what kids should know in science by the end of grades 2, 5, 8, and 12 by logging on to the Science NetLinks "Benchmark" section at *www.sciencenetlinks.com*.

Then, let the benchmarks guide you as you work on science activities at home with Newton. Just about any topic that fascinates Newton relates directly or indirectly to one of these topics. Use them to fill in the gaps in his science learning or to satisfy his natural inquisitiveness.

Fifth Grade Science Topics

These are some of the topics kids should be familiar with by the end of fifth grade:

1. *The Nature of Science*
   Specimen observation and collection
   Investigation of results from activities and experiments
   Use of evidence to back up claims
   Clear communication of data

2. *The Physical Setting*
   The purpose of a telescope
   General characteristics of planets and stars
   The properties of gravity, air, liquids, gases, and solids
   Rocks and minerals
   Geologic forces on landscape
   Structure of matter
   Energy transformation
   The laws of motion
   Magnets and electricity

3. *The Living Environment*
   Organization of living things
   Basic laws of genetics
   Cells, germs, and microscopes
   The interdependence of species
   Evolution of life
   Fossils

4. *Humans*
   Human birth and development
   The skin, the brain, respiration, and nourishment
   Differences between human and insect behavior

Creation of tools to improve life
Use of archeology to give clues to human behavior
Nutrition, disease, and substance abuse
Effect of health on emotions and behavior

5. *The Designed World*
Agriculture
Materials and manufacturing
Energy sources and use

Gather Resources

Then, gather some resources that will bolster Newton's Technicolor interest in science. Avoid scouring bookstores or the Internet for what you hope will be engaging science materials. Get expert opinions instead. Each year, the NTSA and the Children's Book Council publish a list called "Outstanding Science Trade Books for Students in Grades K–12." A review panel of science educators and professionals recommends books that provide clear, accurate, current, and age-appropriate information on topics that range from archeology to life science. The benchmark-conscious books they've selected avoid oversimplification and use facts to support generalizations. Annotated titles on the book list include grade levels and prices. For the complete K–12 list, log on to *www.nsta.org/ostbc*.

Get Newton's Hands in the Mix

Turn your house into a science project! As you stand together peering down into the blender, use these simple conversational guidelines to help Newton understand scientific investigation. The following thirty-minute activity adapts to a wide range of topics and works best with kids ages 9–11.

1. Tap prior experience. Connecting what Newton knows to new knowledge forges a critical link in understanding scientific processes. It also gives him a baseline and starting point for new learning. Hark back to his past experience about mixing colors together. Help him recall what happened in kindergarten when he accidentally colored with his blue crayon over the yellow rays of sunshine. Listen carefully as he retrieves his past knowledge and be alert for misinformation.

2. Formulate an hypothesis. Bite back knee-jerk corrections and pat answers in favor of questions that teach kids how to hypothesize. Instead of ticking off a list of foods best mixed in a blender, ask him about his theory. "What makes you think that a kitchen blender is the perfect place to invent a new color?" Listen to his list of advantages, and then highlight the disadvantages by asking him to compare blending bananas to crayons. "What is it about bananas that make them blend well? How are crayons different? How will they blend?" Hypothesizing not only helps kids articulate theories, but it also helps them reevaluate their motives.

3. Control and manipulate the variables. Don Michels defines that as "putting ideas on a shelf next to several other possibilities, then trying to weed one out from the others." What would happen if Newton added one blue crayon to his red mix in the blender? What would happen if he added turpentine instead of more paint? Explain to Newton that scientific investigation is a constant process of considering, controlling, and eliminating variables until a workable solution is found based on the information at hand, or in the blender.

4. Devise an experiment. Get Newton to consider another method for blending and inventing a new color by devising an experiment with carrots rather than crayons. First, have him grind some of the vegetables raw. Experiment with piece size, grind speed, and time. Next, boil some up and blend a new batch. Ask, "Why is the process different?" Then, talk about its implications for his crayon experiment. Could boiling the crayons instead of blending them produce the perfect new color? Considering alternatives leads kids to learn the awesome power of new evidence.

5. Steer clear of pat answers. Because scientific investigation is an ongoing, ever-changing pursuit, don't allow Newton to believe that because he found one solution, his investigation should end. Demonstrate how variable scientific information can be by working out your own solution to his problems while he works. Then share your methods.

6. Defend his conclusions. As Newton stares blissfully down into that nonstick pot and watches how his colors come together in a startling new way, talk to him about why boiling is better than blending when it comes to inventing a new crayon color. There's no more powerful booster rocket to a kid's self-worth than when he's asked, "What makes you think that's true?" and he can answer, "Because I have the evidence right here in this pot to prove it."

7. Extend his learning. Play a game called, "What is wrong with this picture?" to help elementary schoolers generate a joy of thinking and a stronger ability to develop their own hunches about an idea. Invite Newton's little sister to inspect your red-and-purple-splattered kitchen cabinets and figure out what happened. What does she think the splatters are made of? What details give her some clues? Make science investigation a sensory experience by having her touch the splatters or smell them. How does she think the splatters can be removed? Discuss how different solvents will affect waxy crayon material and cabinet surfaces. Play "What's out of place?" outside too, when you and Newton see a sneaker hanging from a telephone wire or Grandma's purse in the freezer.

Take advantage of Newton's natural curiosity to teach him the things he needs to know not just for school, but about the world around him. Scientific investigation gives kids more than a way to find the perfect color. It also teaches a life lesson. It shows them how to look at problems as gateways to new solutions. And it can also transform a crayon-grinding kid into the solar physicist who figures out how to recover a satellite behaving badly one million miles from earth.

16

How to Help Kids Improve Their Math Skills

Mention math and Albert's eyes glaze over, his head rocks back, and the moaning begins. For him there's nothing worse than a worksheet filled with long number problems waiting threateningly for answers.

By the end of fifth grade, Albert should be computing fluently with whole numbers. *Fluently* means he knows efficient and accurate ways to add, subtract, multiply, and divide those numbers and can demonstrate and explain what he is doing. His work should reflect that he understands relevant math concepts well, like the ten-based number system. In grades three to five, he also should be developing his understanding of fractions and decimals. He'll work on developing fluency with fractions and decimals in grades six through eight. You can help Albert divide and conquer, even if you've hated math since you were back in Mrs. Leftover's fifth grade.

Keep Your Negative Feelings Private

You can start by keeping your negative feelings to yourself. "Would you tell your kids you hated reading and that you were never any good at it? No! And for very similar reasons you should not tell them that about math," says Johnny Lott, President of the National Council of Teachers of Mathematics and a math professor at the University of Montana in Missoula.

"If you really want to help your kids in math, let them see the math you do every day, like comparing price per ounce, cost per unit, or comparing box sizes when you are shopping. If you can't make math fun, make it interesting," says Lott. Playing games, such as the ones described below that are full of math learning opportunities, will engage Albert while subtly developing his skills. You will bolster Albert's confidence and ignite his motivation. They just might restore your faith in your own math ability.

Do the Tables

Because more complicated division problems rear their ugly heads in fourth and fifth grade, memorizing the multiplication tables is crucial now. However, don't drill Albert to death or have him write the nine times table nine times. Mimicking and memorizing do nothing but make kids lose interest in math, fast. Your goal is to get Albert interested in playing with numbers. Try these ideas instead:

• *Use a square or rectangular array.* Make square or rectangular shapes out of dots to help Albert "see" basic multiplication facts. Though this might seem too elementary for a big fourth grader like Albert, the objective of this exercise is to give him a "visual fix" on the product of the two numbers he's multiplying.

You'll need a pencil or colored markers and graph paper. Start very simply by making a 3 x 3 square with dots. Pick a special color to make this key square. Place the first row of three dots in a horizontal line close to the bottom left corner of the page. Then layer two more rows on top of this row, spacing them equally above each other. Now you've made a square array. You can also do this with pegs and a Peg-Board. This gives Albert a visual fix on what the product nine looks like. Using another color pen, have him make new equations by layering numbers across the top or down the side of this array. Concentrate your efforts on tables that give him trouble, like the sevens or eights. He can also use this method when he has to determine the volume or area of a shape.

- *Use a hand trick.* Because fourth and fifth graders are fascinated by tricks of all kinds, use one to help Albert remember the nine table. Have him spread out both hands palm down, and then name each finger 1–10, from left to right. To show the answer for 9 x 4, for example, bend finger number four. Looking on either side of the bent finger, count how many fingers are left. There are three fingers to the left of it and six to the right, making the product 36. This works for equations 9 x 1 through 9 x 10.

Add, Subtract, Multiply, Divide, and Conquer

- *Target a number.* To give Albert some practice with problem-solving skills using the four major number operations, play "target a number." On paper, write the number 2, the target number, at the top of the page. Underneath, write the following challenge numbers: 9, 3, 2, 8, and 4. Ask him to try to reach the target number by using all the challenge numbers in the second line. He can add, subtract, multiply, or divide. He must use all the challenge numbers, but only once each. He can work them out in his head, but must record any correct solutions that result in the target number, which in this example is 2. The answer to this example is:

$$4 + 8 = 12$$
$$12 \div 2 = 6$$
$$6 \times 3 = 18$$
$$18 \div 9 = 2$$

Do the exercise with him and compare answers. There can be more than one correct answer.

Create more target number exercises by starting with a set of challenge numbers and then using a reverse engineering process to arrive at a target number for that set, as follows:

1. Jot down a set of any four or five different challenge numbers, for example 2, 4, 8, 6, and 3. Use small whole numbers. Note that exercises with four challenge numbers tend to be easier to solve than with five.

2. Select two of the challenge numbers and apply one to the other using a math operation; for example, $2 \times 4 = 8$.

3. Pick another challenge number and apply it to the previous answer: $8 \div 8 = 1$.

4. Pick another challenge number and apply it to the previous answer: $6 \times 1 = 6$.

5. Take the only remaining challenge number and apply it to the previous answer: $6 \div 3 = 2$. So, 2 is a target number for this challenge number set.

If you want to put a different spin on the exercise, let Albert create a target number and challenge number set following the steps above, and then give that exercise to you to solve. He'll be thrilled if he can stump you, so don't feel like you've got to win this one to save face. The goal here is to get him motivated to play with numbers.

• *Play a calculator game.* Johnny Lott believes the calculator is a good math teaching tool. He recommends the following calculator game to help Albert work with multiples and determine winning strategies. You need a calculator and at least two people to play. The object of the game is to add to reach a target number. "To begin, let the target number be a multiple of four, like 24," says Lott. Begin by setting the calculator to zero. The first player inputs the number 1, 2, or 3, and then hits the add button and passes the calculator to the second player. The second player inputs 1, 2, or 3, and hits add. Players continue adding and swapping until the target, in this case 24, is reached. The first player to get there wins the round. Does it make a difference who goes first? Play several rounds to see if Albert guesses the winning strategy that "if you play second, you can control the game," says Lott. The same kind of game can be played without a calculator by using marbles, coins, or bottle caps.

Get an Estimate

• *Read it in the paper.* Estimation is an excellent companion to computation skills. It also helps Albert decide if the answers he comes up with on paper, in his head, and with his calculator are reasonable. Ask him to guess the number of tiles on the kitchen floor or the spokes on his bike wheels. Lott recommends an estimating activity using a newspaper. "Take a newspaper and rip out the sports and stocks pages, which are obviously filled with numbers," he says. On a page of remaining text, "let kids estimate how many times written numbers, numbers written in words, or number symbols will be used on the page," he says. This kind of exercise "gives kids a feel for the fact that numbers are a part of everyday life," says Lott.

- *Make the cookies count.* Make estimating engagingly delicious by cooking together. Cooking involves the four basic math functions and fractions. A successful result hinges on proper sequencing—all the skills Albert needs for working complicated multiplication and division equations. Ask Albert to calculate approximately how many cookies he'll make if he triples a recipe. How will that number change if he uses a teaspoon, not a tablespoon, for measuring the dough? How many cookies will fit into a cookie jar? How many will fill up the party tray if he places them edge to edge? What if he overlaps them? To monitor his computational skills, have Albert work out his estimation activities aloud. Add to his store of computation strategies by working his problems yourself and sharing your methods.

Get Help

- *Call in the experts.* Just as you'd go to an expert when you need a root canal or a new deck on your house, get a math professional to bolster Albert's math esteem. Interview math tutor candidates until you find someone who has a sense of humor Albert will enjoy. Laughter takes the ragged edge off math. Meet with the tutor at least once a week. And insist that his classroom teacher and tutor coordinate their efforts. If Albert and his tutor make a great match, keep them together for the long haul through middle and high school. See Chapter 24 for details about choosing the perfect tutor.

- *Find a tutoring group.* If private tutoring is unavailable or beyond your budget, then talk to Albert's teacher. If time permits, teachers often tutor kids individually or form small remedial groups before or after school. If this is not an option, contact another parent whose child has trouble with math and offer to share the expense of a private tutor.

• *Get math tutoring yourself.* If you can't seem to get beyond the memories of choking on long division in Mrs. Leftover's fifth grade, find your own math tutor. Check local tutoring agencies to see if they offer sessions for parents. Or check with Albert's school. Many schools schedule math familiarization events for parents in which the math program and materials are explained in depth. Montgomery County Public Schools in Maryland provides math booklets for parents called *Mathematics at Home.* Check to see if your school district might, too.

• *Build a math-loving support system.* If Albert's math problems are only periodic, seek help for him among family, friends, and neighbors. Was Grandpa great at algebra or Uncle Charles a whiz with geometry? Ask if they might have the time to help Albert fight his way through fractions. "Retired teachers are great, or retired anybody who worked with math," says Lott. But, he cautions, "Look at temperament, too." A math loving support system can only be built with kid-loving people.

Check Out the Sites

The Internet abounds with sites for parents who want to help their kids with math. Explore these excellent ones below:

The National Council of Teachers of Mathematics: The first professional organization to develop and introduce national math standards in 1989, they provide lessons and activities for all grade levels, found in the "Families" section at *www.nctm.org/families/.*

The Math Forum: Sponsored by Drexel University in Philadelphia, this site offers comprehensive math information and activities for parents of kids in kindergarten through college. Puzzled about how to do the math? Ask "Dr. Math" at *www.mathforum.org.*

Hit the Books

Get math help from a cognitive psychologist in *Math Coach: A Parent's Guide to Helping Children Succeed in Math* by Wayne and Ingrid Wickelgren.

Or snuggle up with your third, fourth, or fifth grader and read stories filled with math. Lott recommends the following titles, which are ranked by grade-level ability in math:

- *Below grade level: The Doorbell Rings* by Pat Hutchins. A story about factors of 12.

- *Grade level: A Grain of Rice* by Demi. A folktale from India.

- *Anno's Mysterious Multiplying Jar* by Masaichiro Anno and Mitusumasa Anno. Pictures teach factoring.

- *Above grade level: The Number Devil: A Mathematical Adventure* by Hans Magnus Enzensberger. A twelve-year-old in Alice-in-Wonderland-type adventures that teach math concepts.

Half the battle in helping Albert become proficient in math is overcoming the knee-jerk fear of failure that he's associated with managing numbers. Playing with numbers in the context of a game or daily routines makes math less of a public choking exhibition before his classmates and more of a simple intuitive exercise in recognizing number patterns. Eventually, he'll connect the dots and see that the same pattern recognition and counting skills that he uses to dominate his older sister in playing all forms of card games applies directly to classroom math challenges. Don't forget that the success you bring to Albert is a direct reflection on you. Take Albert by the hand and face math together. Maybe by helping him you'll prove to yourself what Mrs. Leftover knew all along, that you aren't so bad at math after all.

How to Help Kids Improve Research Skills and Write Reports

Lorraine spent three hours coloring the cover for her report on China. Then fifteen minutes copying two pages straight from the encyclopedia in bloated, space-gulping handwriting. She hoped this was what her teacher meant by "a three-page report."

Research reports are to fourth and fifth graders what reading and handwriting are to first and second graders—big challenges and big opportunities to synchronize skills and make great leaps in learning. But if the prospect brings tears to Lorraine's eyes, step up and help.

If she can't remember details or recall them in order when she reads, lend a hand. If she doesn't know how to take notes or understand why you need paragraphs when you write, you'd better slap on your coach's hat.

You don't have to be Charles Darwin to help her successfully complete a long-term report. The following plan helps you isolate areas that need practice at home or more support from her teacher. Don't rush the process! Two weeks will make it comfortable. Many steps can be done while you're cooking together, waiting in the orthodontist's office, or riding in the car to her best friend's house. Keep it chatty and friendly and enjoy watching her grow.

Step One: Check Lorraine's Deep-Reading Skills

Begin with a thirty-minute guided reading session, using a book that matches her assigned topic and her reading level. Chances are, if the report has been assigned, Lorraine will already have a suitable book from school. If not, ask her teacher, tutor, or school librarian for appropriate titles. Then, sit down beside her and ask her to silently read a page of the book. When she's finished reading, use the following questions and tips to get a snapshot of her skills:

1. Can she pick out the main idea in a paragraph? Repeated words or synonyms often give clues to the main idea.

2. Can she explain what she just read in her own words? She'll more likely put it in her own words if you ask her to look at you, not her book, when she's speaking.

3. If you ask her a detail about what she just read, can she skim the first sentence of each paragraph or look for repeated key words to find the answer, or must she reread every word on the page?

4. Can she remember details or events in order? Encourage her to use her fingers to tick them off. Fingers are natural prompts for helping kids recall ideas in sequential order.

5. Can she find the cause of an event she just read about? Can she explain the effects of this event? The relationship between cause and effect is often signaled by words like *and then* or *because*.

6. Can she express an opinion about what she just read? Can she supply details that support her opinion? To avoid pat answers like "I liked it," don't ask "if" she liked a topic, but

instead ask her "why" she liked it, or why not. Two or three supporting details will show you she's effectively processed the topic.

If she responds confidently to all the above reading challenges, she can independently use research materials on her reading level. Make yourself available, however, for the next phases of her report.

If she has difficulty with two or three of these skills, support her reading. If she can't recall details, for example, point out some interesting ones and read them to her. Then give her a hint to help her find the next one. Or use the key words above to help her locate causes and effects until she answers without prompting. If she's in fourth grade and still not a strong reader, you'll need to support her by citing examples and practicing whenever long-term reports are assigned. Or you might consider a homework tutor.

If, however, she has difficulty with more than four of these skills, talk to her teacher about customizing the assignment or allowing Lorraine to team with a classmate with complementary skills. Reluctant or tentative readers greatly benefit from private tutoring. Some schools now offer tutoring programs after school or during the summer. Check also at community centers, public libraries, churches, or senior citizen groups. Many offer inexpensive or free programs for neighborhood kids.

Once Lorraine can work independently or has the kind of academic support she needs to complete the reading aspects of her research assignments, move on to the next section.

Step Two: Show Her What the Best Looks Like

Next, show her what good research looks like. Some teachers use former students' work to show kids how a good assignment should look and how it will be graded. At home, scan newspapers or magazines for research-based topics written in an interesting style or from a unique vantage point. Read them together, or read them to her and then use these questions to take them apart.

> Does this author punch up her work with catchy words and phrases?
> Do the graphics and color enrich or detract from the topic?
> Did the writer interview some interesting people?
> How would Lorraine have written it differently?

Teachers call this critical reading and focus on it in the upper elementary grades. It shifts perspectives and elicits opinions which deepen comprehension, and it fosters the development of a personal writing style. Then turn to the specifics of the report she must complete.

Step Three: How Will Her Report Be Evaluated?

Discuss together not only the due date, length, and formatting characteristics but also how the paper will be evaluated. Will spelling count? Will her grade suffer if her handwriting is illegible? Must she use three references to get an A? Advance thinking springs old traps and helps young writers avoid them. Visualizing a finished product hones focus and boosts creativity, too.

Step Four: What Does She Know about China?

If Lorraine has to write about China, what does she already know? Teachers call this learning step "tapping prior knowledge," psychologists call it "metacognition," and both use it to help kids evaluate what they already know. Use this when she says, "I don't even know where to start." This esteem-boosting, clarifying exercise provides a more confident, secure launching pad even for kindergarten students. Ask Lorraine questions that get at her experiences of the Chinese culture.

> Does she eat Chinese food?
> Did her aunt visit Beijing?
> Does her grandmother do Tai Chi?
> Does her dad get acupuncture treatments?

These kinds of questions also spark curiosity, uncover misinformation, and help Lorraine narrow her topic for writing. Use snapshots, postcards, or videos to trigger her memory.

Step Five: Determine the Audience

Who is her audience for the report? The larger the audience, the more motivating the task. Thinking about the audience for writing is now taught in language arts classes as early as third grade. Will Lorraine read her paper to a class of second graders or make a presentation at Grandparents Day? Making kids aware of their audience forces objectivity and naturally corrects the course of theme development. Gently remind her about her listening audience when and if her ideas veer off course.

Step Six: Manage the Project

Make a project plan together. If the teacher doesn't provide a checklist to track the phases of work, make one together. Schedules are highly important to fourth and fifth graders. They will happily recite by heart their own school schedules, and everyone else's, and are none too tolerant of interruptions, even for thunderstorms. To visually reinforce her work plan, use colored markers and a large erasable calendar. By fifth grade, she'll be comfortable with a plan about ten days long and divided as follows:

1. Three to five days for reading books and online resources and making note cards

2. One day for adding to or correcting her note cards

3. Two days for making a rough draft of her report

4. One day for proofreading her draft and making additions or corrections

5. Two days for producing a final copy and a cover

Step Seven: Use Resources

Now's the time to guide Lorraine's research skills using tools like the library, the Internet, and the interview process. Where does she think she can get the materials she needs? How does she function using different resources? Take her on a trip to the library, or sit down together at the computer and analyze her skills using the following questions:

At the Library

Can she use a traditional or electronic card catalogue?
Can she locate book sections or specific titles?
Can she use the library's computers to do her research?
Does she know how research librarians can help her?

To reinforce library skills, make weekly trips to the library a routine. Go more often during holiday and summer vacations and when visiting authors come to town. Remember that research librarians are happy to help, and teach.

On the Internet

According to the National Educational Technology Standards of Learning, "technologically literate" students should, by the end of fifth grade, be able to use web research tools to produce products that inform audiences inside and outside the classroom. If you don't have the technical know-how to help her or own a home computer, check with your school. Many offer Saturday or after-school classes for families and kids who don't have access to computers at home. Look also for summer computer programs at community centers, churches, or local day camps.

Watch Lorraine on the Internet to see if she can do the following things. If your computer skills aren't up to evaluating hers yet, take this list to your next conference and discuss them with her teacher. You might also ask her school's media center specialist or your favorite research librarian at the local library to watch Lorraine do an Internet search and give you feedback on her skills. Can Lorraine do most of these things comfortably?

CAN LORRAINE SEARCH THE INTERNET?

1. Access the Internet through a modem connection or high-speed line.

2. Locate a search engine like Google, Excite, or Alta Vista.

3. Launch an Internet search. If she's writing about Chinese diets, what words does she use to command the computer to search for information? Does she simply type in words like *Chinese* and *diets*?

4. Refine her search terms to get the best search results. Can she refine her search by adding the words, *eating habits, Asian,* or *children* to *Chinese* and *diets*? The more exact her

search criteria, the more closely the search results will fit her needs. Most large search engines like Google or Lycos rank search items by how closely they align with the search criteria.

5. Consider the source. Teach Lorraine to look for the most reliable resources by directing her to the synopsis or Internet address of each search item. To assure herself that she's getting the accurate information she needs for her report, have her look and select only dependable sources like universities, educational organizations, museums, professional organizations, and local, state, and federal education departments.

6. Keep her on track. Does she spend more than ten minutes scanning each page of the search? A productive search takes about 30–45 minutes. Bring her back on task when she gets sidetracked or distracted.

7. Download and print pertinent graphics or text. Does she know what types of files her computer can't read, like Mac or Adobe if she has an IBM?

8. Reboot if her computer crashes.

9. Make a simple diagnosis of what went wrong. Did she click the mouse too many times? This can cause a program to freeze. Or ask the computer to do too many things at once? Or open too many windows at the same time?

Conducting Interviews

To broaden her research skills, have her investigate resources beyond the routine. Does she know how to make like a journalist and conduct an interview? The owner of the Asian grocery store might be able to give her information on a typical Chinese diet or favorite snack foods for kids. Illustrate a simple interview format by asking her about her favorite brand of protein bars or chicken barbecue sauce. Then test her fledgling interviewing skills by listening to her grill her brother and his best friend about how they got those massive matching holes in their brand-new backpacks.

Step Eight: Take Notes, Sequence Tasks

Kids need tools for putting their collected data in a logical, understandable order. Can Lorraine record newly learned information? Does she know how to take notes and sequence her work?

Use the following process to show fourth and fifth graders how to take notes and sequence their tasks. The process starts by skimming the page of a book or the screen of an Internet resource.

1. Have her read only the first line of each paragraph on the page.

2. Have her select only those paragraphs which seem like they will contain the information she needs to write about in her report on Chinese diets. Use Post-it bookmarks to highlight them.

3. Ignoring the paragraphs that aren't helpful, return to the "meaty" paragraphs and have her read aloud a detail she finds interesting.

4. Have her write this detail *in her own words* on a 4 x 6 note card. This is the perfect time to talk about plagiarism and copyright infringements. She cannot copy word for word from a book or Internet resource and claim it as her own— this is plagiarism. Nor can she use any graphics, pictures,

or illustrations without giving proper credit to the source—this is a copyright infringement.

5. At the bottom of each card, have her jot the book title or web address for later reference.

6. Repeat this process with the number of book or Internet resources she's required to use for this assignment.

7. After she's collected ten or more cards, spread them out on a table. Ask her to decide if there are cards that can be grouped together.

8. Put them in separate piles. Then determine an appropriate title for each one and make a title card for it, like "Chinese vegetables," "Holiday meals," or "Food traditions." Tell her she's just determined her subtopics.

9. Lastly, have her arrange the subtopics in the order she wants to write about them in her report.

10. When she's produced 10–15 note cards, have her check her progress with her teacher. She might already have enough to begin a rough draft.

Step Nine: Drafting and Final Copy

Lorraine is now ready to draft and finalize her report. According to our plan, this could take a fourth grader a week to complete. Use the following ideas to guide her through:

1. Help her begin a rough draft by copying sentences from note cards arranged in her predetermined order. Point out that paragraphs will change whenever she moves from one note card pile to another. By fourth grade, she should be able to comfortably write three-sentence paragraphs.

2. Now have her add a paragraph in the beginning. She can begin by explaining that the reason she chose to write about Chinese diets is because she loves dim sum.

3. Next, instruct her to add a concluding paragraph. This is a good place for her to make statements about whether or not she believes the typical Chinese diet is healthy.

4. Now do the proofreading. Reading aloud is crucial here for making grammatical corrections, clarifying points, and smoothing out the flow of words. See if she self-edits her spelling, repeated words, awkward sentences, and grammar. If she stops in confusion while reading or if you have to ask her to clarify what she means, she will probably need to rewrite that part. When the draft is as long as required and sounds smooth when she reads it aloud, move on to the next step.

5. Set her down to write or type up the final copy. Lorraine's teacher might allow her to type it on the computer or write in pencil. The final copy should be free of errors. Offer to be a "reader" for her. Tell her that most professional writers have at least one.

6. "Publish" it. In school, students can read it aloud to the class or pin papers up on the bulletin board. Lorraine might publish by reading it aloud to her grandmother or sending it by e-mail to her grandfather.

7. Put a cover on it. Lorraine probably won't need your help for this final part. Then make sure she hands it in on time!

Don't be afraid to intervene during long-term assignments when Lorraine seems hesitant about reading, computer, or writing skills, or when you're asked. Show Lorraine, in conversational tones and with gentle guidance, how to give her work thought and consideration, search out the best resources, put it all together, and then model it before an appreciative audience—now her grandparents and, later, the world.

PART FIVE

Middle School:
The Hormone-Hammering Years

18

How to Help Middle Schoolers Study

Heather Whatever has headphones for ears. When she finally hears that you're asking about homework, she flutters her iridescent fingernails in your face and cranks up the volume on her favorite rude rap song.

Welcome to middle school! Those parental hair-tearing years between elementary school and high school when your dimpled moppet morphs into monosyllabic, hormone-harassed, emotionally challenging Heather, the Queen of Whatever. Don't despair. You can help Heather study better and survive her middle school experience with a full head of hair.

Hormonal Background Noise

Before we get to the study tips, know that hormonal background noise will play constantly throughout middle school. Sometimes it plays so sweetly and softly you'd hardly notice. Other times, it blares so loudly you'll need the same kind of sound-muffling headset a construction worker wears for drilling a hole through concrete with a jackhammer.

Though the adolescent years can be hard on adults, no one has a tougher time than the kids. Blame it on the growth spurt. Between the ages of eleven and thirteen, kids go through physical changes more quickly than at any other time in their lives. Their noses grow, their feet spread, their bodies blossom and lengthen, and their voices squeak out of control. It's no wonder they spend so much time focused on themselves and staring dumbfounded or horrified in the mirror. Only Alice, back in Wonderland, had it worse.

It's all so, like, totally embarrassing. Classmates' constant comparisons to each other's physical appearance compounds a complex mix of psychological, emotional, and social challenges. Especially if Heather is not developing at the same rate as her friends. Reaching full physical maturity can take two years for some, and for others, as long as five or six. Those who mature quickly tend to be more athletic, more active in school, and more socially skilled. Late maturation, on the other hand, can make Heather defensive, temperamental, and hypersensitive. "Regardless of whether they mature early or late, all young teens worry to some extent about their physical attractiveness," says counselor and educator, Ann Vernon of Janesville, Iowa.

So, what's a parent to do? "Keep a level head. Remember that the outbursts aren't about you; they are usually just the natural consequence of the hormonal eruption," says Vernon.

Being present will help. According to the *MetLife Survey of the American Teacher, 2002: Student Life: School, Home & Community*, which surveyed over two thousand three hundred seventh through twelfth grade kids and over one thousand middle and high school teachers, students are more successful when parents are interested and informed about their school lives. In fact, the study found parent involvement had a direct affect on grades. "Students who are failing or nearly failing are more likely than 'A' students to report that their parents are not aware of key aspects of their lives," the study reports. In other words, though she'd rather have root canal than admit it, Heather Whatever craves your attention the same way she did when she was your dimpled little girl.

Get on the Study Track with Parent's Night

Parent's Night or Back-to-School Night is your bright red Ferrari on the twisty road of middle school. Held early in the fall of every school year, this event is planned especially for parents. It gives you a fast-forward report on the doings in the place that reigns supreme over Heather's days. It's designed by teachers and administrators who, by choice, surround themselves with hundreds of Heathers. Think of that. Better yet, change your plans or your business trips and be there. This event yields a huge return for a modest investment of time. Here's how to make it work for you:

Get practical. Parents traditionally follow an accelerated, abbreviated version of their child's schedule, so dress for comfort and wear shoes for walking, sometimes sprinting, long hallways and lots of stairs. Take a pen, Post-it Notes, paper for noting details or questions, and a folder for collecting handouts.

Get the facts. In the ten minutes or less provided for each class, teachers will outline their curriculum plan for the school year. Note in your notebook areas of emphasis and expectation, homework requirements, and deadlines for major projects and book reports. If teachers don't announce them, raise your hand and ask for a schedule of quizzes, tests, book and research reports, and standardized tests, which are routinely given to sixth and eighth graders each year. Ask also about where you must drop off assignments left on the kitchen table. Take notes, and then mark dates on your calendar at the office and home.

Get names and e-mails. Write down the names of Heather's homeroom and subject teachers, guidance counselor, bilingual advisor, principal, and vice-principal as they apply. Jot down a memory hook (patch over one eye, handkerchief stuffed up her sleeve) about their appearance so you'll recognize them later when you meet in the hallways, at conferences, and school events. Don't forget to jot down their contact information. Most teachers provide parents with their school phone numbers or e-mail addresses. Some offer home phone numbers. Jot them on Post-it Notes so you can easily transfer them to your address book at home or your appointment book at the office.

Get the scene. Since middle school is likely the first time Heather will change classrooms for all subjects, note the location of her homeroom, locker, subject classrooms, cafeteria, auditorium, and gymnasium. Later, Heather and you can strategize the most efficient ways for her to get to class on time. Find the school office, too. This is the most likely place for dropping off books, lunches, or assignments she left at home.

Now that you've been to Parent's Night, you can engage in Subtle, Informed, Parent-engineered Dialogue (SIPED). Use it daily to steer you safely not just through academic subjects but through social and emotional issues, too. Keep the volume normal and constantly tuned to Heather as she makes her way through middle school. Now that you know Mr. Corduroyjacket (skinny, elbow patches on his sportcoat) gives social studies quizzes every Thursday, you'll arrange your schedule to offer your homework services every Wednesday night.

A Campaign for Homework Coaching

The homework-coaching campaign for middle schoolers is not an open invitation to sit beside Heather through every homework assignment every single night. Forget that. Work with her only when you're invited or if she's confused or overwhelmed by an assignment. She will undoubtedly let you know.

Keep tests tops on your list. Whenever you work with Heather, your efforts will pay off in points if you keep in mind the four major areas evaluated in the annual standardized group tests now federally mandated for sixth and eighth graders.

Vocabulary: Measures the extent of the words she can understand and use when she reads.
Verbal ability: Examines her skill in using words to associate, relate, reason, infer, remember, and think.
Mathematics: Measures numerical activities taught in the classroom.
Quantitative ability: Reflects math potential by probing her insights into numerical relationships and strategies.

Get a verbal chronicle. While you're studying together, encourage Heather to think out loud. Verbal chronicling demonstrates how she self-monitors, self-corrects, comprehends, analyzes, strategizes, and reasons. It also forces Heather's eyes and attention to stay focused on her task.

Play dumb like a fox. Nothing inspires conversation in middle school kids better than setting a befuddled adult straight. As she explains what she needs to study for her social studies quiz tomorrow, play dumb, like a fox. Make it clear that it's not her, but you, who needs the help. Employ the following dumb-like-a-fox phrases to reveal whether it's the work itself or her own abilities Heather's questioning.

--------------- **DUMB-LIKE-A-FOX PHRASES** ---------------
FOR HOMEWORK COACHING

I'm not sure how you got that answer.
Did you mean to put an 8 there, not a 7?

Please do it for me again. I didn't get it the first time.

I can't tell what you're thinking.

I might understand better if you put it in your own words.

Help me remember the details.

How did that happen?

What happened first?

What happened after that?

What happened in the end?

Can you explain it another way?

Listen for clues. Listen carefully as Heather explains what and how she will study for her quiz. Listen for clear clues like "I don't understand this," or more subtle ones like "He didn't explain that very well," or "This doesn't make sense." Note recurrent weak spots and make a teacher phone call or conference to strategize how to get Heather Whatever the help she needs to succeed. To help her focus, clear her desk of all unrelated materials.

Yuk it up. Attentive listening is the most important study skill, so don't be afraid to have fun when you're helping Heather study. If she's laughing, she's listening.

Chunk it up. Together, review her assignments, figuring how many steps they will take to complete. Decide how long each step will take. If it's a lengthy research report, make up a plan sheet and schedule days for each step. Make two copies so you can monitor her progress together.

Link it up. Probe Heather's prior knowledge to show her that learning is a dynamic continuum and that she's developing a body of knowledge all her own. Is there anything in this assignment that she's seen, done, or heard of before? Then, since middle schoolers have no shortage of opinions, ask Heather her views and her feelings about the topic she's studying. And offer your own. Kids retain information better when they feel that learning is a familiar, personal thing.

Dig deeper. Probe beyond details to get at Heather's verbal ability. When working on a book report, for example, if she describes the main character as brave, ask for examples from the book which describe him or her acting bravely. Then ask her to do something for which middle schoolers are famous—making predictions about their friends. Given what she knows about a character in her book, can she predict how he or she will handle an impending situation? This also tests forecasting skills, a major indicator of verbal ability.

Sensory-Smart Study Ideas

"No one is too old for sensory integration activities. Neuroplasticity, changes in the way the brain receives and interprets information, continues until we die," says occupational therapist Diana Henry of Phoenix, Arizona. "The 11- to 13-year-olds can verbalize and tell you what their behavior is all about. Then tell them they aren't clumsy, bad, dumb, or lazy, and that they are not alone." When thoughts of homework send Heather reaching for her headphones and her rambunctious rappers, the following activities provide more constructive sensory input.

Use music. Heather might become more productive if you capitalize on her love for music by using it to help her study. Experiment with different types of music like rap, rock, country, classical, or soft jazz to see which masks distracting outside noises and helps her concentrate better. Test her physical response by having her listen to different selections while she simultaneously reads an assignment. Use a timer to determine how long she concentrates. When she starts to fidget, turn the music off and talk about it.

How long did she concentrate? How did it make her feel, twitchy, ready to dance, or calm? Were any background noises still annoying? Sample different musical styles to determine which she can listen to and still effectively concentrate. If rude rap works for her, accept it and be very grateful for your jackhammer earmuffs.

Visualize it. For developing vocabulary, draw her a picture of a word she needs to memorize. For example, if she needs to memorize the word *lugubrious*, which means sad and mournful in an exaggerated way, draw a person crying a river of tears. Or use the letters as a base for drawing. Make a long and trailing track of tears pouring out of the letter *i* near the end of the word. This will give her both a definition and a spelling clue. You'll only have to do one drawing as an example. Doodle-happy middle schoolers will take right over.

Use maps. Programming and transferring information to long-term memory occurs best when information is personalized, organized, and based on something Heather already knows. Make a written road map of ideas in a chapter. Then link ideas together and amend the map as more material is read. Make vocabulary maps, too. To make *lugubrious* part of her writing and testing vocabulary, print and encircle the word in the middle of a page. Make six spokes and attach a circle to the end of each one. Label them as follows: definition, part of speech, synonym, antonym, example, and sentence. Discuss each and then fill it in. This is also an excellent exercise for learning concepts like prejudice, culture, or diversity, which middle schoolers will encounter frequently in writing assignments and on standardized tests.

Use color. Use bright markers to highlight the important parts of the map. Use brightly colored Post-it Notes to post vocabulary words all over her room and throughout the house. Use them to mark an important spot in a research book. When it's been a while between laughs, post one on your forehead.

Do some yoga. When leaning over the books too long makes Heather achy and cranky, show her how to do a yoga warm-up exercise. Have her lie flat on her back on a soft mat or carpeted floor. In this exercise she will gently clench all her muscles in sequential order, relax, and breathe. Starting with her toes, have her curl them under gently and squeeze all the muscles in her feet, and then move to the calf, knee, thighs, buttocks, stomach, chest, neck, arms, fingers, and hands. Remind her to keep breathing throughout this exercise! When all her muscles are tense and tight, tell her to release them all at once and breathe deeply from her belly three times, feeling all her muscles go soft and warm. Have her relax quietly for 30–60 seconds, then return refreshed to her work. She can also do this while sitting in a chair at home or school.

Sensory-Smart Homework Games

Sensory Sentences. Because grammar is an important part of the sixth grade English curriculum, help Heather figure who did what to whom with a sensory sentence game. The object is to match parts of speech, physically construct a sentence, and then "activate" it. This activity works best with a group of classmates, campers, cousins, or friends. Supplies needed are 4 x 6 cards, a marker, and a dictionary. Elect one person grammarian; the others are the sentence makers.

Print the following parts of speech on separate cards: subject, predicate, direct object, and indirect object. Place those cards in a line on the floor in the order above. Think of highly visual sentences like "The waddling bird gave a wiggling fish to the trembling turkey," or "A growling tiger put a laughing gorilla on the sofa." Write each word in your sentence on its own card. Then, shuffle the cards and distribute one to each player. To control the game, don't reveal the sentence to the players ahead of time. Ask players to match their word to its part of speech, then walk over and stand behind it. The grammarian then reads the sentence that's formed. Are words correctly matched to their part of speech? Does the sentence make sense? If not, have the sentence makers shuffle around until everything is correct and logical. When it reads correctly, the grammarian gives the order to "activate!" If time permits, ask the group if they can shuffle themselves around to make another logical sentence. Read and activate this variation. Then move on to a new sentence and repeat the progress.

Wave the flag. "Slow, rocking, rhythmic, repetitive movements are relaxing," says Dana Henry. Borrow the classic military semaphore flag signaling system for calming, focusing, and increasing visual skills. Letters and numbers are signaled across the classroom or the backyard using color and wide arm movements. "Make sure kids cross their hands across the midline of their body because it integrates both sides of the body," says Henry. Instead of the standard red and yellow flags, Heather might wear two different colored gloves. Better yet, use one-pound hand weights in two different colors. Henry believes that age-appropriate heavy lifting can be calming even for middle school-aged kids. Heather can use this system to spell confounding words or practice her Spanish vocabulary words. Find the semaphore alphabet at *www.anbg.gov.au/flags/semaphore.html*.

Wrap it up. When the work is done, the report is in, and the test is over, establish a ritual of approval. Slide Heather a soft high five, put your fingers in your mouth, and whistle long and loud, or do a victory dance with an *A* printed on a Post-it Note and plastered to your forehead. Do this every time she's successfully completed a difficult task, and your silly, sweet, honest gesture will become its own reward.

19

How to Motivate an Underachiever

Dino's been on the sofa so long he'll need surgery to have it removed. He's convinced that no matter how much homework, studying, or paying attention in class he does, he won't get good grades. He thinks that lucky thing happens only if the teacher is in a good mood.

Unfortunately, Dino is no longer your ever-enthusiastic and constantly curious preschooler. He lives in Hormone City now. Unlike blemishes and a squeaking voice, however, underachievement is not something he will outgrow. Don't doubt yourself when you first start questioning whether Dino is an underachiever. If you're questioning, it's probably because he's displaying some worrisome signs.

Michele J. Sabino, who teaches a freshman remedial English class at the University of Houston Downtown, believes that "a lack of motivation is typical of kids who push buttons and have images instantly flashed back at them on a screen." Though there is no consensus about the cause or causes for low motivation and underachievement, certain factors and behaviors in combination contribute to Dino's lack of achievement.

If too many factors in the box below describe your middle schooler's life, or these behaviors have persisted through one marking period, your sofa-bound Dino is probably headed straight down the underachieving track.

-------- **FACTORS AND BEHAVIORS COMMONLY** --------
ASSOCIATED WITH UNDERACHIEVERS

Commonly associated behaviors

Has his social circle outside school

Seeks out low-achieving comrades

Disparages the value of school, teachers, and goals

Adopts alienated fashions, mannerisms, language, and demeanor

Has low self-esteem

Has a learning delay

Feels he has low academic ability

Is easily bored or distracted

Is hypersensitive and critical

Has low or nonexistent motivation and effort

Dislikes book-work or academic challenges

Dislikes structured activities and timed exercises

Forgets, misplaces, or loses textbooks or assignments

Organizes poorly time and materials

Has poor self-management skills

Has a learning style that does not match the teaching style

Is disruptive in class

Possesses poor test-taking and study skills

Gets low or failing grades

Thinks good grades are the result of luck or favoritism

Takes on limited extracurricular school activities

School factors

Morale of student population is low

Teacher/student relationships are poor or ineffective

Contributing Factors

What is getting Dino down? The following ideas elaborate on some critical elements that might be contributing to a low-achieving cycle. Each contains suggestions to implement if you think they apply to your middle schooler.

HEALTH AND DEVELOPMENTAL CAUSES

Certainly, hammering hormones add moodiness, irritability, and resentment to Dino's hair-flattening sofa experience. But it might be more. Check out the most obvious thing first, his physical condition. Investigate whether food or environmental allergies, sensory integration dysfunction, or hormonal or metabolism changes might be making him less productive. Take him to a trusted health care professional for a complete physical evaluation. Do not, however, spend any precious time searching for a magic potion. Nobody has bottled motivation yet.

POOR SELF-IMAGE

With health concerns eliminated or under control, check his school environment next. Maybe it's a self-image problem that's got Dino stuck. Has anything uncomfortable happened in school recently? Did he, perish the thought, wear the wrong kind of shirt to school? Middle schoolers think and function in a constantly comparative mode that few, other than cancer researchers, do with greater microscopic precision. Teasing, taunting, and bullying are common currency, and even popular and well-adjusted kids can be adversely affected by it.

Seeking Dino's input is a critical first step to understanding his lack of motivation. Find a subtle and gentle way to initiate a conversation. Use a third person, nonconfrontational opener like "I hear that some kids in your school are . . ." If that gets you exactly nowhere, try the direct approach like "I am ready to talk anytime about things that are going on with you in school." When that fails, too, turn to his friend who always tells you everything. If together you determine that Dino's lack of motivation and low achievement have their basis in his school environment, set a conference immediately with his school guidance counselor, his favorite or homeroom teacher, or the school principal. Don't let teasing, taunting, or bullying persist any longer than the first minute you hear about it.

FAMILY-BASED PROBLEMS

A lack of motivation and low achievement can also result from negative or stressful family dynamics. Is something going on at home that's stressful or abusive? Has there recently been a traumatic event, like a death, divorce, or move from a school he loved? These can negatively affect even middle schoolers with great fortitude.

With a middle schooler, however, family matters don't have to be drastic to cause a lack of motivation. It could be your attempts to inflate his ego by constantly praising, congratulating, thanking, or rewarding him for something he knows he should be doing anyway. No age group is more sensitive to misplaced flattery than ultrasensitive middle schoolers. Dino's sofa siege could be his reaction to your well-intended action.

Now is the time to swallow the patter. Be tactful, frank, and honest about his habits instead. Kids appreciate that kind of feedback and seek it consistently from loving and resourceful adults. It also eventually restores credibility to your words of praise.

If, however, you can't change your obsequious ways, it is time for a family-dynamic tune-up. Start with someone you trust who will give you an honest answer about whether your habits might be adversely affecting Dino. If he or she says, "Yes, indeed," ask for suggestions about how to improve your interaction, dialogue, and behavior.

Or turn to Dino's pediatrician, your faith counselor, his school counselor, or another parent. Consider family counseling with a licensed clinical social worker or psychologist. Note that if you seek the advice of a mental health professional, make sure he or she has deep experience with academically underachieving adolescents. Be specific about the situation. The more honest you are about Dino and your family dynamic, the more effective a therapist's help can be.

LEARNING PROBLEMS

Learning problems can also make Dino's achievement drag. Get to any root learning issues by talking first to his middle school teachers or school counselor. It could be a difficult subject, a specific academic challenge like a long-term project, or a personality clash with a teacher that's causing Dino's stall.

If you or his teacher suspect a learning delay, take him to an educational diagnostician or licensed psychologist for cognitive and achievement tests, especially if he's never had one or the last one was more than two years ago. The Woodcock-Johnson Psychoeducational Battery is an example of one such test. Combined with family and individual interviews, such tests yield a comprehensive picture of current academic and processing skills and give an indication of future performance. Finding out what Dino is truly capable of is a comfort if he has been boring a hole through the sofa with his head. The counselor will also make specific recommendations for getting him on the move again. Remember that if his public school agrees to conduct a psychoeducational test, there is no cost to you. Consult his middle school guidance counselor for eligibility and guidelines in your school district. Refer to Chapter 8 for details about individual standardized testing.

TEACHER SENSITIVITY

If Dino is underachieving, it might be because he is a teacher-sensitive learner. Some kids get good grades even if their teacher has one eye, spits when he talks, and rides a red wagon. For some kids, however, there is a direct correlation between their feelings about the person standing in front of that classroom and the grade they get in that subject.

Though with middle schoolers every teacher will be a one-eyed monster at one time or another, listen closely to the nature of Dino's remarks. If you're hearing a negative theme repeated over a period of weeks, or if it seems, even to you, that he's being singled out or reprimanded unfairly, make a conference with that teacher and bring Dino. As you sit face to face with his teacher, listen first to the other side of the story, and then be forthcoming about Dino's role in the current dynamic. Strategize ways to refresh the relationship. Set a conference date for two weeks later and reassess their progress.

Periodic clashes between teachers and kids can put a hitch in the achievement flow even if a kid is not the teacher-sensitive type. If you are aware, or Dino makes you aware, that an uncharacteristic personality tangle is contributing to underachievement, set a conference but don't bring Dino. Sit down, look the teacher in the eyes, and say, in your gentlest voice, "Look, I know you're having a problem with my kid right now. Sometimes I have a problem with him, too. How can we work through this together?" This is an icebreaker better than any axe. With honesty and openness paving the way, you can swap comradely war stories and strategize ways to pry Dino off the sofa. You've also just gained an important ally at school.

Tips for Rousing Underachievers

Whether you are involved in activities with Dino in the classroom, on the soccer field, or beside him on the sofa in the living room, employing some of the following ideas will stoke unmotivated middle school students to learn again:

Don't wait another minute to act. If you let his lack of motivation last one marking period, you can bet his grades won't reflect his potential when his report card arrives. Because you are an important adult in his life, you are also a powerful change bringer. Having the gumption to change what you do and say and how you instruct Dino in your own home is the first, critical step toward helping Dino find and maintain his most productive mode of learning. Be kind, be honest, but be the boss.

Give him some face time. Personal attention is an honestly flattering thing that even the most dubious middle schoolers take as a compliment. Carve time out of your own schedule and give it to him, one to one. Do this every day, especially when he's sofa-suffering. But do not fawn.

Do something different. To shock him out of the doldrums, do something out of character like standing on your head. Or if you've never done it before, sit down next to him on the sofa and play a video game together or watch his favorite blood-and-guts movie. Comment on his video playing technique or his analysis of the villain's cruel intentions. Do not inflate his skills; instead be on the alert for comments that provide a natural transition to a suspected trouble spot in his life, and then jump on it. If you can move your conversation to the kitchen to make dinner or out to the car to pick up the pizza, you've broken the momentum of that day's downward spiral. This is the middle school version of what you did with a cookie when he was two.

Use one success to build on the next. When he's procrastinating about reading his book report book, remind him that the fast reflexes and good eye-hand coordination he displayed while playing video games means he must have excellent predicting skills when he reads. Tell him you have time right now for a little demonstration.

Invite his friend over to study. If Dino does not want you to explain his homework or help him study for a test, he might allow his friend to do it. And if it happens to be your favorite friendly informant, be sure to snatch an update about that teasing situation at school.

Make your house like a classroom. Show Dino that his problem is your problem, too, by doing things that can turn a one-eyed monster into a favorite teacher. Give him a second chance to prove himself when his first attempt is a miss or a dismal failure. Use his mistakes as a window of opportunity to teach him something new. And when you finally get him off the couch and on his homework, be a good homework detective. See Chapter 9 for details.

Life can be difficult when you're a kid, and most adults would agree that they were fortunate to have survived their tumultuous adolescent years with so few psychological scars. It would be a disservice to you and Dino to oversimplify the causes and the remedies for his lack of motivation. But do something about it and do it on all fronts. Do not let your paralysis in dealing with Dino become an example for dealing with his own issues. Sometimes all it takes is a few well-placed nudges to loosen a kid like Dino from the couch for good.

20

What to Do When Kids Have Trouble Studying

Vinny thinks studying means getting facts to stick in your brain, so he straps his math book to his head and waits forty-five minutes. When he gets an F on his test, he blames his teacher, his mother, and his cat. It never occurs to him to blame his methods.

You can help Vinny develop a personal plan for studying that goes beyond the outmoded methods he devised during elementary school. If you draw on his daily routines, learning style, and organizational habits, he will develop the sophisticated and productive personal resources he needs for middle school.

According to the US Department of Education, most teachers agree that two to two-and-a-half hours of homework is appropriate for kids in seventh grade and above. This can bring on a book-induced headache in kids who have strong reading and writing skills, let alone those who are struggling. But just like Vinny can learn more efficient ways to read, he can learn more fruitful ways to study.

The Root of Study Skills

To succeed in these years of constant and increasing academic demands, Vinny needs to think about how he's thinking. Educators call this "metacognition," and it's his bird's eye view on how he's reflecting, appraising, strategizing, monitoring, and evaluating himself while he studies. It's that elemental self-probing most adults do spontaneously when facing new experiences or challenges. Have I ever seen this before? Do I know anything about it? How do I do it? Do I need help to get it done?

Research studies show that learning increases when kids are taught metacognition skills. It's even being taught to college freshmen. Michele Sabino, visiting assistant professor at the University of Houston Downtown, requires all her freshmen developmental-reading students to develop a plan for how they will learn the required material for her course. She notes, "The ones who were able to develop their own plan for learning were the ones who learned."

"Study skills can't be taught in isolation; they're a bore. Underneath all these isolated study skills is the 'metacognition.' That is what has to take place. Study skills need to be incorporated into good teaching and reinforced repeatedly," says educational diagnostician Carol Springer of Wake, Kendall, Springer, Isenman, Schweickert, Weintraub & Associates of Washington, DC. "Kids need to be responsible for their own progress in school," Springer adds.

Develop a Personal Plan for Studying

Allow 20–30 minutes daily over the period of a week to help Vinny develop a personal plan for studying, one he will eventually be able to use spontaneously for complicated assignments or long-term projects. The key is to listen to how Vinny thinks out loud and talks to himself when he's studying. The better the impression you have, the more consistently you can correct and reinforce how he thinks to make the work he does more effective and successful. Monitor this process for a month to six weeks.

Don't hesitate to intervene when stress threatens to sabotage it. Enlist the aid of his favorite aunt or a homework tutor if you feel you and Vinny would benefit from the input of an objective voice in this important process.

ACCOUNT FOR DAILY HABITS

Base Vinny's personal plan for learning, first and foremost, on his daily living needs. Ask him to describe a typical day in his life. Since you never know how the hormones are hammering and changing him today, don't assume you know the answers. Is he a morning person or a night owl? What perks him up? What foods satisfy his hunger best? Does he get tired during the day? What helps him fall asleep? Talk about ways to accommodate his needs for food and rest to his needs for studying. You might find that working on spelling in the morning with a bowl of bananas and milk is his round-trip ticket to an A.

ACCOUNT FOR LEARNING HABITS

A quick test of Vinny's learning style is to watch how he teaches someone else. Ask him if he knows how to use the new jar opener or a handheld computer. Does he point and draw an example, lecture, or pick it up in his hands and show you how to use it? Remind him to rely on this method whenever cantankerous concepts cause him to forget. Use it yourself whenever he asks for your help.

Getting Vinny's Mind around an Assignment

Now that you have a general idea of when and how Vinny will study most productively, analyze a specific assignment together.

Sample pre-study questions, in italics in the following section, are based on the work of Wilma H. Miller, Professor Emeritus of Education at Illinois State University.

- *Do I understand why I have to read this material? What do I already know about this subject? Can I make some predictions about this material even before I read it?* These first questions help Vinny focus his attention and make a conscious appraisal of what he already knows about the project ahead. They link learning, concentrate his efforts, sidestep time-consuming and unnecessary repetition, and force him to make predictions. Don't accept short answers to any of these questions. If it's a report, how many pages? If there are math questions, how many? Specifics force him to reflect and project. How well he predicts also demonstrates how well he makes thinking links to visual clues.

- *Do I know all that I need to know about this? Do I know where I can get some more information?* Can Vinny do the work alone, or will he need another person? Sharing ideas helps kids verify, clarify, expand, or correct their thinking. Encourage him to enlist the support he needs by keeping handy the phone numbers or e-mail addresses of reliable classmates, tutors, or his grandfather in Florida who speaks Vinny's language when it comes to math. Ruminating about the kind of help he needs also teaches flexibility and resourcefulness.

- *How much help am I allowed to have?* Don't be hoodwinked into believing that middle school teachers give assignments to parents or let best friends study for Vinny's tests. What parts of the assignment must Vinny legitimately do by himself, and what specific parts are you or his study partner permitted to assist with? If he doesn't know or suddenly forgets, call or e-mail his teacher and get clarification.

• *What are some new strategies and tactics I can use to learn this?* This makes Vinny think of new ways to utilize his talents to fulfill ever-growing academic demands. This is where creativity kicks in. If his social studies teacher is amenable, he might choose to erect a model of an ancient polis instead of reading chapters about Greece and writing out the questions at the end. Teachers know that the greater the choice and stake kids have in their own learning, the greater the motivation and final outcome. Allow ten minutes for strategizing and developing tactics. Repeat this as often as assignments change.

Try some of these tactics: Instead of laborious note taking, have Vinny write only the most important point of each paragraph. As a hint, tell him to look for main ideas in the first or second line of each paragraph. Have him make up quiz questions for each chapter and then quiz his best friend. Make rhymes to link important names and dates. For example, "in 1903, Orville and Wilbur flew above a tree."

• *When is the work due?* This simple question forces Vinny to think about time management. How many thirty-minute homework sessions does he think he can fit into his schedule before the project is due? It might even inspire him to get advance notice about assignments, tests, and quizzes.

• *How much time will I need to do or learn this?* The time element doesn't occur to most kids until 3:30 a.m. Time limits provide critical milestones for kids with attention or behavior disorders to set a realistic pace. Set short-term goals at first so Vinny can experience success faster. Set the kitchen timer, or use a grandfather clock or his wristwatch alarm to sound at fifteen-minute intervals. How many math problems did he complete in that time? Setting concrete time limits even helps kids with strong discipline and skills to stay focused and on task. For long-term reports, teach him to use the "new task" and calendar features in the office program standard on most computers. Periodic reminders can be set to sound off whenever he boots up his computer. By the end of middle school, he should be able to work steadily through three thirty-minute sessions with only short get-a-drink breaks.

• *How do I submit it?* This encourages Vinny to think about presentation and organization. Must the finished piece be typed or handwritten? In what format and how should the pages be bound? Is the teacher a stickler for spelling? Then talk about how he prepares for school the next day. Does he have a routine place for stashing completed assignments that must be submitted in the morning? What is the best location for his backpack? His lunch money? Sports equipment? Does he have a trick for remembering to stop off at his locker on the way to science class or health class to get his textbook? Conduct a walk-through of assignment requirements and submission strategies to ensure against forgetting, careless omissions, and misplaced or lost work. The best way to get Vinny to plan ahead is to guide him to think ahead.

Bringing the Assignment to a Close

Asking questions will help Vinny monitor himself for mistakes and evaluate his work whether it is a composition for English class or preparation for a test in ancient history. Reviewing material immediately after reading, writing, or reporting makes the information stick to his brain.

After producing written materials, he should ask himself, "How can I spot an error if I make one?" Vinny's best bet is reading aloud. If he's confused after reading a paragraph, it's most likely because he misread something. Have him read a sample section aloud for you to see if he self-corrects. If not, point out errors. Make notes to share with his teacher or tutor about repeated phonetic, visual tracking, or comprehension mistakes. Also, there's no better way to proofread compositions and reports than by rereading them aloud, even to his cat.

After studying for a test, he should ask himself, "Will I be able to answer questions correctly in class? Will I be able to answer them on a test or quiz?" Simple oral questioning or answers jotted on a piece of paper will reveal whether his thinking, strategizing, and timing have been effective. Teach him to dissect errors by talking aloud to you or a friend about how he arrived at an answer. Thinking aloud about his methods is as powerful as reading aloud for detecting and correcting misinformation.

Debriefing Vinny's Study Plan

After a month or six weeks using his personal plan, debrief its efficacy. Debrief and revamp whenever stress blows holes in the process.

- *How can I revise my plan if this one is not working?* Conduct a three-step review, first by asking Vinny to think about the assignment he just completed. Did he complete the work in a reasonable amount of time? Was he able to participate in class? Get a good test grade? Ask his opinion about his most successful thinking strategy. Was it thinking out how to budget his time to get to his locker and back to science class in time to submit his paper? Was it a wasted effort to set the kitchen timer when his new bedroom wall clock works better? Debrief his personal learning plan, have him make notes, and transfer his best thinking strategies to his next assignment.

A Self-Reflection Checklist

The following checklist condenses the questioning process for developing a personal plan for study for middle school students. Make copies for yourself and Vinny. Add, delete, or change questions to accommodate his changing needs and academic demands. Have him use this before and after all major assignments until he can do it spontaneously.

----- **CHECKLIST FOR THINKING ABOUT STUDYING** -----

Thinking before I study

Do I understand why I have to read this material?

What do I already know about this subject?

Can I make some predictions about this material before I read it?

Do I know all that I need to know about this?

Do I know where I can get more information?

What are some new strategies and tactics I can use to learn this?

When is the work due?

How much time will I need to do or learn this?

How do I submit it?

Thinking when I finish studying

How can I spot an error if I make one?

Will I be able to answer questions correctly in class?

Will I be able to answer them on a test or quiz?

How can I revise my plan if this one is not working?

A final and very powerful way to get Vinny to think about his thinking is to think aloud yourself. Strategize aloud as you shop in the supermarket, buy a new car, fix dinner, or figure out how to get him to the dentist after the soccer game and home in time to let the cat out. Metacognition prompts self-reflection, forces clarification, and paves the way for self-correction. Show Vinny, with a thinking checklist and by your own good example, that forty-five minutes of self-monitored ruminating is the best study method he can strap to his brain.

21

How to Increase Reading Comprehension

When you ask Millie what she just read, she says it was about some-body who did something, somewhere a long time ago, maybe,,like, you know. The only thing she can recall in vivid detail is the sequin design on the main character's shoes. Millie's reading comprehension skills are flapping and full of holes.

Middle school is not too late to help Millie improve her reading comprehension skills. Much like little kids who want to snuggle up together with a good book at bedtime, older kids with uneven reading skills often welcome support when reading demands sur-pass their skills. Reading is a thinking and imaginative experience that involves learning new ways to identify unknown words and build image-rich contexts for learning. You don't have to be a reading teacher to help Millie.

Reading Is Based on Language

"Reading is an interactive, language-based process," says teacher educator and author Wilma H. Miller, Professor Emeritus of Edu-cation at Illinois State University. You can help Millie increase her comprehension if she's still having trouble with phonics. "There is an overstress on phonics. It is important, but the context is the single most important way to identify new words," Miller says.

In the language-based method of reading instruction, teaching Millie to use context clues goes beyond phonics by linking her background knowledge to the words on the page. Neighborhood house or garden tours, museum exhibits, poetry readings or storytelling presentations, scientific experiments, cooking and craft classes, and educational TV and videos are all language-based learning experiences that effectively expand Millie's background knowledge. They are image-rich, vocabulary-packed, and loaded with sensory details. They lay the groundwork for the best and least expensive method for improving reading comprehension— making predictions.

Based on Wilma H. Miller's reading comprehension strategies, use the following language-based reading methods to increase Millie's comprehension as you, for example, tour Toronto's unique Shoe Museum.

Use Context Clues

Experience clues. When Millie can't figure out the word *stiletto*, remind her that her aunt Elaine used the word as she modeled her new pink party shoes.

Association clues. If Millie knows the word *odor*, use it to help her read the word *malodorous*.

Synonym clues. As you read the guidebook or a textbook together, look for clues to meaning in the same sentence. For example, "modern-day women frequently consult with a podiatrist when they have trouble with their feet."

Previous contact clues. Was there a word she read in previous sentences that is similar to an unknown word? Draw her attention back to it. For example, "many modern-day women have become firm believers in the benefits of podiatry."

Compare/contrast clues. Draw Millie's attention to words that compare or contrast to an unknown word. "The woman's feet were hot and dry, and their torrid condition made her walking tour miserable."

Make Predictions

Making predictions about a book before reading enables Millie to assemble her prior knowledge about the topic. It lays the context for absorbing new, related information and piques her interest for learning more. To guarantee her engagement, start with topics she loves. Borrow or buy a book about shoes, for example, and read it yourself before sharing it with her. Millie might enjoy one that reviews the shoes at the Victoria and Albert Museum in London, called *Shoes*, edited by the curator, Lucy Pratt.

1. Skim or read the book to find the key concepts. Does it cover construction, style, pattern, and design of shoes in a historical context?

2. Without asking her, think about what Millie already knows about some of these important concepts.

3. Pique her interest by musing aloud or writing up at least three of these concepts, in the order covered in the book. Give her enough information about the key concepts without giving away the answers. For example, "I think the way women kept their shoes out of the mud in the fourteenth century was very efficient," "you'd be surprised when the first slip-on mules were invented," or "you'd never guess what kind of shoes Queen Victoria wore."

4. Elicit her reaction to your statements. Can she guess about mud protectors, mules, or slides? Does she have any ideas

to add? If she makes a statement, for example, about the queen's pointy shoes, ask her to defend her ideas.

5. Now, read the book together. Look specifically for the key concepts you discussed together.

6. Clarify or verify her predictions. Then, discuss how her trip to the shoe museum helped her make accurate predictions about this book.

Take Comprehension Higher

Language-based methods of teaching reading comprehension also include asking increasingly more difficult questions to develop more sophisticated levels of comprehension. As you read together, be sure to ask these kinds of questions, ranked from easiest to hardest.

Literal comprehension. "Right There" questions. Ask her details, main ideas, or sequences that can be found right in the text.

Interpretive comprehension. "Think and Search" questions. Ask Millie to draw conclusions, make predictions, and summarize what she read.

Critical reading. More "Think and Search" questions. Ask Millie to compare and contrast, determine fact from fiction, and recognize propaganda.

Applied comprehension. "On My Own" questions. Have Millie utilize her personal experience and background knowledge to arrive at new understanding. Apply her understanding to problem solve, write poetry, write a play, or cook a meal after reading about it.

Visualizing and Verbalizing Method

If Millie has all her language skills in order and still only remembers the sequin designs on the shoes when she reads a story, it might be a problem with her ability to visualize concepts. Difficulty in this basic thinking process could cause her to remember only parts, not the whole of what is read. The Lindamood-Bell method of teaching reading comprehension, called "Visualizing and Verbalizing," developed by Nanci Bell, shows Millie how to "apply language to something that is representational," says Paul Worthington, Executive Director of Research and Development and School Services at Lindamood-Bell Learning Processes in San Luis Obispo, California. The method takes Millie from visualizing pictures, to words, to sentences, to whole paragraphs, and then finally whole-page imaging.

Try some of the following ideas adapted from Nanci Bell's book *Visualizing and Verbalizing for Language Comprehension and Thinking*. Lindamood-Bell and Visualizing and Verbalizing are registered trademarks and service marks of Lindamood-Bell Learning Processes, a California corporation.

1. Hand Millie a fashion magazine and ask her to find a picture of a shoe. Make sure it is one you have not seen before. Now, ask her to describe it to you in detail. From her description alone, describe it back to her, using the Lindamood-Bell phraseology, "Your words made me picture . . ." Finally, look together at the picture and discuss which elements she omitted in her description. Then reverse the process by describing a shoe to her.

2. Lindamood-Bell suggests using "structure words" to prompt oral description. Use these words to trigger Millie's recall, especially when she's having trouble remembering details:

what, where, when, movement, mood, size, color, number, shape, sound, background, and perspective.

3. Or have her try making "mental movies" to form a visual map through the material and reinforce memory. It starts by identifying key words. Select and read one of Millie's middle school reading assignments. Skim through the selection and pull out important words, especially ones ripe with imagery. Make a list on paper. Discuss with Millie the images she visualizes when she says each word. Then have her read the selection orally to see if her images reflect the material. A variation on this strategy is to read the selection aloud to her. As you're reading, she places a colored square on the table each time a word produces an image in her mind. She then uses her squares as memory jogs to retell the story.

The most effective learner is the one who understands how to go about learning. So, as you go through each set of questions and exercises described above, point out to Millie the different types of comprehension each approach elicits. Noting the varying levels of comprehension illuminates for her the depth of her own understanding. For a shoe-loving girl like Millie, the dawn of comprehension might come with a full-page illustration of a pale pink satin eighteenth-century dancing slipper with a black bone buckle and a froth of lace.

22

How to Help Kids Improve
Creative Writing

Talking with her friends, Sally spins stories just like J. K. Rowling. However, her English teacher reports: "Sally writes at the most basic level and shows a limited ability to compose complex thought." Translation: Though Sally thinks in Technicolor, her writing ability is still in black and white.

Creative writing is the meeting place of a complicated set of cognitive skills. It's where imagination, grammar, spelling, handwriting, keyboarding, visualization, description, and logical sequencing all come together. And if you can throw great storytelling skills into the mix, all the better. Because so many skills converge here, creative writing can develop slowly or unevenly throughout elementary school and into middle school—especially if Sally is a poor speller, labors over handwriting, dislikes reading, or has an attention deficit disorder or a learning delay.

But it is not unusual for an otherwise bright, organized, and efficient middle schooler to experience frustration in creative writing. That's because the writing process is also a revealing and deeply personal process. Which is what makes it the perfect subject for teaching middle school kids like Sally.

A Good Fit for Middle Schoolers

"Middle school kids are dealing with who they are anyway. They are cognitively and emotionally ripe to talk about themselves. This is when they should be writing creatively about their world. Descriptive and narrative writing in which they can make use of their experiences is thus more appropriate and nourishing for this age group than abstract, idea-based formal essay writing," says Eva Dömötör, one of Washington, DC's, Queens of Creative Writing.

According to a recent report by the National Commission on Writing called, *The Neglected "R": The Need for a Writing Revolution*, the amount of time students spend writing in school should at least be doubled, more out-of-school time should be used to encourage writing, and parents should review students' writing with them.

You can help Sally learn to write better without being J. K. Rowling. When you coach writing at home, with infinite tact and honest cheering, Sally will learn that writing is a vital form of communication that shares a person's heart, mind, ego, and senses in a self-satisfying and creative way. It will deepen her perception of herself and the world around her. She'll also gain new respect for the skill, insight, and artistry of other authors. This is no small thing, given the amount of books Sally has to read in middle and high school.

Try some of the following ideas for challenging writers in middle school:

Coaching Guidelines

Put the red pencil down. "Amateur writing should not be overly corrected; doing so might well make the child stop writing. If the child writes a lot, she will outgrow some of her technical problems," says Dömötör.

Cheer, honestly. "Cheer from the sidelines. As a parent, your job is to admire. Creative writing is wonderful because it so deeply satisfies our psychological need to have a sense of ourselves and to create out of that sense. What could be more wonderful than a person, let alone a parent, who resonates to what we write. So, do tell your child which word, which phrase you found particularly delightful. Be specific in your praise. 'I loved this,' rings hollow because it is too general. Something like, 'Wow, I loved the word exploded over here—so powerful,' is much more nourishing," Dömötör says.

Don't limit Sally to pencil and paper. To keep her focused on writing, without putting pencil to paper, ask her what story opener she might write as she watches the carrots in the blender erupt on the kitchen ceiling or as a large hawk swoops over the car on your way to Philadelphia to visit Aunt Ev and Uncle Chick. The creative writing process can begin whenever and wherever sensory stimulation is surprising and rich.

Take it in small doses. Do the actual drafting and rewriting process when Sally's rested and receptive to help. Don't work longer than thirty minutes at one session. Take several short, nondistracting breaks, especially those which force her to gaze over a long distance. This helps rest the eyes and lessen the strain of too much close work.

Support her writing arm or typing arms. Sometimes a lack of desire to write is fed by physical discomfort. Make the act of handwriting less laborious by seeing that Sally supports her writing arm, from wrist to elbow, on her writing surface. At the keyboard, place a gel-filled or foam pad under her wrists and set the monitor screen level with her eyes. Don't let body aches get in the way of her creative flow.

Be the hands behind the brain. To completely remove handwriting or keyboarding stumbling blocks, offer to write or type Sally's rough draft or revisions for her. Say to Sally, "You be the brain; I'll be the hands," advises Dömötör. Then, "you can be right there when the creativity happens, and you can help keep the creative process going through the warmth of your interest and sometimes even with a tactful question," she says.

Give Writing a Sensory Start

"The challenge to parents is to make the child aware of her five senses. The ability to write a good descriptive piece has to do with the sensory skills of seeing, hearing, touching, tasting, and smelling. Someone who writes description well does so because she is able to put into her description concrete detail, then appeal to the senses," Dömötör says.

Create a verbal still life. Sixth graders, in particular, would benefit from producing a "still life" says Alan Cheuse, novelist, journalist, National Public Radio's book commentator, and creative writing professor at George Mason University in Fairfax, Virginia. "Have them describe an object as an artist would paint it—the color, surface, shadows it creates, odor, sound, and taste, if any. This develops 'sense-memory,'" he says. "Teach them to find the right nouns and verbs of the sense they are trying to record. The modifiers come later," he adds.

Create sense-memory recollections. From a past memory, ask middle schoolers like Sally to "reconstruct a room they've been in; how it feels, smells, sounds, looks. They approach it the way they approach an object," says Cheuse. Have her describe the sun porch at Aunt Jane's on tape or over dinner, then write it up. Now Sally will be able to use flashback when she writes!

Read Charles Dickens. "Read a paragraph as an example and have her list the senses," says Dömötör. And there's no one quite like Dickens for creating rich, sensory word soups. Read aloud the following excerpt from *Oliver Twist*, which describes market day. To give it full impact, practice before you read it to Sally. When you finish reading, ask her to list, by category, which words and images made her see, hear, feel, and smell the scene. Remind her of each sense as she crafts her own creative pieces.

--------------- **A DICKENS OF A DAY** ---------------

A description of market day from **Oliver Twist** *by Charles Dickens, published by Dodd, Mead and Company.*

It was market morning. The ground was covered, nearly ankle-deep, with filth and mire; a thick steam, perpetually rising from the reeking bodies of the cattle, and mingling with the fog, which seemed to rest upon the chimney tops, hung heavily above. All the pens in the centre of the large area, and as many temporary pens as could be crowded into the vacant space, were filled with sheep; tied up to posts by the gutter side were long lines of beasts and oxen, three or four deep. Countrymen, butchers, drovers, hawkers, boys, thieves, idlers, and vagabonds of every low grade, were mingled together in a mass; the whistling of drovers, the barking dogs, the bellowing and plunging of oxen, the bleating of sheep, the grunting and squeaking of pigs, the cries of hawkers, the shouts, oaths, and quarrelling on all sides; the ringing of bells and roar of voices, that issued from every public-house; the crowding, pushing, driving, beating, whooping and yelling; the hideous and discordant din that resounded from every corner of the market; and the unwashed, unshaven, squalid, and dirty figures constantly running to and fro, and bursting in and out of the throng; rendered it a

stunning and bewildering scene, which quite confounded the senses.

Writing Exercises for Middle Schoolers

Have her write first about her feet. There's nothing that interests middle schoolers more than themselves, so tap this boundless topic to inspire Sally's writing. Ask her to orally describe her feet, without looking down at them. Ask about the shape of her toes, toenails, instep, heel, skin, size, length, and width of her foot. Then, take a photo of her foot or have her trace it on paper and write an accompanying description of it. "Publish" her work by e-mailing it to her grandmother in Phoenix who loves her down to her toes.

Put a face on her characters. Though by sixth grade, most kids know about and use graphic organizers or mapping techniques of all kinds, they are essential when kids are stumped about how to develop a character beyond a physical description. Focus on personality and behaviors by showing Sally how to use a face map.

Find a large close-up of a man, woman, or child in an old magazine and cut it out. This is her face map. Can she imagine how this person thinks, acts, or talks? Build vocabulary by asking if the woman with the wrinkled brow might be optimistic, confused, or argumentative. Across the forehead, have Sally jot the words she thinks will apply. Make notes near the eyes about how this character perceives. Does she look at her friends through rose-colored glasses? Use the nose to scribble traits like inquisitive or meddlesome. Across the lips note whether this character talks too much (loquacious) or sadly whines out all her words (lugubrious). Use the chin to talk about perseverance, fortitude, and gumption. A face map filled with high-octane words not only gives depth to

Sally's characters, but it builds sentences and concepts far beyond that reportedly "most basic level." It also increases the storehouse of words she can draw from for answering vocabulary questions on standardized tests.

Plan the plot. To make sure Sally includes all the elements that are typically part of good creative writing compositions, ask her the following critical questions:

> How many characters will there be in your story?
> How are the characters related to each other?
> Who starts the action and who receives it?
> Where does your story take place?
> When does it take place?

Start her off with one or two characters, advancing the number as her narrative ability grows.

Roll the action. This is the part where Sally establishes and follows a story line in her writing. What is the main conflict, or conflicts, in her story? How are they solved? If Sally is stalled or has trouble sequencing abstract thought, personalize the crafting process by asking her to recount the latest installment of her favorite TV soap opera or a recent social episode at school. To simplify the process, have her talk into a tape recorder, and then listen to her retelling together.

Jot notes as you listen. Be alert for sequential "action changing" words like *first, second, third, next, also, another, before, after, during, earlier, finally,* or *later.* Listen, too, for the verbs that follow each action-changing word. For example, if Sally relates, "First, Jenny poured out the peroxide. Then, she put it on her hair," your notes should say: "first/poured, then/put."

Build the story. Using your notes from Sally's anecdote, point out how she constructed her story in a specific sequence. Have her use this same sequence for constructing the action in her next creative writing composition. Make a simple map by drawing a line from the top of the page to the bottom and then inserting transition words down that line in the order she used them, leaving room for notes between each one. To layer on more action, prompt her with some of the action-changing words noted above. Remind her that each action-changing word can start a new paragraph. To visually reinforce the sequence of her story, have her circle each one as she proofreads her story.

This method also gives her a self-checking devise for determining if her plotline develops logically from "first" to "finally."

Set a time. As Sally's writing confidence grows, occasionally toss her a topic and ask her to write it up in twenty minutes. This gives her test-smart practice in probing a new topic, generating ideas, organizing her thoughts, and writing a complete composition within a given time frame. She'll need this skill for answering essay questions on tests.

This skill will come in handy as the number of tests that require examples of student writing increases. Many state tests are currently emphasizing writing, and in the 2005 school year, a writing sample will be added to the Scholastic Aptitude Test (SAT).

Write together for the fun of it and to help your middle schooler expand her internal and external horizons. It's a sure way to add color to her work.

RESOURCES

Find free, online tutoring at Purdue University's Online Writing Lab at *owl.english.purdue.edu*

PART SIX

High School:
Where the Party Starts

23

How to Handle Teacher Conferences

James struts with a downbeat on the first note, low-slung jeans and baggy T-shirt framing his angular adolescent form. If he isn't downloading music on the computer, he's instant messaging his girlfriend about Friday on Monday night. Unfortunately, his freshman report cards don't reflect his percentage of coolness achieved.

Unlike some elementary and middle schools which schedule parent-teacher conferences after every marking period, many high schools schedule only one per year. However, with kids like James who put parties before books, you need one hundred per year! Set a date for one today.

Before you go, do some preconference homework first. Advance preparation gives you the chance to prepare for a worst-case scenario. It also puts you in the best position for volleying suggestions and making crucial decisions. The more you know and share, the more strategic advantage you and his teachers will have.

Common Teenage Issues

Though much of the hormonal tensions of middle school eases as James moves into late adolescence, life can still be an emotional and philosophical taffy pull for you both. After all, if he is only fifteen, you could well be forty, which naturally gives you both de-cidedly different ideas of what's important.

What's pulling at him and his grades are common teenage is-sues. First and foremost, fifteen- to eighteen-year-olds firmly be-lieve they are fully capable of parenting themselves. Ironically, though, they feel both a raging desire for, and a secret fear of, in-dependence. Though it's often the result of their still-developing sense of self-confidence, high schoolers often make their families and teachers the monkeys in the middle.

High schoolers also often have big ideas that have no relation-ship to reality. James knows for sure he wants to be really rich some day, but when you ask him how he plans to achieve this, he goes blank. Under pressure, he might mumble, "I might have to, like, maybe work or something."

All the while you're working hard on him, kids like James are pumping every waking ounce of intellectual and creative en-ergy into parties, best friends, girlfriends, driving your car, the Internet, or conversations on the telephone. Because these dis-tractions have undoubtedly impacted his grades, it's conference time.

Preconference Homework

Interview James. No evaluation is valid without the input of the person involved, so get your high schooler's point of view about his poor grades. First, discuss how he views himself as a student. Take your hands off your hips and ask questions like you are in-terviewing a famous rock star, and you might spark his interest long enough to get an answer beyond a grunt. His opinions about himself might surprise you. His opinions of his own abilities and efforts have tremendous impact on his production and how you and his teachers gear your plans to increase his self-confidence.

The more James is involved in the conference process, the greater his stake in the outcome.

- *What does he think about his study habits?* Watch for his reality-free perceptions here. If he thinks he's a scholar, but you think he's a dabbler, ask for proof of his opinion. Or ponder aloud about when he got started on his persuasive writing assignment because you know you heard him on the phone from the time you started dishes until his little brother went to bed at 10:00 p.m. Stock up on seemingly innocent observations, complete with time frames and associated facts whenever James needs a nonjudgmental reality check.

- *What are his hobbies and sports interests?* What percentage of his time is devoted to pursuing them as opposed to studying. If it's over thirty percent of each day and his grades are sliding, it's time for him to plan on cutting back. Help him devise specific ways and means and advise his teacher of this sign of his good academic intentions.

- *How does he cope with stress and problems?* Is he a procrastinating worrier or just a laid-back partying kind of guy? If his grades reflect his level of motivation, see Chapter 19 for ways to get him moving again. Then, get specific about what he can do to get back on track.

- *What is happening in the classroom that is jamming up his grade?* Talk about the classroom dynamic, his participation, teacher reactions and expectations, and his tardiness or absences, which all can negatively impact grades. What does the teacher say or do that he can't understand or cope with? What is the best thing about this class?

- *What about assignments?* Are there too many? Too complicated? Are too many based on a book he never understood in the first place? Does he need more time to complete them than the other kids because his reading skills aren't as strong? If he's having trouble writing essays because his spelling stinks, see Chapter 26 for tips.

Find a mole. What you need when kids are having trouble with course work or with anything in high school is a friendly informant. If James has stayed in the same school district, this could be that middle school friend who told you everything. If, however, you don't have one, it's time to suggest he bring some friends home for dinner. Then, casually interview the most opinionated one (there's always one). Ask some general questions about classes, teachers, schedules, and activities both inside and outside school. The more interested you are in his friend's opinion, the more likely you will be to get them. Such communication often leads to confidences, and when you've reached that level, you have found your mole. Use your Deep Throat source to get a consistent third party opinion about James's progress. This is not an underhanded suggestion. There is nothing but good to be gleaned from another perspective on James and his high school dynamic. Find yourself a mole today.

Rehearse the worst-case scenario. Plan for the worst possible feedback from his teacher at the conference you've just scheduled. Will she suggest psychological counseling, drug rehabilitation, or summer school? Get the gasping out of your system ahead of time by rehearsing different hairy scenarios and brainstorming alternative solutions you can offer for improving his situation. Though what the teacher says might make that desk appear like a yawning pit between the two of you, that person, more likely than not, is on your side when it comes to your kid. Keeping that foremost in your mind will fortify you as hysterical fantasies thrash around inside your head.

Construct an anecdote. More powerful than your most fervent declarations and pledges is a short narrative to share with the teacher about James, particularly if the teacher is building up a negative opinion of his efforts. What episode in his recent past best illustrates his gifts, talents, personality strengths, or skills? Did he carry a large package down the steps for the crankiest old lady who lives in your apartment building and deliver it with a smile to her waiting car? Let his actions paint a promising picture for his teacher. A good anecdote can be a powerful antidote.

Make arrangements to meet. If there is not a regularly scheduled conference when you need one, set one by calling or e-mailing the teacher or teachers in the subjects where James needs the most help. Conferences typically last 20–30 minutes and are held most often before or after school. Be accommodating. Remember you are the one asking for help. Rearrange your schedule accordingly and mark it in your appointment book. Ask if anyone else should be included. The guidance counselor or assistant principal? If you don't already have some, request to see two examples of James's English class work—his best and his worst. Class work tells a better tale than homework. These two papers show range of ability. The best one gives you both an opportunity for honest praise; the worst provides the focus point.

Take a pal along. During that call also mention that you will not be alone. Take your spouse or James's favorite aunt along to ask all the questions that go straight out of your head when the teacher says things you knew you would dread hearing. Don't hesitate to ask tutors, mentors, or educational counselors to attend teacher conferences with you. Kids in academic trouble need all the advocates you can find. Adding the voice of another committed family member, particularly one that he respects like a favorite aunt, can be helpful especially if you and your spouse's relationship with James is currently strained. In the car on the way to the conference, agree on key areas and important points and make some last-minute notes.

Do a background check. Who are the people teaching James? Contrary to James's opinion, his English teacher does not weigh five hundred pounds and sound like a turkey with a sinus condition. Ask your mole, your local PTA, neighbors, friends, or James's former teachers to brief you on the philosophies, teaching techniques, or sticking points about the teachers at your conference for James. Background information gives deeper meaning to their recommendations and allows you to formulate your requests based on their known strengths and habits.

Set your agenda. Think about your plans and objectives for the conference and jot them down. Don't discuss wishes, hopes, and dreams of Harvard; focus instead on what is appropriate for James today. Does he need a math tutor? Does he need Internet resources or book titles for independent reading? Include a list of your special requests, too. How can the teacher support James's need to balance his course work with his sports activities? Would you like him or her to focus on helping James overcome his anxiety about speaking in front of the class? Limiting yourself to three items helps align your conversation to the short conference time allotted.

Make a folder. In addition to your James interview and mole notes and your own three-point agenda, include copies of excellent work the teacher might not have seen. Did James write a convincing and successful letter to the manager of your apartment house explaining the tenants' need for new storm windows? Include copies of educational or psychological testing results or former teacher evaluations. Include in your folder note paper, a pen, and your business card or personal contact information.

Leave the sweats at home. You are there to take care of business, so dress for it. To make the best impression possible, leave the holey sweatshirt, drooping jeans, and running shoes at home. Let your appearance underscore the importance of this meeting for James and you. Arriving on time and respecting the scheduled time also wears well on teachers.

At the Conference

Behave yourself. Thumping on the desk, demanding, or threatening is the fastest way to get absolutely nowhere with a teacher. Set the tone with kind words about a recent assignment or a common interest you learned about during your background check. Don't let negatives send you both fleeing in opposite directions. On the other hand, don't be surprised if your kudos leave the teacher dumbfounded and eager to go the extra mile for James. And if you know his English teacher is a chocoholic, take some chocolate chip cookies to munch together while you're talking about James. Be prepared to listen to what the teacher has to say, and don't drop crumbs all over the floor.

Be honest. Let the teacher talk first. When the teacher is finished talking, make your case for James. If you need to overcome an unreasonably negative perception, start by sharing your illustrative anecdote about his gallantry to that cranky neighbor. Share your notes about his skills and learning methods. Show her his letter to your building manager. Then be honest about the habits, attitudes, and weak skill areas that you know are getting in his way.

Talk about clashes. The best time to deal with student-teacher clashes of any kind is during a private parent-teacher conference. Come clean, too, if you believe there might be a mismatch be-

tween James's learning style and the teacher's instructional methods or the two personalities. Talk about alternatives. Will she allow him to tape her lectures instead of relying on his poor
note-taking skills? Openly discuss what James does that is particularly irritating to him. What does he do, in turn, that makes
James ornery or disrespectful? Sometimes merely the honest ac-
knowledgement of common human interaction problems will
open the door to soothing irritating interpersonal relations. See
the section on "Teacher Sensitivity" in Chapter 19.

Ask the right questions. What does James need to know? How
does his class work and homework compare to his classmates'?
How does his testing compare? What, specifically, can you do to
help him with this problem? Ask questions that will clarify your
role, illicit helpful comparisons, and demonstrate your willingness to help. Listen, take notes, and make sure your mouth is
closed when you chew your cookies.

Agree on a plan for helping James. This is the final critical step in
any good parent-teacher conference. And never more important
than when you and his teacher disagree about how to handle a situation. Set your individual differences aside and focus on James,
together. Establish action steps, assignments, and a time frame in
which James must accomplish the goals you've set. Include interim goals that act as stepping-stones toward overall improvement and as an early warning sign if he misses a progress marker.
Take notes about the action plan while the teacher is talking, and
then quickly review to make sure you've heard correctly and included everything. Set a date for a progress report by e-mail,
phone, or another meeting face to face.

After the Conference

Review the meeting with James. In the same way that you prepared for the teacher conference, have a James conference. Do it the same day while your impressions are fresh and James's interest is piqued. If his aunt accompanied you to see the teacher, be sure to include her in this conference. Give an honest rendition, using your notes as a reference. If applicable, ask his aunt to describe the meeting from her vantage point. You brokered a deal with the teacher on James's behalf, so run down the action plan and the roles that you, James, and the teacher each have in that plan. Ask James if there is anything in the action plan that was overlooked or misconstrued from his vantage point. Were the issues he raised in your initial interview with him addressed? Review the milestones and interim goals in the plan so that he is clear about the entire plan.

Display the nice manners your mother taught you. Be sure to thank the teacher for his or her time and efforts by mail, e-mail or phone. Reconfirm your mutual course of action, and promise to keep him or her posted.

Put the plan in action and follow it up. Together with James, mark the milestones and interim goals on James's personal calendar that's posted in the kitchen. Or if he's a techno-guy, he can log the dates on his handheld computer. If he has a cell phone, he can enter dates and set them to beep using the calendar programming feature. Do this to ensure that he participates in his own "change equation." Then, follow up by phone, e-mail, or letter on the recommendations made during the conference. Did you contact that creative writing tutor? Are you helping James study for social studies quizzes by implementing the teacher's idea to construct a visual timeline? Demonstrate that you valued the teacher's suggestions by acting on them.

Maybe the most shocking way to get James's mind off music, cars, and girls and back toward schoolwork would be to put this chapter on teacher conferences in his hands and have him do the entire thing himself. Teachers have been known to change grades when a student takes initiative, makes changes, and works hard to show he's got the will and the drive to make it happen. This approach would gives James the self-control and independence a fifteen-year-old yearns for within the safe parameters a forty-year-old adult can live with. Then when his grade point average exceeds his percentage of coolness achieved, you'll both have something to party about.

24

What to Do When Kids Don't Want to Study

Ruby's got the academic ability, but her study habits are too lax for success in high school. Pearl's situation is quite the reverse. What they need to get high school right is a balance of knowledge and *skills.*

The trouble with helping high schoolers learn to study better is that by this age most of their work habits are entrenched, including the ones that are faulty, counterproductive or outgrown. However, if your high schooler displays even a glimmer of interest in changing her habits, you can intervene at this late date to help her change her ways and get improved results.

Depending on her "academic profile," there are different strategies you can pursue. If Ruby has poor study habits, but her math, comprehension, and composition skills are on grade level, you can help her by tapping her intuition and by teaching her to think like a teacher and keep records like a research librarian.

If, on the other hand, she's motivated but has weak basic skills and a history of poor grades, or if she does not seek or want your help, get her a tutor. Employ the step-by-step process prescribed below for locating the best and most qualified individual for your Pearl.

Whether you have a Ruby or a Pearl, all the following ideas will help your high school gem. And if you decide to throw a "Study Party" like the one recommended at the end of the chapter, you will find it adds a little sparkle to you, too.

Ruby: High Academic Ability, Low Skills

Start by teaching Ruby how to harness her intuition to improve her study habits. Intuition is characterized by the ability to detect subtle signs, symbols, clues, and emotions and link them into patterns. "One of the telltale signs of naturally intuitive students is that they are able to see the big picture when given bits and facts," says Harvey Brightman, Professor Emeritus of Decision Sciences at Georgia State University in Atlanta. "Intuits bring pattern to chaos even when there isn't," he says. The following techniques will help a bright high schooler like Ruby generate her hunches and develop her intuition into a study-enhancing tool:

Help her construct linking mind maps. Brightman finds that his students build better cognitive maps when they are asked first to compare and contrast elements of a topic. This highlights the patterns and builds the concepts, "which aid intuition," he says. Though people can only hold "five to nine chunks of knowledge in their mind at any given time, if they can make linkages between facts, then the amount of knowledge is almost unlimited," he says. Find endless and unusual mapping devices that span curriculum and personal problem solving from Critical Thinking Products at *www.criticalthinking.com*.

Run a worst-case scenario. You've had experience with this if you've done your preconference homework for James. Now it's time to teach Ruby. Is she sure she's going to fail her Modern History test? To help her practice her impulses and analyze them, have her imagine the worst possible results on a given test and then think backwards to guess which issues caused the bad results. Which images or questions flash in her mind and make her sweat? That dreaded map of 1870s Britain? Or a time line she must create showing major textile inventions during the Industrial Revolution? Teach her how to focus her studying today by analyzing the source of the sweat on her brow created by an imagined problem.

Translate the people cues. Punch up Ruby's hunch ability by teaching her to go beyond visual clues to detect significant sounds or gestures that people unknowingly provide or that situations reveal. Does Mrs. Cottongin always clear her throat just before she asks someone to explain what she just taught the class? Does she hold up her fingers as she ticks off the important elements in a topic? Make Ruby aware that seemingly minor human sounds or finger-underlined signals can alert and prepare her to answer or to add something obviously important to her notes.

Make sure she's getting feedback. Make notes yourself and ask Ruby to monitor her own intuitive skills. Monitoring, of course, means that you have to pay attention and track her progress as closely as she lets you. Was she right about that dreaded 1870s map appearing on her history test? Did Mrs. Cottongin clear her throat and then call on Ruby in class? Tracking her positive hunch history builds Ruby's self-esteem and encourages her to continue trusting her intuition as a studying tool.

"Tell her to think like a teacher," says former teacher Barbara March-Smith of Chevy Chase, Maryland. Especially when Ruby is reading and studying for final exams, ask her to imagine what important information her teachers might want her to know for the test. Have her "formulate a key question about every paragraph that she reads," advises March-Smith. Note key questions on index cards and place them in order by chapter in a small file box, color matched to all her other social studies materials. After the test is over, have her return to her card box. Which hunches were accurate? Place a star on cards that hit the mark and correct those slightly off the mark. Save these cards and use them to study for final exams. "Note cards can be a key to [students'] success if they are done well," notes March-Smith. And if a final grade happens to be teetering on the edge, a recipe box filled with key cards about the Industrial Revolution also provides Mrs. Cottongin undeniable proof that Ruby is working hard on her study skills.

Pearl: High Skills, Low Academic Ability

Many high school kids have the desire and the motivation to get ahead but not the basic skills or academic stamina it takes to get there. Some Pearls invent elaborate but completely ineffective ways to study. Other Pearls don't have the confidence to try new ideas even if the old ones stopped working in fourth grade. If your Pearl is a kid with the willingness to learn but not the skills to get there, get her a tutor to develop her academic ability and help her focus her good efforts more effectively. If you have a Pearl who refuses your offers of help, a tutor can be the answer you both need.

Though a tutor might be critical for a Pearl, one can also help a Ruby do better in high school. Many academically strong students benefit from a tutor who helps with homework coaching, preparation for the SAT, advanced placement testing, and final exams, or with the essays many colleges require for admission. The following step-by-step process will help you locate the best person to work with students at any grade level.

How to Pick a Good Tutor

Make the plan. Mrs. Cottongin probably already told you more than you ever wanted to know about Pearl's performance in modern history, but don't forget to ask Pearl's opinion when identifying the areas where she needs help. What is the hardest part of a troublesome course for her? The compositions or essay questions on tests? Poor basic calculation skills, reading comprehension problems, or shaky note-taking or study skills? Pinpoint specific tutoring goals. What do you both want? A passing grade in a particular course, better study habits in general, or better organization of materials and studying processes? Define and refine exactly what Pearl and you need from a tutor.

Decide your place or theirs. Before you interview candidates to tutor Pearl, decide when and where it's most convenient to conduct the tutoring sessions. They typically last sixty minutes and take place after school, once or twice a week.

Duration of tutoring. Assume that Pearl will need at least a one-hour session per week for six weeks before you see an improvement reflected in her tests and assignments. As much depends on the skills of the tutor as on Pearl's willingness to accept help, her desire to change, and your support of the process. Take into account, too, how much time Pearl will need to dedicate not just to weekly sessions but to any homework the tutor might assign.

Shop around. Just as you'd never take Pearl to a medical professional without a trusted referral, don't start tutoring without one. Start with her school. Ask Pearl's teacher, guidance counselor, a PTA member, an educational diagnostician, or a friend who found a great tutor for his kid.

Get background. When you talk on the phone, ask about teaching credentials and tutoring experience. Talk about prior experience and request a reference or two. Many tutors provide contacts by phone or send information by mail or e-mail.

Go wide. Try to find a tutor who has teaching or tutoring experience in more than one subject. Ask what other resources the tutor can bring to Pearl. Does the tutor write or speak a second language? Is he passionate about computers? Is she a writer or poet or someone with editing experience? A tutor with secondary skills can provide benefits far beyond a student's initial needs.

Go for the click. Look for a personality that works with Pearl's. The right combination yields another positive adult in a kid's life.

Have an exit plan. Tutoring should help a kid grow. However, it can become a difficult process if Pearl's attitude is negative or trust does not develop. Agree ahead of time to review the tutoring relationship monthly. If it's working, keep going. But if tutoring is not moving Pearl ahead or if the tutor becomes the target of her frustration, plan ahead to give both parties the right to bow out gracefully.

Make the connection. Put the tutor in touch with Mrs. Cottongin so they can coordinate planning. This is the ideal situation, but it doesn't always happen. Some classroom teachers see outside tutoring as a direct affront to their experience or skill. However, if you see a private tutor as the best way to help Pearl, do not let this stop you. Soldier on.

Stay in the feedback loop. Seek feedback immediately after the first session with the new tutor. What is his opinion of Pearl's needs? How long does she think it will take before some improvement will become evident? Is tutoring appropriate now? If it is, check back in three weeks. By that time, a good tutor will know Pearl's strengths, weakness, and ineffective study habits and should have suggestions about how you can provide additional support.

After about six weeks of tutoring, you should begin to see some positive changes in how Pearl assimilates information and in the materials she produces. This is the time to decide the next course of action. What will be the next area of focus? Does tutoring need to continue at all? For about how long? Reevaluate her progress at least every six weeks after that.

Respect the process. Whether you have taken on a tutor to help Pearl pass a class or to sharpen Ruby's skills for taking the SAT, tutoring is serious academic business. Show your respect for the person and the time you've reserved by making sure Ruby and Pearl arrive and are picked up on time. Just as you would for a doctor or dentist, call ahead if Ruby or Pearl won't be able to make it. If she's sick or is absent from school for illness, don't send her for tutoring. The greater the support and respect you show for this important process, the greater the likelihood Ruby and Pearl will respect it, too. Set a good example.

FACTS ABOUT TUTORING

Tutoring is a wise long-term investment. The contacting, negotiating, and scheduling of tutors is usually a parent or caregiver's responsibility. Most public and private schools provide referrals for local individual tutors and tutoring organizations. Know, however, that school policy often prohibits teachers from tutoring kids in their own classes or school.

Tutoring fees depend on the experience and credentials of the tutor employed by you. Some work independently and others work through tutoring organizations. If tutoring costs are an issue, you can reduce costs by finding a tutor who is willing to let you share time with another student or is willing to form a tutoring group. Many community centers, senior citizens groups, churches, or youth-related organizations provide tutoring services for free or at reduced rates. Check at your local YMCA. See Chapter 6 to learn more about free intergenerational tutoring programs.

Be aware that according to the federal education act called "No Child Left Behind" by the 2005–2006 school year, public schools that have not achieved proficient scores in reading and math for three years must offer supplemental services such as tutoring.

PRIVATE TUTORING SERVICES

Learning centers. Some provide both tutoring and psychoeducational testing services. They often want to do their own diagnostic testing before tutoring begins, so check first on up-front costs. Normally, you take Ruby to their facility. You pay the center; they pay the tutor.

Tutoring agencies. They employ teachers to tutor. Tell them your needs, and they decide who fits the bill. Typically, the tutor comes to your home. In many cases, you pay the agency, and they pay the tutor.

Independent tutors. Teachers at all stages of their careers become independent tutors. Recommendations from satisfied clients or your school are the best sources for finding private tutors. In some communities, college students provide tutoring services. Check with the private and community colleges near you. Typically, you pay the individual directly.

COMPUTERS AS TUTORS

The market abounds with tutoring aids for all academic subjects. Check out your local computer superstore for popular educational titles in areas where Ruby needs help. Sometimes that software is already loaded on a demo machine in the store, so try it out. Seek recommendations about online tutoring programs from the media specialists (research librarians) at your local or school library. Many universities provide online tutoring help for their students. This kind of resource might help Ruby and Pearl learn how to write a better long-term report and give them a preview of what is expected of a college student.

Throw a Study Party

"Teenagers like the social aspect of studying together. Study groups are good for test preparation, events, assessments, debates, or speeches," says Richard E. Bavaria, Vice President of Education for Sylvan Learning Centers and a former high school English teacher. They work like a charm for both Ruby and Pearl.

Study groups help kids hone their skills, learn together, even "organize each other," says Bavaria. Ruby's teachers can also play a role in home study groups. "Teachers can give verbal cues, encourage groups to form, and remind students when they should meet," he says. Here's how to set one up for your high schoolers. This example is based on writing a research paper.

When. A month before that English research paper is due, encourage Ruby or Pearl to invite four or five friends over to write their introductions together.

Who. Include kids with "mixed abilities, especially those who don't mind sharing their knowledge," Bavaria says.

What. Set study boundaries to make the gathering productive and keep it focused. Limit the study group's time to your high schooler's regular study hours.

Where. Hold it in a place conducive to parental walk-bys and snack service, like the dining room or kitchen. Provide a table, chairs, and study materials like a dictionary, thesaurus, pencils and paper, or a computer.

Special guests. Invite an outside expert. Uncle Fenimore, the family historian and writer, might be the perfect guest for idea bouncing, sentence wrestling, and researching tips.

Individual work. Of course, it's important for study groups to not only encourage everyone to help each other get clear on the concepts, but also to encourage students to articulate the concepts in their own words. Mrs. Cottongin wouldn't appreciate nearly identical work from the kids in a study group. Once the study group successfully launches everybody on his or her task, let Ruby finish on her own in her own words.

Post-mortem. Have the same study group convene again to do a post-mortem after the finished papers have been graded. This works best when the study group is a bunch of very good friends. It's very instructive to see what composition elements worked and which tanked. Learning does not stop when the homework is graded. Often the most valuable lessons are learned in the aftermath. An evaluation of past work is incomplete and partly wasted without using the evaluation to refocus your next goal. Think of a successful study and work pattern as being circular: goal, action, and evaluation, revised goal, action, and evaluation. And then repeat.

A major benefit of devising personalized study techniques for high school kids is that they gain critical insight into how they learn and how to critique and amend their own methods—two of the most valuable qualities your high school gems can possess.

25

How to Deal with
Serious Emotional Problems

Jason argued with his teacher about his chronic tardiness and got suspended for it. When he got caught speeding, he ripped the rearview mirror off his father's new car. And when he was grounded for losing his license, he pitched his best friend's camera against a wall. Holes are forming where Jason's relationships used to be.

When problems metastasize in a kid's life, nothing fits anymore. The school is too big, the house is too small, and the family pinches in all the wrong places. In eighteenth-century France, some kids with problems were abandoned in the woods. Some believe that it was the capture of one such "wild child" in 1799 that started the whole notion of teaching, not abandoning, these kids.

Several centuries later, there are specialized programs that take kids with serious emotional problems back to the wilderness to find themselves. "The wilderness of today is anything but abandonment," says Georgia K. Irvin, an independent educational consultant in Chevy Chase, Maryland.

Serious Emotional Disturbances

A serious emotional disturbance can show itself in many ways, such as

Eating disorders
Chronic low self-esteem
Relationship problems
Antisocial behavior
Angry, defiant, or violent behavior
Depression
Learning problems
Serious withdrawal
Drug or alcohol abuse
Internet or video game abuse

However, many seriously emotionally disturbed kids have superior intellectual ability and are often highly creative. Their performance, though, is erratic, and their grades are often middling to poor.

What behaviors or patterns are disrupting your family life or Jason's progress in school? It might be time to ask yourself some blunt questions about him, and about the family environment. The more honestly you evaluate Jason's situation, the faster you can set him on a path that will lead him out of the woods. The following suggestions will get you off on the right foot.

Consider Therapeutic Alternatives

If Jason's problems are consistently disrupting your home life or his progress in school, consider a "therapeutic" school that specializes in treating kids with similar problems. "You do not need to suffer the dangerous, acting out behavior these children display," Irvin says.

Such schools are called "therapeutic" because "they have group therapy and behavior modification methods that can have a therapeutic effect on a child," says independent education consultant Ethna Hopper of the School Counseling Group in Washington, DC. They are also called "emotional growth" schools. "There is something in every school that can be used for a child," says Hopper. However, these are not schools for students with mental deficiencies or those who are psychotic.

Therapeutic programs typically last six to twenty-four months, serving mostly thirteen- to seventeen-year-olds. Both coed and single-sex settings are available. Programs normally have five components: education, therapy, psychiatric or medication management, supportive environment, and recreation. Academics are highly structured and adaptable to a range of abilities, learning styles, and attention spans. Examples of such programs are Lindamood-Bell, Orton-Gillingham, or Precision Learning. If Jason is academically talented or highly motivated, it might even be possible for him to accelerate his high school course requirements during his stay in a therapeutic program.

Therapeutic programs can, however, be very expensive, many charging $4,000 and up per month. "There are some private programs available that offer financial assistance, but there aren't many," says Hopper. Some are even county funded. "Go to your school. Ultimately the school makes the recommendation," Hopper advises parents.

The type of program you should choose depends on how much intervention he needs to get back on the right path. At one extreme are small, private hospitals staffed by medical professionals. At the opposite end of the spectrum, students who need the least amount of intervention attend day schools with highly structured academic programs. In the middle are therapeutic boarding schools and wilderness programs.

Consider Wilderness Programs

Though wilderness programs have recently received some negative press, both Hopper and Irvin often recommend them to their clients because they provide a unique type of therapeutic experience. Irvin feels strongly about the people who staff them. "They are the saints of our time. They are experienced, intuitive, committed, and compassionate. They are often wounded healers," she says. She also believes a wilderness program can be time-efficient. "It reduces the time in an emotional growth boarding school. You can go so much farther with a child in the wilderness," Irvin says. She prefers wilderness programs that use the national parks, "for the safety services and security they provide, like helicopters."

These programs remove kids from toxic family dynamics, destructive friends, and negative situations, and pit them, instead, against nature, where actions and consequences are stunningly obvious. If you don't learn to make a bow-drill fire, for example, you eat a cold dinner. Wilderness programs range from the strict, in-your-face management style to more gentle methods, some based on Native American tradition. In some programs students plant and maintain vegetable gardens or care for domestic or farm animals as part of their therapeutic treatment.

Whether or not Jason is an athletic or outdoorsy kind of kid, a wilderness program might provide the kind of open-air therapy he needs to get a better sense of himself. For six to eight weeks, but often as long as three months, students trek off into the wilderness with a group of experienced counselors.

For example, a three-month program at a West Virginia therapeutic school begins with a twenty-eight-day wilderness experience that identifies primary issues and establishes working relationships between six students, their instructors, and their therapists. The next phase helps kids make connections between beliefs and actions. In the final phase, in the school's therapeutic high school, students learn how to learn, again. Individual and group therapy and parent and sibling workshops reinforce each phase.

Follow-up is critical and should be extensive like the one at a residential treatment program in Utah. Their aftercare program includes parent phone conferences, weekends back at school for parents and kids, parent support groups, individual and family therapy, transition groups, and monitoring of new school placements.

Despite high tuitions, however, the beneficial effect of these programs can wear off quickly if a kid returns home to the same toxic family dynamic, destructive friends, and negative situations. "If they are snarled up in the same pain, anxiety, [and] fear, then the likelihood of reversal is great," says Irvin. Despite all your good intentions and willingness to pay high tuitions, conducting consistent reality checks to see if you are contributing some kind of poison to Jason's mix is the key to sustaining his improvement.

Set Your Criteria for a Therapeutic School

What critical components must Jason's program have? The following are some of the elements he will need in his new school. Think about them *before* you start looking for programs and keep them handy when you investigate schools by phone.

Put safety first. Ask about what special precautions are taken to ensure that Jason will be physically, emotionally, and socially safe. Get specific. Don't be afraid to ask what measures are in place to guard against drug use or purchase and sexual encounters that could lead to sexually transmitted diseases.

Go beyond structure. Jason needs more than a structured environment to find his path out of the woods. If he has Tourette's syndrome, for example, find a therapeutic program that specializes in working with kids who have that disorder.

Ask about therapy. Is there only group therapy, or is individual therapy available, too? Is there art, music, dance, or movement therapy? Are there therapy programs for parents and siblings?

Ask about lessons. Jason doesn't need to learn basket weaving; he needs to learn coping mechanisms and healthy-thinking techniques he can use for the rest of his life. What kinds of self-help skills are taught? How is self-esteem built? How do they teach kids to trust? To build relationships? To cope with stress? Do they use programs, like the twelve-step program, to deal with chemical addictions?

Ask about the daily schedule. This sorts bad programs from good ones. A good program gives Jason lots of opportunities to talk and interact each day with healthy young adult counselors and teachers. A poor program allows plenty of time for students to sit around trading horror stories.

Ask about staff credentials and experience. Are there licensed professionals among the medical, psychological, and guidance staff members who will be working with Jason? Irvin stresses the importance of experience. "What you are looking for is people with experience with these children," says Irvin. Some wilderness programs employ staff members who, rather than possessing credentials, have only personal experience. "Many are graduates of these programs themselves," Irvin says, adding, "They are an intensely personal, engaged, nurturing, caring community of adults." Follow your heart about the level of professionalism and experience you need in the people who will care for your child.

Ask for references. These the school should happily provide. Communicate especially with the parents of other students who have already been through the program.

Ask about the "after the therapeutic stay is over" program. Remember that follow-up to any therapeutic program is equally important as the program itself. A strong one guards against repeat performances.

Consider Private Therapeutic School Options

After you've pondered about what you want, you are ready to investigate individual therapeutic schools. Use the Internet or seek help from an independent educational counselor or school placement professional. When you find one that feels right, grab your criteria list and make a phone call. Inquire about arranging a visit.

Search hundreds of schools and wilderness programs at the National Association of Therapeutic Schools and Programs (NATSAP) at *www.natsap.org*. You can also search schools by a specific disturbance, like bulimia.

If you can't see the forest for the trees in your hunt for a therapeutic program for Jason, don't hesitate to seek professional, objective advice. See an educational diagnostician, educational or child psychologist, licensed clinical social worker, school placement counselor, school psychologist, or independent school counselor. Find independent school counselor referrals for thirty-eight states at *www.educationalconsulting.org*. Resources, however, may be limited in the Midwest.

Consider Public School Alternative Programs

If you can't afford a private therapeutic high school, seek advice about "alternative" public high school programs from Jason's guidance counselor or school psychologist. Alternative public education is, strictly speaking, any type of education outside the mainstream curriculum, like special education. However, it also applies to school-affiliated programs provided for students with social, emotional, behavioral, or drug- or alcohol-abuse issues.

Though specific regulations vary from state to state, Jason

normally does not have to have a diagnosed learning disability nor have an individual educational plan (IEP) in place to qualify for alternative school placement.

Alternative schools generally have a smaller pupil-to-teacher ratio and highly trained staff. Some programs are held on school grounds, others in community buildings. Students are still required to follow the established high school curriculum. Some alternative programs have work-study options or opportunities for kids to earn college credits. Investigate what your school provides.

If nothing is available that addresses his needs within the public school system, placement is sometimes made in a private school and paid for by the public school system. Be aware, however, that these placements rarely happen unless Jason has been diagnosed with a special need and has an IEP in place. It's still worth checking out.

Get educated about alternative programs and other special education services at the National Information Center for Children and Youth with Disabilities (NICHCY) in Washington, DC. Its patient and knowledgeable information specialists provide parents and professionals with details and referrals, in English and Spanish, for every state in the union. Call 800-695-0285 or go to *www.nichcy.org*.

The US Department of Health and Human Services provides comprehensive information on substance abuse and mental health. Log on to *www.health.gov* or call 800-662-HELP.

Adopt Some Native American Techniques

To improve your communication with Jason, adopt some time-tested techniques like these, drawn from Native American cultures.

Avoid "combustible" words. What words set Jason off into his negative patterns? Compromise? Feelings? Responsibility? Family? At a hiking and camping therapeutic program in Arizona, they substitute Nez Perce words for words that set kids off. Get out the dictionary and find synonyms without a negative connotation to use in your conversations with Jason. Or borrow words from your native or favorite foreign language. Changing synonyms frequently helps you sidestep word-triggered explosions and increases his vocabulary, too.

Give him obvious short-term goals. At an outdoor program in North Carolina, for boys aged twelve–seventeen, they walk the medicine wheel to chart their progress. The medicine wheel symbolizes the circle of life in many different Native American cultures. Paths and circles within it mark passages and changes in people's lives. In rituals and ceremonies, tribal members "walk" the circle. Though you might not go so far as to construct a medicine wheel in your backyard, you might assign chores that provide obvious feedback quickly. Ask him to pitch at least five old boxes blocking the door to the toolshed. The next day ask him to heave five more. When the shed is empty, dance with him around the newly empty space and decide together how you will fill it up again. Then have him mow the lawn in stages, starting with the wilderness encroaching on your front door.

Ask a question, and then tell him you'll be back later for an answer. This ducks the arrogance and boastfulness that often fuel first responses. Called "wait time," it increases the depth and substance of responses and encourages class interaction. For a literary lesson in the perils of arrogance, download free "Ipani Eskimos: A Cycle of Life in Nature" by James K. Wells, at *www.alaskool.org*.

Save the doing for last. Contrary to hands-on experience, Inupiat (Northern Eskimo) hunters gathered knowledge about and studied the techniques and learned skills for sea-ice conditions before they traveled across it. "Doing is the back end of the educational

experience in traditional life," says Inupiat educator Paul Ongtooguk of Anchorage, Alaska. Utilizing this method might mean
taking notes for Jason when he has to read a long chapter in his bi-
ology textbook. Why not quiz him about what he thinks is important to remember about cell mitosis? Teacher- or parent-prepared
notes, especially for kids experiencing serious emotional distur-
bances, can cut through distracting information in books and
websites and give them accurate study materials as well as models
they can use later for taking their own notes.

Make him part of the community. "In Inupiat society, it is through
participation that a person becomes part of the community. In
fact, in Inupiat society, high status is acquired through sharing.
Boys learn to prove themselves through helping others," says
Ongtooguk. Can Jason share his fine reading skills by reading
Harry Potter aloud each week to a group of senior citizens in the
assisted-living community near your house? Or contact your local
hospital to see if he might do some of his famous magic tricks or
play his guitar each week for patients in the pediatric wing. The
shine of gratitude on the faces in the group will provide another
light on his way through the forest.

Maybe what Jason needs is an "environectomy" to remove
negative situations, destructive friends, toxic family situations,
and maybe even you from his environment for a while. Change
the trajectory of Jason's life by changing his vantage point. Consider a school where success is measured by walking in places
where cacti are tall and canyons are wide. Success is not guaran-
teed. Reversals can happen. But the cost of not acting, not taking
advantage of the options now available to help you tame your
"wild child," can be even greater yet.

26

How to Help Kids Who Are Poor Spellers

Spelling is the junkyard dog in Chip's high school work—it's erratic, it's wild, and it stinks.

Spelling will always bite if Chip's phonics are weak or if he limits his reading only to what is required for school. If he is new to speaking and writing English, spelling will be cantankerous, too. If he has an attention disorder, chances are he'll have little patience for concentrating on which letter goes where. Nor will poor memorization skills tame that cranky spelling dog.

Sometimes the problem is one small sound bite, like the "uh" sound vowels can make called "the schwa." You hear it in the *a* in *zebra*, the *e* in *siren*, the *i* in *disease*, the *o* in *bacon*, and the *u* in *supply*. It might be small, but it's everywhere and it's confusing when Chip goes to spelling.

But what about students who are strong in most subjects and even read for pleasure and still can't spell for *beens?* Maybe it's the English language.

English has 400 different ways to spell 42 sounds. The long-*e* sound, for example, is spelled twelve different ways. And though English has 90 basic spelling patterns, 84 of them have exceptions, like "put the *i* before the *e* except after *c*." Then there are exceptions to the exception, like *weird* which is totally weird. To make matters worse, at least 3500 of the most common words in English do not follow the 90 basic patterns. German, on the other hand, has only 800 such junkyard words. Spanish has 600 and Italian has just 400. Unfortunately, it's English he needs most of the time in school.

Though we can't change phonics or the language Chip needs for school, we can improve his spelling ability by taming his most troublesome spots. You can help him even if you've never come close to winning a spelling bee. The following tips work for high school kids of all abilities. Adapt them for elementary and middle schoolers, too.

Teach Phonics, Incidentally

Bring phonics howling back when kids have trouble with spelling. To help you isolate exactly which sounds Chip has trouble associating with the correct letter, insert a seemingly incidental phonics lesson into his normal routine.

1. Listen for annoying, repeated, unusual sounds around him like Buster, the ever-howling mutt who lives next door.

2. Draw Chip's attention to the sound.

3. Imitate the sound yourself.

4. Then say, "I wonder how you'd spell that sound? I think I'd write it this way: a-r-r-a-w-o-w-y-i-p-y-i-p-i-p."

5. Ask him, "How would you spell it?"

6. Make sure he listens to the sound, and then ask him to write it.

7. Discuss how your sounds and spellings differ.

8. Make each other's sounds.

9. Reverse the process by first writing out a sound, then asking him to mimic it. If his sound doesn't match your intention, say it your way for him. Which part is he saying differently? This might be a clue to an incorrect letter-sound match. Turn to the pronunciation guide of any dictionary to settle the dispute and review that sound bite again.

--- **MORE INCIDENTAL PHONICS FOR GOOD SPELLING** ---

Cough it up. When either one of you coughs, sneezes, groans, moans, or wails, ask him how he spells that. Try to spell it yourself.

Take it outside. Try to spell the sound of a motorcycle changing gears, a truck backing up, or a fire siren sounding. Ask him if he agrees with your spelling, or can he go you one better?

Read the funnies. Ask him what the sound "eeeeuuuuwww" in the bubble over a character's head might sound like. Vocalize the sound yourself. Who does the dictionary deem the winner?

Make it roar. Spell out the orchestra of animal sounds during a trip to the zoo or a pet store. Inform curious strangers that it's for the sake of your kid's spelling.

Make it electronically hiss. Ask him to spell the sound or "wav" files on his computer. Jungle sounds are particularly phonetic.

Train the Ornery Parts

Let him invent spellings. Use this old elementary school technique to diagnose where Chip is making mistakes in words. Patterns will often appear like misheard vowel sounds or confusion about how a word changes when an ending is added. Then, make like a tutor and focus your work on his weak patterns.

Doodle that dog down. Take advantage of high schoolers' love of doodling. If you find that Chip has trouble with a particular spelling rule, like *i* before *e* but not after *c*, ask him to draw a cartoon to illustrate it. He might picture, for example, a heavy-footed *c* walking toward *i* and *e*, who are standing together. Because the *i* and *e* see him coming, insert a word bubble over their heads that says, "Hey, here he comes. Quick, switch places with me!"

Put a tail on it. Encourage Chip to add doodles to the words that make the most trouble for him. In the word *administrative* for example, he might draw a pair of glasses over the two *i*'s in the middle of the word. The glasses visually reinforce the vowel sounds and hint at the word's meaning.

Croon it. In the animated movie *Pinocchio*, Jiminy Cricket taught a whole generation of kids how to spell *encyclopedia* just by singing it. As a high schooler, Chip is probably used to your embarrassing yourself, so go ahead, croon a tune when he encounters a hard word like *obsequious*, making sure to elongate the vowel sounds by raising and lowering your voice. Nudge him to invent his own version. Then hum it in his ear every time he has to spell that word.

Point it out. As coincidence would have it, Chip's spelling words will suddenly appear as if by magic in magazines, newspapers, or books. Don't let any occurrence go by unnoticed and unmentioned. Repeated sightings of the word glue it to his memory.

Take a shot. Instead of singing it, telling him outright, or sending him off to the dictionary, encourage Chip to try to spell a perplexing word two or three different ways. This accomplishes two things: it helps him develop a sense of what the correctly spelled word looks like—the first step toward correct spelling. And it identifies in a flash nagging phonics and spelling rules. The spell-checking program on his computer is a superb tool for working this strategy.

Do not pooh-pooh automatic spell-checking programs! Though a spell-checking program won't correct homophones like *to*, *two*, and *too* and doesn't correct when a word is used incorrectly in context, it *only* makes corrections *after* Chip "takes a shot" at the word. If his attempt is too wild, he will not get a signal that the word is incorrectly spelled, nor will the program provide correct spelling options. A computer spell-checking program is also a great way to practice for the "pick the correct spelling" questions in the language arts section of group standardized tests, now required annually for students in public school grades 3, 5, 8, and 12.

Piggyback it. Once Chip masters a word, build his spelling inventory by adding a prefix or suffix or making that word plural. Or show older kids like Chip that by merely replacing the *p*'s with *t*'s, a porpoise becomes a tortoise. Use a known word to carry him correctly to other words with the same pattern, like *poise*, *counterpoise*, and *equipoise*. This double-dip trick punches up spelling and vocabulary.

Relate it. Encourage Chip to look for clues in the words to help him remember the spelling, like looking for the "sign" in *signature* or the "finite" in *infinitesimal*. If he has to spell the word *abstain*, give him a hint that the final syllable is spelled just like *rain*.

Leave it out. Play the old hangman game particularly with words that have repeated or unsounded vowels like *amateurism*. Write only the consonants and have him fill in the vowels. Then write only the vowels and have him fill in the consonants. This aides memory because it isolates and highlights the orneriest places in the word.

Invent new nonsense words. Put phonics and word parts together by playing with words that make no sense at all. Invent new root words like "merp" or "glat" or "poot." Then make a list of actual prefixes like *pre-*, *en-*, *anti-*, or *dis-*. Make a third list of real suffixes like *–ation*, *-ous*, or *-ly*. Then, select three parts and construct a new word, like *antimerpation* or *prepootous* and have him read it. Are his phonics correct? Next, say the word *disglatly* and ask him to spell it. This is a good game to play during plane or train trips, bus rides, or road trips. Corporate consultants and advertising executives make big dollars cobbling together names in this way for new products and companies. Why not Chip?

Tame the Tails

Pay particular attention, too, when Chip is adding endings on words. "Our research shows that most youngsters and many adults make several errors when they add endings to root words," says Barry Ross, a former teacher and spelling expert from Port Lambton, Ontario. Use the following two rules from Ross's spelling program:

Directer or director? To help Chip get around the *-or* or *-er* ending dilemma, have him check to see if he can add *-ion* to make a correctly spelled word, like *direct*, which by adding *-ion* becomes *direction*. It usually follows then that the person who directs is spelled with an *o* as in *director*. But if you can't add *-ion* to make a correct root word, like *jump* can't be *jumpion*, then you know that the person who jumps is called a *jumper*, not a *jumpor*. Note that this spelling rule works only *most* of the time.

Immediately or immediatly? To help Chip remember when he leaves the *e* or drops the *e* at the end of the word, tell him to examine the letters at the back and the front of the root word and ending he wants to put together. Avoid two vowels coming together.

• *Drop the* e. When the root word ends with a vowel and the suffix begins with a vowel, drop the final *e* on the root word. Is it *comeing* or *coming?* Point him to the end of the root word *come*. It ends with an *e*. Then look at the beginning of the ending he wants to add, *-ing*. It begins with an *i*. If that would put two vowels in a row, then he drops the final *e* on the root word. So, the correctly spelled word is *coming*.

• *Keep the* e. When the suffix begins with a consonant, keep the final *e* on the root word. Is he trying to attach *move* with *-ment?* Again, point him to the ending letter on the root word and the beginning letter of the ending he wants to add. If one is a vowel and the other is a consonant, he keeps the *e* on the root word to correctly spell *movement*.

Get at the Roots

In Ross's spelling system, all root words are broken into syllables to help in the spelling of unknown words. Do this when you are working with Chip, especially if the word is long and complicated or just sounds like it. The word *extraordinary*, for example, is easy to spell when you break it apart and show Chip that it's just *extra* and *ordinary* joined together.

A rule of thumb about breaking words into syllables is that the number of syllables is roughly equal to the number of vowels. For example, the word *elementary* has five syllables and five vowels. However, because this is the English language, this rule does not always hold true. To be safe, check the dictionary.

Latin and Greek word parts abound in the words we use every day. Pointing them out to Chip and discussing their meaning not only aids his spelling, but it gives him a leg up on figuring out the meaning of a word. The prefix *dys-*, for example, comes from the Greek language, and it means bad or difficult. Can Chip guess then what *dysfunctional* means? Find two hundred roots and three thousand words in *Merriam-Webster's Vocabulary Builder* by Mary Wood Cornog.

Though Chip might be able to use computer spell-checking for research papers, compositions, and reports, he can't use it on classroom or standardized tests or to write a note to a classmate. Poor spelling is not the message he wants to send. So start howling and tame that spelling dog in him.

RESOURCES

Find an excellent list of various spellings of the same sound at the American Literacy Council at *www.americanliteracy.com/ variations.htm*.

Animal sounds can be found at *www.georgetown.edu/faculty/ballc/ animals/*.

Spelling animal sounds can be found at *www.georgetown.edu/ faculty/ballc/animals/animals-spelling.html*

27

How to Help Kids Who Get Confused by Science

Tessie thought she knew everything about chemical reactions from Chemistry I class. But when she dyed her blond hair with hydrogen peroxide and powdered drink mix, sure she'd get streaks of Madwoman Magenta, what she got was splotches of Purely Pathetic Pink.

As her pink hair fiasco proves, Tessie's grasp of high school science needs work. Capitalize on her hair hysteria to channel her in a more effective direction. At the minimum, it might result in successfully Madwoman Magenta–streaked hair. And it might give her an indelible lesson in the methods of scientific investigation.

Strictly speaking, understanding how to best dye your hair is no different from any other field of scientific inquiry and investigation. Chemistry, for example, studies substances like earth, water, and powdered drink mixes and the "hairy" changes and interactions they undergo under different conditions.

Changes can be natural like the burning that results when lightning strikes a tree, or man-made like the washed-out pink that happens when Tessie doesn't add enough Pink Fandango coloring agent. Even if Tessie is not taking a separate class in chemistry, she will need scientific investigation and inquiry skills in the other science classes she might encounter in high school, like astronomy, consumer science, earth science, geology, meteorology, or oceanography.

Questioning Is the Key

Questioning is an integral part of scientific inquiry. The right kind of questioning can lead Tessie to guessing, which in turn can lead to thinking about results. "I wonder if I waited long enough? I figured it would take at least fifteen minutes to get a really Madwoman Magenta. Maybe forty-five minutes would have been better." It's through this unique process of questioning, predicting, and evaluating results that Tessie is able to figure out her next move. "Now, I need a hairdresser."

When science classes like chemistry and physics prove hairier than Tessie or you imagined, there are things you can do to help. "Engagement is the most important thing," says Eric Mazur, Professor of Physics and Applied Physics at Harvard University. Little kids engage themselves naturally by looking at the world around them and constantly asking, why, why, why? But, somewhere around middle school, "their curiosity gets turned off. From that point on, people concentrate on facts," Mazur says.

To get older students to ask why, why, why again, Mazur developed a simple teaching technique in use at Harvard since 1991. Called "ConcepTests," its purpose is to "exploit student interaction and focus attention on underlying concepts." High schools and colleges across the country report ConcepTests improve student performance. Mazur's studies show gains even on conventional exams.

The first section below provides questioning strategies based on ConcepTests. Use them at home with high school kids. These suggestions build on the methods for fourth and fifth graders covered in Chapter 15. The second section brings investigation home with some lab work to "dye" for.

Bring Back the Curiosity

Listen to her theories. How Tessie questions what happened and develops theories reveals her ability to sequence critical events. It also reveals her understanding or misconceptions about basic concepts like chemical reactions. In ConcepTests, students are required to develop individual theories and then "sell them" to other students. Share your scientific theories at the dinner table. If Tessie thinks her hair disaster occurred because she should have used another flavor dye, ask her what led her to that conclusion. What evidence does she have? Don't accept her opinions unless she supports them. This is what responsible scientists do.

Don't fear all the whys. When Tessie's why, why, why gets beyond the scope of your scientific knowledge, have no fear; use three methods Mazur uses with his students at Harvard:

- *Turn her questions back on her.* Why does Tessie think her hair turned pale pink? Not enough coloring agent, peroxide? Wrong flavor? This technique also gives you time to think about where you can turn together to find in-depth answers, like her textbook, the Internet, or an e-mail to her teacher.

- *Divert her questions.* When she asks you why her hair only turned a pale pink, ask her how long it took before she noticed a change. Or what did she do after putting the ingredients in her hair, sit in the sun? These kinds of diversionary questions teach her to question the phenomena from a variety of angles, which is how scientists go about learning more.

- *Ask somebody else.* Since you don't have one hundred and seventy students in class to rely on like Mazur does, find an informal team of consultants to help when Tessie is confused by science. Take all her accumulated whys to a group of sympathetic friends at a study party or in her dance class and brainstorm them together.

Pump up the question quotient by reading ahead. Increase Tessie's curiosity and questioning by having her do some "pre-homework"—skim ahead to the next chapter in her chemistry or science book *before* it is covered in class. What is difficult or confusing? Have her jot her questions on Post-it Notes in the chapter. Since Tessie is under no pressure to listen and take notes like she must in class, she can skim, ponder, and pose questions at her own pace. Mazur routinely uses this method with his students.

Bringing Science to Bear on Highly Flavored Hair

Setting up and conducting simple experiments to get to underlying concepts in chemistry is just what Tessie should be doing in high school science. According to the National Science Standards, by the end of grade 12,

> Students should formulate a testable hypothesis and demonstrate the logical connection between the scientific concepts guiding a hypothesis and the design of an experiment. They should demonstrate appropriate procedures, a knowledge base, and conceptual understanding of scientific investigations.

Use Tessie's failed attempt as a starting point to help her learn how to invent lab procedures at home consistent with the National Science Standards recommendations. Keep the materials and equipment simple. The point here is to make her consistently question the phenomena, to reveal basic concepts in their clearest colors, to revise her assumptions based on each test outcome, and to provide practice opportunities that will make her more confident in doing science work at school. At-home labs also demonstrate how she's really thinking in science, not how you or her teacher assume she is. You do not have to be Louis Pasteur to be Tessie's lab partner at home.

An Experiment to Dye For

The following outline will help you structure an at-home experiment. It will help Tessie understand how variables affect the hair-dying process and hone her scientific investigative skills at the same time. Adapt this approach for other topics and gear it to your high schooler's interests.

The goal is to identify the variables that could affect the outcome of the dying process and, in particular, result in that perfect Madwoman Magenta color. Through the guided questioning and why, why, whys described above, help Tessie list the variables that could have possibly led to that pathetic result. In the interest of time and simplicity, help her narrow down and consolidate the list to the four most significant factors.

1. Materials (original hair color, powdered-drink colors, conditioners, acids, water, aluminum foil)

2. Condition of the hair (wet, dry, greasy, clean)

3. Applied heat (none, some, sunshine, hair dryer)

4. Time (how long to apply materials, how long the effect lasts)

Next, Tessie will test the variables. The more she can isolate each variable when testing, the better she can identify the impact of each variable. To save her hair, and her nerves, from another hysterical dye job, conduct her experiment on bunches of white or beige wool yarn. To make the experiment more realistic and fun use an old human hair wig in a light color. Note that synthetic hair will not take dye. Look for wigs or hair pieces at flea markets or secondhand shops.

Using pieces of aluminum foil, divide the yarn or wig into approximately 16–24 bunches of hair. Wrap each bunch with aluminum foil or clear plastic wrap to isolate those strands for each of the seven following experiments. Number each bunch with a permanent marker. Create a log where Tessie can document the variables applied to each of the yarn or hair bunches in each experiment.

The desired Madwoman result will be achieved when she reaches the preferred conclusion. Tessie needs, therefore, to test, adjust, retest, develop procedures, draw conclusions, build a knowledge base and conceptual understanding, and, finally, make logical links between variables. In the end, she will know how to best apply each variable to achieve the end result she desires.

Experiment 1 (Materials): Original Hair Color vs. Bleached

Leave one bunch of hair or yarn its natural color. Bleach another bunch so that it's almost white. Mix the powdered drink with water until it is the consistency of mud. Apply the same powdered drink mix for the same amount of time to each. How does the starting color of the hair affect the results of the dying? Why? Draw a conclusion and choose the preferred strategy: fair or bleached hair results in more saturated colors. Darker hairs develop sheens but are not saturated with the powdered drink color.

Experiment 2 (Condition): Greasy vs. Degreased

Put hair conditioner on one bunch of hair or yarn and rinse. Shampoo a different bunch to remove hair oil and do not apply conditioner. Apply the powdered drink. How saturated is the color? Why? Is the hair shaft more open to receiving the pigment if less covered with oil? Draw a conclusion and choose the preferred strategy: the cleaner the hair, the better the color saturation.

Experiment 3 (Condition): Color Duration

Shampoo the same two bunches used in Experiment 2. Which bunch retains more color? Why? Does hair oil reduce the penetration of the pigment? Draw a conclusion and choose the preferred strategy: the cleaner the hair when dyed, the longer the color will last over repeated washings.

Experiment 4 (Heat): Temperature of the Dye

Prepare two identical mixtures of powdered drink mix. Put one in the refrigerator to chill and gently warm the other. Apply each to a different bunch for the same amount of time, then rinse. How saturated is the color in each? Why? Draw a conclusion and choose the preferred strategy: the hotter the mix, the more saturated the color.

Experiment 5 (Heat): Temperature of the Hair

Prepare two identical mixtures of powdered drink mix that are the same temperature. Apply each to a different bunch for the same amount of time; however, leave one bunch wrapped in aluminum foil at room temperature while wrapping the other in aluminum foil and then applying heat from a hair dryer (be careful not to overdo the heat). Rinse. Or instead of using a hair dryer, wrap the second bunch in plastic food wrap and let it sit in the sunshine. How saturated is the color in each? Why? Draw a conclusion and choose the preferred strategy: the hotter the hair, the better the color saturation.

Experiment 6 (Time): Time of Dye Application

Prepare one mix of powdered drink but apply it to two different bunches for different amounts of time. For example, fifteen minutes on the first bunch and forty-five minutes on the second bunch. How saturated is the color in each? Why? What if you allowed one batch to sit overnight for maximum saturation? Draw a conclusion and choose the preferred strategy: the longer the dye is applied, the more saturated the color.

Experiment 7 (Materials): Using Vinegar or Peroxide

Prepare two identical mixtures of powdered drink mix that are the same temperature, except use peroxide or vinegar to mix one and just water to mix the other. Apply each to a different bunch for the same amount of time. Rinse. Shampoo both bunches. Which bunch retains more color? Why? Draw a conclusion and choose the preferred strategy: the peroxide or vinegar fixes the color and it lasts longer.

Experiment 8 (Conditions): Confining the Dying

When you are preparing the powdered drink mixes for the above experiments, use leftover mix to measure the effect on your skin. Cover one finger with Vaseline and dip it into the mix for five minutes. Do the same thing with another finger that has been washed and is free of oil. Which finger retains more color? Why? Draw a conclusion and choose the preferred strategy: smear Vaseline on your ears, neck, and forehead (but not hair) before applying the mix to your hair. What Tessie wants are Madwoman Magenta streaks, not ears.

As Tessie learns how to systematically investigate, she will be less dependent on and less content to simply ask why, why, why of her teacher or her mother. She will be equipped with a skill set that will help her figure out the world around her for herself. Then she can transfer her knowledge not only to her science exams, but her life. Who knows? Sometimes when kids systematically investigate, they encounter wholly unexpected discoveries and solutions that are better than anything they had anticipated at the start. Tessie might decide after some lab work at home that the best solution of all is to leave her beautiful blond hair natural and just wear her highly flavored wig.

PART SEVEN

Beating the Summertime Blues

28

What to Do When Summer Gets Boring

Two weeks into summer vacation, Harry dons his best pitiful face and turns it on you. "I'm really, REALLY bored. Are you listening to me, Mom? Dad? Anybody?"

Banish boredom from your house this summer with activities that cross-pollinate and resonate with your Harry. Adventures that complement each other put skills and knowledge in a broader, more real-life context. When projects are related or are natural outgrowths of each other, that initial spark of interest jumps from one activity to another. That moves projects along and gives them a better chance of lasting to conclusion.

Below are some interactive, sensory-stimulating, whole-body, whole-family summer activities. Some are cross-pollinating summer-long campaigns. Others you can do when you have fifteen minutes to spare. They are all designed to keep academic skills perking during those long breaks from school. Copy this entire chapter and paste it on the refrigerator before Harry can begin singing his old boring song. Age appropriateness is noted throughout.

All-Summer-Long Activities

Have a family book club. Read the same book at the same time. Schedule club meetings at two-week intervals to discuss the books, maybe over dinner. Which characters did you like best? Did the story keep you interested? What was effective about the author's style? When pressed for time, select shorter books to give everyone time to complete them before the next club meeting. The frequency and quality of the book discussion is almost as important as the book selections. This activity helps kids learn to critique story elements and authors' styles—exactly what elementary through high schoolers need for writing book reports at school.

Start a family newsletter. Put Harrys of all ages in charge of keeping in touch with family and friends by e-mail this summer. Younger kids can focus on individual e-mail messages. Older ones can put together family newsletters and distribute them by e-mail. Most word processing software gives computer-savvy or more ambitious Harrys the option to lay out the newsletters and insert images. This reinforces more sophisticated computer skills. At the least, this activity strengthens keyboarding, composition, grammar, and spelling skills.

Make a family history. Designate Harry the family historian. Put younger ones in charge of maintaining folders or scrapbooks of summer events like movies, museum trips, family parties, or vacations. Paste photos, postcards, movie stubs, museum brochures, party invitations, travel itineraries, and receipts for favorite new toys in this permanent family record. These scrapbooks make for excellent sharing when Harry returns to school. Younger kids can also practice handwriting and creative skills by writing a narrative for each set of items.

Older students can sort family photos by person, date, or event. Put a scanner in Harry's hand and have him scan the photos and move them into page layouts. These two steps alone could take all summer. Ask him to collate his pages to add to his younger brother's family history scrapbooks. Frame and send individual pages as gifts for the entire coming year.

Teach cooking. Find math in measuring and determining portions and nutrient contents. Find science behind why yeast makes bread rise and why sparkling water bubbles. Find history in family recipes, art and design in food presentation, and cultural awareness in preparing ethnic meals. Planning meals, budgeting, buying food, preparing, and serving also demand organizing and that most important skill of all, cleaning up the mess. Cooking can even instill responsibility. Those who learn to cook over the summer can make a weekly dinner for the family during the school year.

Note that microwave ovens are prime opportunities for younger, computer-reluctant Harrys to learn to operate a simple computer program. Computers and microwave ovens have lots in common. They both have computer chips and preloaded software and controls so Harry can tell the device what to do. The microwave, however, is simpler because it has only a few controls like a timer and a clock.

Work on food allergies. A summer cooking project might also provide the perfect opener for investigating your suspicions about whether your child's hyperactivity might be food related. Harry can become his own food-allergy detective with a simple elimination diet. You can help by planning cooking projects around his new foods. Find excellent guidelines written for elementary-aged kids in *Tracking Down Hidden Food Allergy* by William G. Crook, M.D. Available to order at 800-227-2627.

Learn a foreign language. Summer is the perfect time for learning a second language together. Access the many computer programs available free online. Select trips, television programs, ethnic grocery stores, museum exhibits, local festivals, and events that highlight the language of your choice. Be on the lookout for words in your chosen foreign language in newspapers, books, and magazines. Borrow or buy books in two languages, and then read the dialogue aloud in both languages to learn grammar, sentence structure, and vocabulary. Incorporate foreign expressions in your daily conversations and cook meals from regions that speak your new language. Bring all your efforts together by having a family book club discussion about your Chinese book selection while eating Harry's interpretation of *chow mein*.

Build endurance. Involve Harry in exercises that build strength, stamina, and lung capacity. Go hiking, tree climbing, rock climbing, bicycling, running, jogging, skipping, jumping rope, playing hopscotch, and swimming with kids of all ages. Get a younger Harry a mini-trampoline or set up a badminton court in the backyard and have family tournaments. Harry can perfect his body control and movement strategies merely by learning to avoid the azalea bushes when he lunges for the birdie. These full-body, high-movement exercises are also excellent outlets for kids with attention disorders. Older kids might learn fencing over the summer, which builds strength, stamina, balance, and eye-hand coordination.

Form a visiting artist collective. Ask the parents of four or five of Harry's friends to join you in inviting artists to teach a small group of kids this summer. The artist doesn't have to be a professional. It can be one of the parents in your neighborhood, or a friend or family member who is interested in graphics arts, interior design, jewelry making, beading, weaving, knitting, sewing, quilting, gardening, house or wall painting, pet grooming, bicycle repair, carpentry, wood carving, or picture framing. Classes can meet for an hour once or twice a week. Parents can take turns chaperoning and learn a new art along with the kids.

Organize collections. Whether Harry collects stuffed teddy bears or CDs of his favorite rap groups, organizing, sorting, cataloguing, and storing collections is a great summertime activity. Make it a writing exercise by having him maintain a collection notebook in print or on the computer. This should include notes, comments, and/or opinions about individual items. This could take all summer.

Plant a vegetable or flower garden together. There are many life lessons in gardening that kids of all ages can harvest. Nature is never short of surprising revelations. Gardening also teaches design, spatial and visual planning, sequencing, scheduling and long-term planning, and follow-through—the same skills middle and high school kids need to complete a long-term report. The plant selection process puts kids in touch with weather conditions and soil quality as well as care and maintenance schedules. If it is a vegetable garden, it will also show Harry where vegetables come from. It's not surprising that some kids think green beans come from cans in a supermarket.

This would be also a fine time to teach Harry how to safeguard his health and preserve the environment by investigating and using natural fertilizers and nontoxic pest-killing methods. As a finishing touch, Harry can prepare his harvested vegetables as part of his weekly cooking performance.

Introduce Harry to traditional crafts. Cross-cultural experiences will expand Harry's awareness, spark his creativity and teach him tolerance. Seek out local or large festivals and events that highlight the crafts of another culture. Because traditional artists learn their crafts within their own communities, they provide a personal insight into the culture, too. Check for festivals, events, celebrations, or parades in your local newspaper or on community bulletin boards. This idea dovetails nicely many of the others above. From the Hispanic cultural festival, Harry can learn the recipe for a dish he can cook using vegetables from his garden project and serve it on Tuesdays in the fall when he cooks dinner for the family as they discuss a book everyone just read about El Salvador.

Redesign his bedroom. This is a superb lesson in how to sustain his skills during a long-term project, a skill Harry needs if he's in grade four or above. Designing and planning a bedroom also anticipates the increased homework load for kids transitioning into middle or high school. Have Harry, the junior contractor, prepare a design proposal that includes a color palette, floor plan, window treatments, and floor cover. He should make a budget based on his predictions about supplies and outside contractor needs. His proposal should include a time line for completing each phase, which portions he can do on his own, and those requiring assistance from others. Instead of budgeting for new furniture, challenge Harry to explore what he can accomplish with simple materials like boards, cinder blocks, and boxes, or by refinishing or repainting his old dresser.

Fifteen-Minute Summer Activities

Read books aloud together. Choral reading focuses attention in kids with attention deficits. It provides moral support for shy ones, oral support for stuttering ones, and motivation for those who are reluctant to read. If it is done after a discussion about a character, it makes the character's personality resonate with life. If it's poetry you read together, Harry gets the benefit of hearing rhyme, rhythm, and the beat of language, which will smooth his oral reading skills and enliven his writing. Choral reading works, too, for primary-grade kids or those new to English because it reinforces phonics, pronunciation, and the rules of punctuation. Fifteen to twenty minutes a day provides an entertaining and nontaxing way to keep reading skills sharp all summer long.

Practice handwriting. Though the computer is taking over much of what was once handwritten, there are still critical times, like on standardized tests, when kids of all ages need to put pencil to paper and make legible, meaningful marks. If Harry has a problem with his handwriting, don't let this important skill fall by the wayside, even if he is in high school. Poor handwriting skills can have a negative effect on an elementary school student's self-concept. An inability to write smoothly can also affect a young one's desire to compose his thoughts on paper. Hairy handwriting, like stinky spelling, gives a false impression about an otherwise dazzling kid, no matter his age.

- *For preschool and elementary level.* Do some old-fashioned handwriting activities for 10–15 minutes each day. They help primary graders develop small-muscle control and improve eye-hand coordination. Have Harry make letter garlands across a page of lined paper. Start with one letter at a time, like a whole row of loops that look like the letter *e* linked together. Make a bigger garland using loops that look like the letter *L*. Make garlands with points like in the letters *t*, *u*, and *v*, or humpy garlands with shapes that look like the letters *n* and *m*. Kids begin by making two or three letters together and work up to four or five. This is an excellent exercise for beginning writers and those making the move, typically in second or third grade, into cursive writing.

- *Grades three and above.* Investigate calligraphy. This stylistic writing demands good small-muscle control, posture, and breath control. Colored markers with a wide tip or a piece of chalk held at a forty-five-degree angle will help kids easily achieve the characteristic thin and thick lines of calligraphy.

- *High school:* Though you might never get an older Harry to make garlands or write in calligraphy, you can get him to practice his handwriting over the summer. Insist that he leave written notes about where he is going and when he'll be home. Ask him to write you a note to remind you that you need to take him to the dentist tomorrow, and tell him you'll remember better if he writes the details. If in these notes, you see that he consistently misspells a word, leave him a note that includes that word spelled correctly.

No-Time-At-All Summer Activities

Work on good manners. Use the months of summer to teach elementary and middle school kids how to write thank-you notes, for example. Help Harry create and print appropriate stationery by hand or on the computer. Together, compose a general letter of thanks he can use as a template. Then, make copies, leaving blanks for personalizing each note. Show him how to correctly address, stamp, and mail his letters promptly.

Focus on the small niceties, too. He can learn the proper way and when to open a door for someone elderly or handicapped, or merely another person entering or exiting around him. Or how to answer the phone and write a message down or to be considerate of the time he's on the phone or on the Internet. Teach elementary school Harry table manners, too, like posture, passing plates of food, chewing in public, and the proper use of his knife. Good manners reflect well on the whole family.

Rely on these activities whenever Harry is bored and looking to you for something to do. Use them to bring the family together in entertaining and educational ways. But don't crowd out spontaneity. Engineer some downtime in your summertime, too. If you go where the wind blows and where the creative urges lead, this could turn out to be a summer of adventure and self-discovery not only for Harry.

29

How to Keep Reluctant Readers Reading over the Summer

It's been six years since Robert took his first look around his kindergarten class and said, "Just how much more of this do I have to do?" He still thinks writing, spelling, math, science, and social studies are annoying, but most of all, Robert dislikes reading.

This summer, read Robert the riot act. Read him his rights, read him the directions, the ingredients, the computer manual, and the back of the cereal box. Read to, read on, read up, read around, read along, read with him and through him, but this summer, get reading and Robert together. It's good for him and for you, too.

"Reading is to the mind what exercise is to the body," said Joseph Addison, an early eighteenth century English poet, playwright, and essayist, and centuries later his words are still right on. Especially for beginning and reluctant readers who have more attitude than answers when it comes to this complex skill. Reading consistently and everywhere during any long breaks from school is critical for kids like Robert.

The following tactics will keep reluctant readers involved in books all summer long. Unless otherwise noted, they apply to kids in grades four through twelve. At the end of the chapter, find book titles listed by age level. They are recommended by kids who loved them though they swore they'd never, ever feel that way about a book.

Get the Basics in Place

Lay down the law. The equation is simple: no watering, no tomatoes. It's the same with a reading-reluctant elementary-aged kid like Robert: read books over the summer or else. Stand in front of the tomato plant together and read him the riot act. He's got no options here. His teacher will thank you for it in the fall, and so will Robert, though he might be in high school before you hear it. Be the boss about this.

Give him what he likes. Though there's no option about whether or not he reads over the summer, inform him that he's got plenty of choices when it comes to topics to read about. However, don't assume you know what he is interested in reading. Elementary-aged kids move with lightning speed from one interest to another. Track that ever-hopping spark of interest and be ready with a book that stokes that flame.

Give him a target. In two months of summer vacation, Robert should read at least five or six books to maintain any strides he made in reading during the school year. Determine how many pages he can read in twenty minutes and make that number his daily target. Tell him, "Sorry, Robert, picture pages do not count." Steadily increase the number over the summer until he's reading at least thirty minutes a day.

Balance reading-list books. Many schools provide reading lists over the summer, and some are sure to have titles Robert wouldn't read if they were the last books on earth. When he's laboring through one of these, keep a high-interest title handy so he can switch back and forth between the two during each daily 20- to 30-minute reading session.

Gather your resources. Search the Internet, the library, and neighborhood bookstores for books. Keep your eyes peeled for kid-catching titles at garage sales, consignment shops, secondhand-book fairs, and flea markets.

Spread them around. Put books in all Robert's favorite places so he stumbles upon them at every turn. Put a few on the kitchen table, in the bathroom, in his bedroom, and in the attic where he re-treats to get away from his little sister. Just like you did when he was two, keep a few books in the car.

Book-Work for Adults

Read yourself. There's no getting around the fact that if Robert sees you reading, it speaks volumes about how much you value this skill. Read your own books, your grandfather's books, the cheesy romances your aunt sends you in the mail, magazines, newspapers, weekly local bulletins, cookbooks, and computer manuals. Keep your eyes moving across the printed word all summer long, and do it where Robert can see you. If you have a reluctant reader in your life, make books on his reading level or on his summer reading list your top priority. Read around kids all the time.

Read to Robert, even if he's in high school. Do not make the mis-take of asking him if he wants you to read to him. Do it sponta-neously whenever you encounter an amazing, amusing, interesting, weird, wonderful, tragic story, or hilarious dialogue in the news-paper, a magazine, or one of his books piled on the steps leading to the attic. Inserting oral-reading intermissions into each sum-mer day increases his vocabulary and visualization skills, stokes his imagination, and kicks up his comprehension, in spite of himself. So read to him.

Get theatrical about it. Make googly eyes and strange voices whenever you read something interesting out loud to Robert. Read heart-throbbing descriptions passionately at the dinner table. In the car on the way to his grandmother's, moan and complain about a villain who doesn't get his due. Give him bedtime directions in your favorite character's voice. Warble renditions of your favorite lines. But don't give the endings away. Compose your own instead. Add mouth sounds accompanied by air instruments. But always wiggle your eyebrows and saunter away when he wants to know how that ornery kid in the book turned out. Be embarrassing and shameless in your attempts to get him to read.

Write book reviews. Whenever you read a book that is on Robert's reading list or one that is on his reading level, write a one-line book review and stick it under a magnet on the refrigerator door or the bathroom mirror. Note the title and author, and then make short but enticing comments about the characters, plot, author's intention, or writing style. Your review might simply read, "I can't believe the things Danny dreamed up to drive his parents crazy."

Link the book to the movie to the video to the cassette to children's theater. Go to the library together and find a good book, and then explore it in different incarnations: watch the movie, listen to a cassette, or attend a children's theater presentation. Don't let Robert get away with merely saying he liked the movie better than the book or vice versa. Dive into the details. The ASAP format below works best with strong elementary school readers or those sixth grade and above. Note that this technique polishes critiquing skills for *all types* of literary works.

----- **WHAT'S BETTER, THE BOOK OR THE MOVIE?** -----

Track a story's incarnations using the **ASAP** format below.
Spend 20–30 minutes on this activity.

Add

What did the producer add to the story? A new character? A
  different setting? A different time period? A happy ending?
  A new ending?
Did the producer add a romance where there was none?
Was the movie told from another perspective?
Was there a narrator?

Subtract

What did the producer leave out? A character? An important
  plot element like the death of a character? An important
  relationship in the past?
Did the producer omit or skim over a detail about a character
  that was critical to understanding his or her motivation?

Amplify

Did the producer highlight certain character traits more than
  the author did? Was the character weaker, braver, dumber,
  wiser?
Did the producer play up different plot elements? Was there
  more violence in the movie than there was in the book?

Personalize

How did the setting of the movie compare to the one Robert
  visualized?
How did the characters on-screen compare to his imagination?
Why does he think the producer chose to highlight certain
  traits in a character over another? Certain plot elements
  over others?

What did the author do better than the producer?

What did the producer do better than the author?

How would Robert rewrite the script? Rewrite the ending?

Find a wealth of classic books-turned-movies in films by Walt Disney. Or investigate Weston Woods, a collection of audiovisual adaptations of classic children's stories for preschool through grade eight, in English as well as French, Japanese, Mandarin, and Spanish, at *www.scholastic.com/westonwoods*.

Family Book Projects

Become a theatrical family. This was one way families entertained themselves before television and computers took over. Engage in playacting when kids are reluctant to read. Make it a family production by assigning everyone parts of a play to read. Take it "on the road" by memorizing parts, dressing up, and putting on your play for a highly appreciative audience, like the grandparents. Get pointers by attending plays or children's theater presentations. After Robert has seen several, he'll understand how expressive he can really be and learn some innovative ways to add to your simple one-act play.

Picture it. When reading to younger kids from books without pictures, have them cut pictures from old magazines that look like the characters and settings they visualize. Or make separate sketches and compare them. Did Robert remember that the character always wore blue? Do this before you go to a movie or play based on the story! Put the pictures together so he can "retell" the story to his younger cousins or his favorite uncle.

Make book brochures. Elementary-aged Roberts and older artistic types might enjoy making a brochure about a book they just read. Use crayons, markers, computer clip art, or magazine clippings to design typical three-fold, travel-like pamphlets. Brain-storm which kind of illustrations, photos, graphics and short, engaging descriptions about the plot and characters would tempt someone else to read this book. Book brochures provide fodder for book reports later in the school year. And more importantly, they give elementary and middle school kids early experience in writing persuasively—a big focus of writing in high school English classes.

Make book-based family trips. If Robert is amused by a story that relates how the American colonists kept their teeth white with acid, gunpowder, and sticks of sea coral, take a trip together to see a colonial American exhibit at a local museum. Or read a circus book and then attend one. This reinforces, especially for young readers, that adventures can begin in books. Attend story-reading sessions, oral-storytelling events, or author visits at bookstores, libraries, and community events. See Chapter 30 for details about setting up educational family trips.

Make book-based foods. Make foods together that characters eat. For kindergarten through grade three readers, look for books that feature food as a main ingredient. Then, make the food together. Make chocolate cake with a secret ingredient like in *Thunder Cake* by Patricia Polacco, or make meatballs after you read *Cloudy with a Chance of Meatballs* by Judy Barrett. As you're sharing dinner with family or guests, have Robert tell them the story.

Have him provide reading services. Is there an elderly relative, neighbor, or sick friend to whom Robert can read each week over the summer? An appreciative audience always makes an odious summer book list title a little easier to swallow. It could well be that the affirmation of his skills that he sees reflected in a grateful listener's eye is what will keep Robert reading all summer long.

RESOURCES

Kids with disabilities that prevent them from reading in a normal manner can get free books on tape from the Library of Congress Talking Book Program. Or e-mail the Library of Congress at *www.nls@loc.gov* for a list of cooperating libraries in your area.

Recorded Books Inc. has two thousand tapes to rent or buy for children, young adults, and adults. Call for a free catalogue: 800-638-1304.

The Smithsonian Center for Education and Museum Studies offers, free, the *Educator's Guide to Smithsonian Publications and Websites*, a two-part, one-hundred-twenty-page publication. It includes curriculum-spanning books, films, records, CDs, maps, slides, posters, activities, and teaching kits, many free of charge. Send requests to The Smithsonian Office for Education and Museum Studies, PO Box 37012, Arts & Industries Building Room 1163, MRC 402, Washington, DC, 20012. Enclose a $10 check payable to Smithsonian/SCEMS for shipping and handling.

30

Summertime Trips through History

Mattie, Mike, and Kenny recently got a gander at a photo of Uncle Cyrus, their ancestor who fought in the Civil War. Since then, the Battle of Gettysburg has raged in your family room. Another summer is off to a rip-roaring start.

If your kids are turning your house into a battleground this summer, try redirecting their energies in a parallel scientific exploration of family history. Start with a trip to your grandmother's attic, and then move learning along with some one-day trips through history. You'll be surprised how many archaeological experiences you can have in your grandmother's boxes, trunks, and crates and how much anthropological experience can be gained in the homes, battlefields, and museums that preserve the past so kids can safely live it all over again.

It's a summertime plan that reaches back in time, through the family tree, and across the curriculum. Genealogy makes history studies personal. "Archaeology can be used to teach math, reading, writing, oral presentation, and even creative writing and art," notes Ruth O. Selig, anthropology educator, editor, and administrator at the Smithsonian's National Museum of Natural History. Best of all, she says, "It means adventure."

The following plan maps out an archaeological, genealogical, and anthropological summertime experience that elementary and middle school kids will remember the rest of their lives.

Do Some Pre-Attic Homework

The ideal place to start your adventure is somewhere that holds historical significance for your family or friends, like a grandmother's attic, an old family apartment, or a retiring neighbor's home. If you're lucky enough to have such a place, Mattie, Mike, and Kenny can learn what "the past" means and how to interpret and preserve historical resources. They can learn techniques for analyzing the "artifacts" they find there, and they'll even polish up their organizational skills. However, if you don't have such a place handy, many of the activities below can be done just as successfully right in your own home or at a small local museum.

Give primary grade kids a better sense of history. This idea is similar to marking the height of your kids on the doorway as they grow. It gives an upcoming kindergartener like Mike or an almost second grader like Mattie a better sense of what "the past" means. Supplies you will need are a roll of crepe paper, masking tape, pens or markers, photos, and a package of Post-it Notes.

Use masking tape to fasten a roll of crepe paper along a wall at Mattie's eye level. This is her timeline. Stick seven Post-it Notes in equal intervals along the time line, one to mark each year of her life. Use the pen to number each Post-it Note one through seven. Use additional Post-it Notes to write up some milestones in Mattie's life like her first birthday, her first words, the birth of brother Mike, losing her front tooth, learning to ride a bicycle, and getting Ace, the family cat. Enrich the milestones with photos or use photos in place of written notes. Arrange the notes and photos in chronological order.

Then, ask Mattie to post them on her time line starting with the thing she thinks happened first. When all her notes and photos have been placed in the correct historical order, ask her to slowly walk her time line. Ask her to stop at each milestone for questions. Ask questions that will teach her what the past means by measuring it against her own life. Could she read and write when Mike was born? Ride her bike? Play war games with her brothers when she was two? Where did the family live when she was three?

Make a retro family time line. To stretch her understanding back even further in time, place another time line on the wall *before* Mattie's that charts another family member's life, or a branch of the family. Ask her if that metal-toothed sixth-grade girl could have been a mother back then. Take Mattie back further in time by connecting her mother's time line to *her* mother's time line. If you feel ambitious, keep going backwards in time until Mattie's time line reaches back to Uncle Cyrus.

Define your terms before you go up in the attic. Inform the kids that what they will be doing in Grandma's attic today is the same kind of work an archaeologist does. Archaeologists study things made by humans in the past, often going on expeditions called digs. Anthropologists study people all over the earth, their development, and their similarities and differences in the past and today. Make these terms part of their vocabulary by repeating them as they apply in the following activities for kids in grades K–8.

On-Site in Grandma's Attic

Use primary sources. Once you've gathered in your special place like the attic, use the contents of boxes and trunks to teach the kids about primary historical resources. Anthropologists and archaeologists formulate ideas and theories about ages, economic status, work habits, and lifestyles by carefully examining the context in which people or artifacts are discovered. They look at letters, diaries, documents, and maps to interpret and understand human history. You and the kids can also use old family clothing, furniture, and toys.

Ask Kenny, Mattie, and Mike, for example, to examine old photos for historical clues. What fashions, transportation, housework, or office equipment gives them a clue as to when a photo was taken? Can the kids determine the age, sex, and habits of the kids who wore those knickers or bloomers or used those toys or school supplies? Make photocopies of forebearers to put on the family time line. What do those chew marks on Uncle Cyrus's pencil tell them about his habits back when he was a boy in school? Use Aunt Jennie's elaborately beaded flapper dress to theorize together about the family's former financial situation or social standing.

Draw comparisons between the kids and their ancestors. Ask if they see anything familiar about the desk where Uncle Cyrus is doing his schoolwork. Is it the same one Kenny uses today? Seek familiar objects in old photos to give kids a personal link to the past. Ask them, also, to imagine what kind of person Uncle Oscar or Aunt Jennie might have been. Then compare their guesses with Grandma's memories. If she agrees that Uncle Oscar looked like a pleasant and happy guy, but informs them that he was really a nasty old geezer, the kids will learn two important archaeological and anthropological lessons. First, that the best resources are people who lived the history, and second, that sometimes new or additional information changes everything.

Teach the layers of time. Use great-uncle Charles's trunk to teach Mattie, Mike, and Kenny "stratigraphy." Like a layer cake, deposits of earth and minerals called strata pile up over time. Archaeologists use stratigraphy to find out how old things are. The layer that is the lowest is usually the oldest.

Have Kenny carefully empty the trunk and place each item side by side in a straight line on the floor. Then, ask him to list these things in the same order on paper. Does he think that the first item he removed from the trunk is the oldest? Were items stored in any meaningful order? What can all those fake mustaches mean? Can Kenny re-create a story about Uncle Charles' life starting with the first thing he took from the trunk and moving along to the last item? Again, compare his theories to Grandma's memories. Tape record their conversation, and use it later as the basis for writing family stories for school assignments, for adding new Post-it-Notes on the family time line, or as gifts for family members. By doing this, Kenny is preserving the past for the future, like archaeologists and anthropologists.

Examine actual pieces of the past. Much as kids increase their comprehension by studying pictures and graphics in a textbook, archaeologists and anthropologists study artifacts—things made by human hands. Scientists use them to hypothesize about the customs, habits, technology, and lives of people in the past. Show kids in elementary and middle school how to analyze an artifact the way these scientists do.

Examine it first. Encourage Mike to explore an unidentifiable object with his hands. What does it feel like—lumpy, rough, or smooth? What are its color, shape, and size? How much does it weigh?

Talk about function. What does he think it was used for? Was it made by hand or machine? Could he buy one in a store today? How does he think it works? Does it remind him of anything he's seen before? Does the shape or design hint at what it might have been used for? Who does he think could have used such a thing? When was it used? Did they need something else to make it work, like thread or water or steam? How does he think it might have helped the people of the time?

When you guide kids through this kind of identification process, it often leads to that "Hey, wow, whoa, I know what this is!" moment when all their ideas and impressions and guesses suddenly click into a recognizable form. Now Mike can mentally classify and catalogue this new item and add it to his vast and growing collection of historical information. Just like an archaeologist.

Preserve pieces of history. Teach Kenny historical preservation while reinforcing his organizational skills as you decide together how the attic stuff should be dispersed. What items are important to family history and should be saved, framed, reconditioned, reupholstered, cleaned, tuned, or returned to the other family members? Are there family artifacts that bear further investigation at the library, a museum, or a historical society? Take pictures, keep notes, or tape record lists of things donated or disposed of so that a historical record remains even after the artifact is gone. When the kids return home, have them fill in their time line even further into the past to record the birth of crabby Uncle Oscar, comical Uncle Charles, and beautiful Aunt Jennie.

Take Some One-Day Trips through History

One-day trips can be refreshing, invigorating, and educational experiences for the whole family if you plan ahead. The following suggestions will make a one-day trip through history more enjoyable for you and for kids of elementary through middle school age. It's a comfortable and subtle way to build academic skills.

Pump up the vocabulary. Punch up Mattie, Mike, and Kenny's vocabulary with words like *expedition* or *excursion* instead of *trip* whenever you refer to these educational family outings. Whenever they encounter a new term on these trips, incorporate it immediately into conversation and repeat it often.

Tie it to school. Pick a place that jibes with their social studies or science curriculum. Seek suggestions from teachers, parents, or older students in your neighborhood. Ask the research librarian at your local library. Or refer to the curriculum section of your school's website to see what topics will be covered in the coming school year. Check your family lineage to see if it intersects with something of historical note at a place nearby. From the list you prepared, have Mattie, Mike, and Kenny select the area that interests them the most and focus your trips there.

Do some prep work. Call your local historical society, library, or park service office for suggestions about local destinations. Check with your local librarian to see if there are any books about your area like *One-Day Trips Through History: More Than 200 Museums, Battlefields, Plantations, Colonial Churches, Monuments, Historic Homes, Forts, and Parks* by Jane Ockershausen. Read it with the kids and select some choice destinations together.

Go for the action. Rather than picking a battlefield that is best toured by car, for example, pick a destination where the kids can get their hands and muscles into the action. Many national parks and local historic sites have activities and programs designed especially for kids, so gravitate there. Hiking an actual Civil or Revolutionary war battlefield and listening to a description of the struggle also highlights the dramatic difference between video game exaggeration and real violence. This is a lesson all kids need to learn.

Look for historical reenactments. Check out local historical sites, state, or national parks to see if any reenactments are scheduled over the summer. Reenactments are vivid depictions that breathe life into an era and engage the senses in understanding the human dimension of a conflict or a specific period of time. People who "live" in the period, called "reenactors," not only replay a famous battle, but they also set up authentic camps, cooking areas, and field stores at the site of a battlefield. Reenactors dress in costume down to the very details of haircut, speech, and mannerism. Many talk knowledgeably about news of "their day." These kinds of settings vividly reflect the materials, lifestyle, technologies, and hardships of a specific period of time. Often period arts and crafts, lectures, demonstrations, and food are available. Check with a state or local park service. Or if you have time for a trip, log on to the website of the National Park Service at *www.nps.gov.*

Narrow the choices. Narrow your choices to two or three places and take a vote or select a destination yourself and keep it a secret. Check out a website called "Museum Stuff" for museum listings by state at *www.museumstuff.com*, or log on to the National Register of Historic Places at *www.nr.nps.gov/about.htm* for historical locations near you. Note that some historically registered places are privately owned, or if publicly owned might not provide tours or information.

Do lunch. While on tour, use a picnic or a sit-down lunch as a reward for everyone. Tour guides at your destination can usually suggest safe picnic areas or local, family style restaurants that serve traditional or historical foods. Recap the morning's events over venison stew and apple "pye."

Leave early and keep it short. Most kids focus better and longer early in the day. Keeping on-site visits to fewer than two hours lessens the crash-n-burn factor.

Chunk up the car time. Travel time shouldn't exceed forty minutes between breaks for gas, drinks, and bathroom. Find help for "de-harrowing" the car experience with a deck of cards and the book called *52 Fun Things to Do in the Car* by Lynn Gordon.

Keep a travel log. Use a map to plan the route and calculate miles and travel time. As you drive, have the kids calculate how long it would have taken Uncle Cyrus to walk the same distance, and what he might have done to prepare for such a journey. Appoint Mattie as the scribe who keeps notes on unexpected detours, good restaurants, the best tour guides, things to avoid, and sites that should not be missed. This could be the beginning of her career as a travel writer.

Make a budget. This is an excellent math and organizational skill. Allocate a reasonable amount of money and appoint one of the kids as trip accountant. Consider travel expenses like gas, snacks, tolls, and meals. Kenny, the accountant, should handle all money transactions, including calculating tips and counting the correct change.

Videotape or take photos of the trip. Appoint Mike the photographer of the trip, especially if he has any attention deficits. This responsible job will help keep him focused on a task and boost his self-esteem. It will also provide a record to strengthen collective memory and reinforce everyone's learning. If Mike's videotaping the event, remind him to record atmospheric sounds like a water-wheel turning or the thumping sound of butter being churned by hand. Everybody can take turns narrating the play-by-play action, and Mattie can provide the color. Don't forget to interview the staff.

Conduct research. Encourage the kids to be like scientists and investigate things they don't understand or can't figure out while they're touring a site. If they can't identify the adze, the spindle, or the ink blotter by observation alone, ask the experts like the tour guides at Mount Vernon or the park rangers on the C & O Canal boat ride in Washington, DC. Many Civil War battlefield sites provide workbooks or guides specifically to keep active kids focused on the history.

Don't become a tour guide. Instead, help the kids find answers for themselves on signs or brochures of the park or colonial tavern. Any unresolved questions can be added to the trip travel log for later research.

Play a word game while you hike. To reinforce phonics and spelling, have kids label weather conditions and reformulate words to mirror changes in climate or time. A dark, drizzly day might be called "fizzley" for example. Or invent words to describe the taste of hardtack or Kenny's noises as he hikes up a hill with a "haversack" named Mattie on his back. Add these to the trip's log.

Stand and deliver. Pick an important site on the battlefield, sit the kids down, insist on silence, and read to them from a book like *Broken Drum* by Edith Morris Hemingway, based on the real-life story of a Civil War drummer boy. Let the views around them and the rhythm of your words inspire visualizations of warfare as it really was, involving real people—some old and some just like them, very, very young. Maybe even Uncle Cyrus.

Bring a project home. It could be a collection of leaves or bark or strange looking berries to add to a scrapbook of the trip. Ask tour guides or museum shop personnel for suggestions on cooking, weaving, candle making, or leather projects for extending their learning when they get back home.

Share the knowledge. All three kids can take the tape, the pictures, the video, and the crafts to share with their classes when the topic is covered in science or social studies class. Invite family members to attend multimedia presentations that weave Mattie, Mike, and Kenny's videos, photos, scrapbooks, and crepe paper time lines with their storytelling. And the kids will realize that they have made history of their own.

RESOURCES

Free archaeology and anthropology teaching materials from The Society for American Archaeology, at *www.saa.org*. Or write to SAA at 900 Second Street, NE, #12, Washington, DC 20002.

Get National Park Service information at *www.nps.gov*.

Bibliography

BOOKS

American Association for the Advancement of Science Project 2061. *Atlas of Science Literacy*. Washington, DC: American Association for the Advancement of Science, National Science Teachers Association, 2001.

Bybee, Roger W. ed. *Learning Science and the Science of Learning*. Arlington, VA: National Science Teachers Association, 2002.

Bell, Nanci. *Visualizing and Verbalizing*. Paso Robles, CA: Academy of Reading, 1991.

Cipani, Ennio. *Classroom Management for All Teachers: 11 Effective Plans*. Upper Saddle River, NJ: Prentice Hall, 1998.

Cohen, Cathi. *Raise Your Child's Social IQ: Stepping Stones to People Skills for Kids*. Silver Spring, MD: Advantage, 2000.

Crook, William G. *Tracking Down Hidden Food Allergy*. Jackson, TN: Professional, 1995.

Dempsey, Doris E. *Classroom Discipline Made Easy: A System That Works for the Inner City or Any City*. Denver, CO: Deck, 1996.

Desetta, Al, and Sybil Wolin, ed. *The Struggle to Be Strong: True Stories by Teens about Overcoming Tough Times.* Minneapolis, MN: Free Spirit, 2000.

Galland, Leo, M.D., and Dian Dincin Buchman. *Superimmunity for Kids.* New York, NY: Dell, 1988.

Getman, G.N. *How to Develop Your Child's Intelligence.* Santa Ana, CA: Optometric Extension Program, 1995.

Gray, Carol. *Comic Strip Conversations.* Arlington, TX: Future Horizons, 1994.

Greene, Lawrence J. *Finding Help When Your Child Is Struggling in School.* New York, NY: Golden, 1998.

Hannaford, Carla. *Smart Moves: Why Learning Is Not All in Your Head.* Arlington, VA: Great Ocean Publishers, 1995.

Hanson, Jeanne K. *Your Amazing Body: From Headaches to Sweaty Feet and Everything in Between.* New York, NY: W. H. Freeman, 1994.

Henry, Diana. *Tool Chest: For Teachers, Parents and Students.* Phoenix, AZ: Henry Occupational Services, 1999.

Kalman, Bobbie. *Historic Communities: 18th Century Clothing.* New York, NY: Crabtree, 1993.

Kaufman, Gershen, Lev Raphael, and Pamela Espeland. *Stick Up for Yourself: Every Kid's Guide to Personal Power and Positive Self-Esteem.* Minneapolis, MN: Free Spirit, 1999.

Kranowitz, Carol Stock. *The Out-of-Sync Child: Recognizing and Coping with Sensory Integration Dysfunction.* New York, NY: Penguin Putnam, 1998.

Luckie, William R., Wood Smethhurst, and Sara Beth Huntley. *Study Power: Study Skills to Improve Your Learning and Your Grades.* Cambridge, MA: Brookline, 2000.

MacKenzie, Robert J. *Setting Limits in the Classroom: How to Move Beyond the Classroom Dance of Discipline.* Rocklin, CA: Prima, 1996.

Mazur, Eric. *Peer Instruction: A User's Manual.* Upper Saddle River, NJ: Prentice Hall, 1997.

Miller, Wilma H. *Alternative Assessment Techniques for Reading and Writing.* West Nyack, NY: The Center for Applied Research in Education, 1995.

———. *The Complete Reading Disabilities Handbook.* West Nyack, NY: The Center for Applied Research in Education, 1993.

Murphy, John J. *Solution-Focused Counseling in Middle and High Schools.* Alexandria, VA: American Counseling Association, 1997.

Petreshene, Susan S. *Brain Teasers!* Hoboken, NJ: Jossey-Bass, 1994.

Pierangelo, Roger, and George Guiliani. *Special Educator's Complete Guide to 109 Diagnostic Tests.* West Nyack, NY: The Center for Applied Research in Education, 1998.

Powell, Sara Davis. *Super Strategies for Succeeding on the Standardized Tests: Language Arts.* New York, NY: Scholastic Professional, 2000.

Rathvon, Natalie. *The Unmotivated Child: Helping Your Underachiever Become a Successful Student.* New York, NY: Fireside, 1996.

Roehlkepartain, Jolene L., and Nancy Leffert. *What Young Children Need to Succeed.* Minneapolis, MN: Free Spirit, 2000.

Seiderman, Arthur S., and Steven E. Marcus. *20/20 Is Not Enough: The New World of Vision.* New York, NY: Fawcett, 1989.

Selig, Ruth Osterweis, and Marilyn R. London, ed. *Anthropology Explored: The Best Smithsonian AnthroNotes.* Washington, DC: Smithsonian Institution, 1998.

Vernon, Ann. *The Passport Program: A Journey through Emotional, Social, Cognitive and Self-Development, Grades 1-5, 6-8, 9-12.* Champaign, IL: Research, 1998.

———, and Radhi H. Al-Mabuk. *What Growing Up Is All About.* Champaign, IL: Research, 1995.

Von Drachenfels, Suzanne. *The Art of the Table: A Complete Guide to Table Setting, Table Manners and Tableware.* New York, NY: Simon & Schuster, 2000.

Weinberg, Winkler G., M.D. *No Germs Allowed: How to Avoid Infectious Diseases at Home and on the Road.* New Brunswick, NJ: Rutgers University, 1996.

Wolfgang, Charles H. *The Three Faces of Discipline for the Elementary School Teacher: Empowering the Teacher and Students*. Boston: Allyn and Bacon, 1996.

ONLINE RESOURCES

Blakely, Elaine, and Sheila Spence. *Developing Metacognition*. Syracuse: Educational Resources Information Center, 1990. Available from ERIC, ED 327218.

Cerny, Jerry. "General Principles of Motivation" in Social Studies Web Page. Available from The University of New Orleans College of Education at *http://ss.uno.edu/SS/TeachDevel/Motivat/Motivate.html*.

Children and Adults with Attention-Deficit/Hyperactivity Disorder (CHADD). "The Disorder Named ADHD—CHADD Fact Sheet #1," 24, April 2002. Available from *www.chadd.iwmpcorp.com/fs/fs1.htm*.

Grateful Dyed: American Kool-Aid Beauty. Available from *www.grassmoon.com/gratefuldyed/*.

Missiuna, Cheryl. "Developmental Coordination Disorder." CanChild Centre for Childhood Disability Research, McMaster University. (Hamilton, Ontario, Canada, 1996.) Available from *www.fhs.mcmaster.ca/canchild/publications/keepcurrent/KC96-3.html*.

"Motivation: Helping Your Child Through Early Adolescence." US Department of Education. Available from *www.ed.gov/pubs/parents/adolescence/partx4.html*.

Muir, Michael H. "What Underachieving Middle School Students Believe Motivates Them to Learn." A Thesis Submitted in Partial Fulfillment of the Requirements for the Degree of Doctor of Education, The Graduate School of Education, University of Maine, May, 2000. Available from *www.mcmel.org/DisWeb/*.

The National Commission on Writing. "The Neglected 'R': The Need for a Writing Revolution." The National Commission on Writing, 25 April 2003. Available from *www.writingcommission.org*.

The Simplified Spelling Society. Available from *www.spellingsociety.org/*.

"Student Motivation to Learn." ERIC Clearinghouse on Educational Management. Available from *www.kidsource.com/kidsource/content2/ Student_Motivation.html*.

Tune-Up Lifestyle Facilitations/Workshops for Physical Education. Lifestyle Education Consulting, Perth, Australia. Available from *http:// tuneuplifestyle. com/facilitations.html*.

ARTICLES AND PERIODICALS

Armstrong, Penelope A., and Jerry D. Rogers. "Basic Skills Revisited: The Effects of Foreign Language Instruction on Reading, Math and Language Arts." *Learning Languages*, 2, no. 3 (spring 1997): 20–31.

Association for Curriculum Supervision and Development. *Curriculum Update*. (summer 2003.)

Department of Historic Resources. *Window on the Past: Threshold to the Future, Teacher's Guide*. Richmond: Virginia Department of Historic Resources, 1995. Booklet

Metropolitan Life Insurance Company. Published report *The MetLife Survey of the American Teacher 2002: Student Life, School, Home and Community*. New York: Metropolitan Life Insurance Company, 2002.

Wheeler, Gerald F. "The Three Faces of Inquiry." *Inquiring into Inquiry Learning and Teaching in Science*. (Washington, DC: American Association for the Advancement of Science, 2000.)

Resources

BOOKS

Bromfield, Richard, *Handle with Care: Understanding Children and Teachers*. New York, NY: Teachers College, 2000.

Budd, Linda S. *Living with the Active Alert Child*. Seattle, WA: Parenting, 1993.

Irvin, Georgia. *Georgia Irvin's Guide to Schools: Metropolitan Washington Independent and Public/Pre-K–12*. New York, NY: Madison, 2002.

Johnston, Francine R., Marcia Invernizzi, and Connie Juel. *Book Buddies: Guidelines for Volunteer Tutors of Emergent and Early Readers*. New York, NY: Guilford, 1998.

Kennedy, Dora, Pat Barr-Harrison, and Maria Guarrera Wilmeth. *Exploring Languages: A Complete Introduction for Foreign Language Students*. Chicago, IL: National Textbook, 1996.

Kushi, Michio, and Aveline Kushi. *Raising Healthy Kids*. New York, NY: Avery, 1994.

Muschla, Gary Robert. *The Writing Teacher's Book of Lists*. Hoboken, NJ: Jossey-Bass, 1991.

Parks, Sandra, and Howard Black. *Organizing Thinking: Graphic Organizers, Books I and II*. Pacific Grove, CA: Critical Thinking, 1990.

Paulu, Nancy. *Helping Your Kids with Homework*. Washington, DC: US Department of Education. Available free online at *www.ed.gov/pubs/HelpingStudents/title.html*.

Reeske, Mike, and Shirley Watt Ireton. *The Life Cycle of Everyday Stuff*. Arlington, VA: National Science Teachers Association, 2001.

Wickelgren, Wayne, and Ingrid Wickelgren. *Math Coach: A Parent's Guide to Helping Children Succeed in Math*. New York: Berkley, 2001.

ARTICLE

Lindsley, Ogden R. "Precision Teaching: By Teachers for Children." Available from *www.teonor.com/ptdocs/files/lindsley1990.doc*.

ORGANIZATIONS AND OTHER RESOURCES

Achievers Unlimited of Wisconsin at *www.achieverswisconsin.org*.

American Council on the Teaching of Foreign Languages at *www.actfl.org*.

American Optometric Association at *www.aoanet.org*.

Benchmarks for Science Literacy at *www.sciencenetlinks.com*.

Center for Applied Linguistics and the Brown University Regional Educational Lab at *www.cal.org/earlylang*.

Charter Schools information at the Center for Education Reform at *www.edreform.com*.

Children and Adults with Attention Deficit Disorder at *www.chadd.org*.

College of Optometrists in Vision Development (COVD) at *www.covd.org* or 888-COVD770.

Department of Defense Education Activity (schools for military or government families overseas) at *www.odedodea.edu/index.htm*.

Developmental Delay Resources at *www.devdelay.org*.

Foreign Language in the Elementary School Programs (FLES), the FLES Institute in Baltimore, Maryland, by FAX at 301-230-2652.

Generations United: a resource for 100 intergenerational tutoring programs nationwide at *www.gu.org*. Search by US Postal Service state codes like PA, CA, NJ.

Homeschooling information at *www.eric.ed.gov/archives/homesc2.html*.

Independent Educational Consultants Association information available at *www.educationalconsulting.org*.

International Coalition of Boys' Schools at 216-831-2200.

Kidtest Benchmarked Sequence at *www.kidtest.com/sequencebenefits.html*.

Lindamood-Bell at *www.lindamoodbell.com*.

National Association of Independent Schools at *www.nais.org*.

National Association of Professional Organizers Information and Referral Hotline at 512-206-0151 or *napo@assnmgmt.com*.

National Association of Therapeutic Schools and Programs (NATSAP) at *www.natsap.org*.

National Coalition of Girls' Schools at *www.ncgs.org*.

National Council of Teachers of Mathematics at *www.nctm.org*.

National Information Center for Children and Youth with Disabilities (NICHCY) at *www.nichcy.org*. or 800-695-0285.

National Network for Early Language Learning at the Center for Applied Linguistics in Washington, DC. E-mail at *nnell@cal.org* or call 202-362-0700.

National Park Service at *www.nps.gov*.

National Register of Historic Places at *www.nr.nps.gov/about.htm*.

National Science Teachers Association at *www.nsta.org*.

OASIS Intergenerational Tutoring Program, Nationwide Locations at 314-862-2933 or *www.oasisnet.org*. Ask city program coordinators about local referrals.

Optometric Extension Program at *www.oep.org*.

Orton-Gillingham at *www.orton-gillingham.com*.

Parents Active for Vision Education at *www.pave-eye.com*.

School Match (national and international schools) at *www.schoolmatch.com*.

"Search for Public Schools" at *http://nces.ed.gov/ccd/schoolsearch/*.

Secondary School Admissions Test (SSAT) at *www.ssat.org*.

Society for American Archaeology at *www.saa.org*.

State education resources and services, interactive US map, available at US Department of Education's Education Resource Organizations Directory. Find it at *http://bcol02.ed.gov/Programs/EROD/org list by territory.cfm*.

US Department of Health and Human Services at *www.health.org* or 800-662-HELP.

Tools for Teaching

FOREIGN LANGUAGE

All-in-One Language Fun! CD-ROM for ages 3–12 which uses native speakers, colorful graphics but no reading, writing, or spelling. Available from Syracuse Language Systems at 800-797-5264.

Berlitz for Travelers. Cassette series recommended by foreign language teachers for helping teachers and parents learn proper pronunciation.

Learn Italian Together: An Activity Kit for Kids and Grownups, Ages 4–8 by Marie-Claire Antoine, published by Living Language. It contains an activity book, cassette, and learning stickers. A teacher's guide is also available.

Picture Word Book. Versions in English, French, Hebrew, German, Italian, Spanish. Dover.

Romance Language Resource Page. University of Chicago program uses native speakers to teach samplings of French, Italian, Portuguese, and Spanish at *www.humanities.uchicago.edu/humanities*.

HISTORICAL ADVENTURES AND BOOKS

Gordon, Lynn. *52 Fun Things to Do in the Car.* San Francisco: Chronicle, 1994.

Hemingway, Edith Morris. *Broken Drum.* Shippensburg, PA: White Mane, 1996.

Ockershausen, Jane. *One-Day Trips through History: More Than 200 Museums, Battlefields, Plantations, Colonial Churches, Monuments, Historic Homes, Forts, and Parks.* Charlottesville, VA: Howell, 2000.

Smithsonian Center for Education and Museum Studies offers the "Educator's Guide to Smithsonian Publications and Websites," a two-part, one-hundred-twenty-page publication. It includes curriculum-spanning books, films, records, CDs, maps, slides, posters, activities, and teaching kits, many free of charge. Send requests to The Smithsonian Office for Education and Museum Studies, PO Box 37012, Arts & Industries Building Room 1163, MRC 402, Washington, DC, 20012. Enclose a $10 check payable to Smithsonian/SCEMS for shipping and handling.

MATH

Anno, Masaichiro, and Mitusumasa Anno. *Anno's Mysterious Multiplying Jar.* New York: Puffin, 1999.

Demi. *One Grain of Rice: A Mathematical Folktale.* New York: Scholastic, 1997.

"Dr. Math" at *www.mathforum.org.*

Enzenberger, Hans Magnus. *The Number Devil: A Mathematical Adventure.* New York: Random House, 1998.

"Families" at National Council of Teachers of Mathematics. Available from *www.nctm.org/families/.*

Hutchins, Pat. *The Doorbell Rang.* Parsippany, NJ: Pearson Learning, 1989.

Organizational Skills

Gross, Gay Merrill. *Folding Napkins.* New York: Mallard, 1991.

Montroll, John. *Easy Origami.* Minneola: Dover, DE, 1992. (Beginner book)

Nakano, Dokuohtei. *Easy Origami.* New York: Puffin, 1994. (Ages 9–12)

Reading Instruction

Library of Congress Talking Book Program offers free books on tape for kids with disabilities that prevent them from reading in a normal manner. Available at *www.loc.gov/nls/index_html.*

Recorded Books Inc. has 2,000 tapes to rent or buy for children, young adults, and adults. For a free catalogue, call 800-638-1304.

Weston Woods at *www.scholastic.com/westonwoods.*

Sensory Integration

"A Teachabout." Occupational therapist Diana Henry's specially equipped mobile home is a classroom on wheels that brings sensory integration classes and workshops to schools and groups nationwide. Details at *www.ateachabout.com.*

Semaphore Alphabet at *www.anbg.gov.au/flags/semaphore.html.*

Tool Chest: For Parents by Diana Henry, OT. "Over-the-counter" sensory integration activities that can be tailored to a child's individual needs. Details at *www.ateachabout.com* or by calling 888-371-1204.

Science

Crook, William G., M.D. *Tracking Down Hidden Food Allergy.* Jackson, TN: Professional, 1980. Order at 800-227-2627.

"Outstanding Science Trade Books for Students in Grades K–12," published annually by the National Science Teachers Association at *www.nsta.org/ostbc.*

SOCIALIZATION AND BEHAVIOR

Bellairs, John. *Mansion in the Mist*. New York: Puffin, 1992.

———. *The House with the Clock in Its Walls*. New York: Dial, 1984.

Colfer, Eoin. *Artemis Fowl*. New York: Miramax, 2002.

Miller, Marvin. *You Be the Detective*. New York: Scholastic, 1991.

Parker, A. E. *Clue*. New York: Scholastic, 1996 (18-book series).

Sukach, Jim. *Crime Scene Who Done Its: Dr. Quicksolve Mini-Mysteries*. New York: Sterling, 2003.

Wells, James K. "Ipani Eskimos: A Cycle of Life in Nature." Available from *www.alaskool.org*.

SPELLING

American Literacy Council at *www.americanliteracy.com/variations.htm*.

Animal Sounds available from *www.georgetown.edu/faculty/ballc/animals*.

Cornog, Mary Wood. *Merriam-Webster's Vocabulary Builder*. Springfield, MA: Merriam Webster, 1998.

Spelling Animal Sounds available from *www.georgetown.edu/faculty/ballc/animals/animals-spelling.html*.

STUDY SKILLS

Critical Thinking Products at *www.criticalthinking.com*.

WRITING

Dickens, Charles. *Oliver Twist*. New York, NY: Dodd, Mead and Company, 1941.

Purdue University's Online Writing Lab at *http://owl.english.purdue.edu*.

Book List for Reluctant Readers

Recommended by students who vowed they could never fall in love with a book.

AGES 4–6

Barrett, Judy. *Cloudy with a Chance of Meatballs*. New York, NY: Aladdin, 1982.

Bridwell, Norman. *Clifford Makes a Friend*. New York, NY: Cartwheel, 1998.

Dahl, Roald. *Fantastic Mr. Fox*. New York, NY: Penguin, 2002.

dePaola, Tomie. *Tom*. New York, NY: Puffin, 1997.

Donnelly, Judy. *Tut's Mummy Lost . . . and Found*. New York, NY: Random House, 1988.

Grossman, Bill. *My Little Sister Ate One Hare*. New York, NY: Random House, 1998.

Hargreaves, Roger. *The Mr. Men Books*, series. New York: Price Stern Sloan, 1983.

Hoban, Lillian. *Arthur's Loose Tooth*. New York, NY: HarperTrophy, 1987.

Korman, Gordon. *Liar, Liar, Pants on Fire*. New York, NY: Little Apple, 1999.

Marshall, James. *Miss Nelson Has a Field Day*. Boston, MA: Houghton Mifflin, 1988.

Mayer, Mercer. *Baby Sister*. New York, NY: Golden, 2000.

Pilkey, Dav. *The Adventures of Captain Underpants*. New York, NY: Little Apple, 1997.

———. *Kat Kong*. San Diego, CA: Harcourt Brace, 1993.

Polacco, Patricia. *Thunder Cake*. New York, NY: Puffin, 1997.

Rathman, Peggy. *Officer Buckle and Gloria*. New York, NY: Putnam, 1995.

San Souci, Daniel. *North Country Night*. New York, NY: Doubleday, 1990.

Slater, Teddy. *The Wrong Way Rabbit*. New York, NY: Scholastic, 1993.

Snyder, Zilpha Keatley. *Below the Root*. New York, NY: Tor, 1985.

Warner, Gertrude Chandler. *The Boxcar Children: The Mystery of the Purple Pool*. Morton Grove, IL: Albert Whitman, 1994.

AGES 9–12

Applegate, K. A. *Everworld #1 Search for Senna*. New York, NY: Scholastic, 1999.

Avi. *The True Confessions of Charlotte Doyle*. New York, NY: Orchard, 1997.

Billingsley, Franny. *Well Wished*. New York, NY: Simon & Schuster, 1997.

Christopher, Matt. *The Comeback Challenge*. Boston, MA: Little, Brown, 1996.

Clemens, Andrew. *Frindle*. New York, NY: Aladdin, 1998.

Creech, Sharon. *Bloomability*. New York, NY: HarperTrophy, 1999.

Dahl, Roald. *The Witches*. New York, NY: Penguin, 2002.

Danziger, Paula. *Amber Brown Wants Extra Credit*. New York, NY: Scholastic, 1999.

———, and Ann Matthews Martin. *P.S. Longer Letter Later*. New York, NY: Scholastic, 1999.

Deary, Terry. *Measly Middle Ages*. New York, NY: Scholastic, 2002.

Hansen, Joyce. *I Thought My Soul Would Rise and Fly: The Diary of Patsy, A Freed Girl*. New York, NY: Scholastic, 1997.

Henry, Marguerite. *King of the Wind: The Story of the Godolphin Arabian*. New York, NY: Aladdin, 1991.

Holt, Kimberly Willis. *When Zachary Beaver Came to Town*. New York, NY: Yearling, 2001.

Levine, Gail Casson. *The Two Princesses of Bamarre*. New York, NY: HarperCollins, 2003.

McSwigan, Marie. *Snow Treasure*. New York, NY: Scholastic, 1997.

Myers, Walter Dean. *At Her Majesty's Request*. New York, NY: Scholastic, 1999.

Park, Barbara. *The Kid in the Red Jacket*. New York, NY: Random House, 1995.

Peck, Richard. *The Great Interactive Dream Machine: Another Adventure in Cyberspace*. New York, NY: Puffin, 1998.

Uchida, Yoshiko. *Journey Home*. Glenview, IL: Scott Foresman, 1996.

MIDDLE SCHOOL

Card, Orsen Scott. *Ender's Game*. New York: Tor, 1994.

Dahl, Roald. *Danny, the Champion of the World*. New York, Bantam, 1984.

Farmer, Nancy. *The Ear, the Eye and the Arm*. New York: Firebird, 1995.

Heinlein, Robert. *Citizen of the Galaxy*. New York: Ballantine, 1987.

Jacques, Brian. *Castaways of the Flying Dutchman*. New York: Firebird, 2003.

Keith, Harold. *Rifles for Watie*. New York: HarperTrophy, 1987.

Lubar, David. *Hidden Talents*. New York: Starscape, 2003.

Matas, Carol. *Daniel's Story*. New York: Scholastic, 1993.

Mazer, Norma Fox. *After the Rain*. Portsmouth, NH: Heinemann, 1991.

Merrill, Jean. *The Pushcart War.* New York, NY: Yearling, 1987.

Osborne, Mary Pope. *Standing in the Light: A Captive Diary of Catherine Carey Logan, Delaware Valley, Pennsylvania, 1763.* New York, NY: Scholastic Trade, 2003.

Paulsen, Gary. *Harris and Me.* New York, NY: Yearling, 1995.

———. *The Hatchet* and its sequel *The River.* New York, NY: Aladdin, 1996.

Paulus, Trina. *Hope for the Flowers.* Mahwah, NJ: Paulist, 1984.

Radford, Irene. *The Hidden Dragon.* New York, NY: DAW, 2002. (Series)

Speare, Elizabeth George. *The Sign of the Beaver.* New York, NY: Yearling, 1994.

Spinelli, Jerry. *Crash.* New York, NY: Random House, 1997.

HIGH SCHOOL

Adams, Douglas. *Hitchhiker's Guide to the Galaxy.* New York: Ballantine, 1995.

Anderson, Laurie Halse. *Speak.* New York: Puffin, 2001.

Bauer, Joan. *Rules of the Road.* New York: Puffin, 2000.

Crichton, Michael. *Jurassic Park.* New York: Ballantine, 1999.

Dickens, Charles. *A Tale of Two Cities.* New York: Signet, 1997.

Holly, Emma. *Catching Midnight.* New York: Jove, 2003.

King, Stephen. *The Girl Who Loved Tom Gordon.* New York: Pocket, 2000.

Lee, Harper. *To Kill a Mockingbird.* New York: HarperCollins, 1999.

Lo, Kuan-chung. *Three Kingdoms: A Historical Novel.* Chicago: Foreign Language, 2001. (Four volumes)

Morgan, Robert. *Gap Creek: A Novel.* New York: Simon & Schuster, 2001.

Pratchett, Terry. *The Color of Magic: A Novel of Discworld.* New York: HarperTorch, 2000. (Series)

Pullman, Philip. *Golden Compass: His Dark Materials, Book 1.* New Orleans: Del Rey, 1999.

Salinger, J.D. *Catcher in the Rye.* Boston: Little, Brown, 1991.

Scott, Joanna. *The Lucky Gourd Shop.* New York: Washington Square, 2001.

Souljah, Sister. *No Disrespect.* New York: Vintage, 1996.

Steinbeck, John. *Cannery Row.* New York: Penguin, 1993.

Wolff, Virginia Euwer. *Make Lemonade.* New York: Scholastic, 2003.

BOOKS TO READ ALOUD, AGES 5–11

Garrity, John. *Tiger Woods: The Making of a Champion.* Wichita, KA: Fireside, 1997.

Jordan, Robert. *The Great Hunt, The Wheel of Time, Book Two.* New York: Tor, 1992.

Rushdie, Salman. *Haroun and the Sea of Stories.* New York: Granta, 1991

Index